Straits Chinese
FURNITURE

A Collector's Guide

This 17th/18th-century map of Southeast Asia was drawn by some unknown (Dutch?) cartographer to specifically highlight the relative positions of the various Spice Islands of the East Indies. The titled word 'Moluccae' or 'Muluccao' was the general name given to such islands as Ambon, the Banda Islands, Ceram, Java, Borneo, etc. Notice the position of Malacca in the Malay Peninsula, directly below the words "Pars Indae Orientalis". Courtesy of the National Archives of Singapore.

**© 1994 Times Editions Pte Ltd
Photographs by Albert Lim**

This book is published by
Times Books International
an imprint of

Times Editions Pte Ltd
Times Centre,
1 New Industrial Road
Singapore 1953

Times Subang
Lot 46, Subang
Hi-Tech Industrial Park
Batu Tiga
40000 Shah Alam
Selangor Darul Ehsan
Malaysia

Colour separation by
Superskill Graphics, Singapore

Printed in Singapore

ISBN 981 204 092 7

INSULÆ INDIAE orientalis

Siday
C. de Enganno
Luco
Paga
nſe
Moro Hermoſo
Piutados
Piutados
INSULÆ
do Mudato
Ancon triste
nia
P. de Mau
G. de Matalahombre
date
Paracalle
e Nebui
I. de Cobos
PHILIPPI NÆ.
Ylhas de Princiro
ARCHI
J. Vean
I. Caburao
PELA
I. Abuyo
GUS S.LA
I. de Bidivia
Matalotes

Buvi
Grege
Praian
Gugan
Pagon
Giges
Seuan
Sarpan
Gugelian
Boſaba
Baban

ISLAS DE LADRONES

Mala
qua
Canola
Mi ndanao
Buran
I. de S. Jonnes
ZARI
I. da Palmetas
Candingar

Molucca inſulæ quinque ſunt Iaxta
Gilolo ſita nimirum Ternate,
Tidori Mthr, Machian et
Bachian.

Bangieaz
Manado
I. de Rao
I. de Dai
Dos Graos
Dagoada

I. de Martin
I. de Aues

Tetolli
Cele
Curi
curi
bes
Cian
Gilolo
Gilolo
inſul
Buorno
Camafo

Hic hybernuit Geor.
ogius de Meſes

Dos Mar
tilhos
La Balhena

Amboino
I. Genaon
Banda
Ceiram I.
Os Papuas
I. de Don de
Moneſes

De las Virgenes
S. Andreo Buerto
S. Tiago
P. Primiro De laGpada
C. de Buena De ſeo

Burro
Batolaia
Bahumbar
I. Daru
A qui imbernoa Martin
Afonſo de Melo
NOVÆGUINEÆ
PARS

Batura
Terra alta
Timor

Milliaria
Germanica

| 15 | 30 | 45 | 60 | 75 |

Straits Chinese
FURNITURE

A Collector's Guide

Ho Wing Meng

TIMES BOOKS INTERNATIONAL
Singapore • Kuala Lumpur

For Fui Len & Alexis

Acknowledgements

It is unavoidable that in writing a book of this nature, I have had to rely upon the knowledge and expertise of many different people who, over the years, enabled me to formulate my ideas more clearly and coherently than they would otherwise have been. But naturally, I alone am responsible for all the errors and shortcomings in this book. I have been fortunate that those people – among them, dealers, collectors, friends and acquaintances – with whom I discussed the various aspects of antique local furniture were more than forthcoming in initiating me into some of the lesser-known facts about the customs and practices of the Baba community. I thank everyone who has helped me in one way or another. I also wish to express my deep appreciation to the following: Mr Kee Tak Lip of Keris Woodwork Sdn. Bhd., Malacca, Dr Eunice Thio, Mr Peter Wee of Katong Antique House, Prof and Mrs Yusoff Talib, Mr Johnson Tan, Mr Albert Teo, Miss Rosna Buang and the National Museum of Singapore. My wife Fui Len deserves a special thank you for many years of unstinting effort in facilitating my research and travels.

Contents

Prologue

We tend to take for granted anything which happens to form a regular and abiding feature of our daily life. This applies not only to farmers living in the valleys of the magnificent Swiss Alps, but also to the Nepalese who dwell in Pokhara, at the foot of the towering Himalayas. To the Swiss farmer, as Arthur Koestler once remarked, tourists who regularly come to gape in admiration at the snow-covered peaks are foolish people. For him, a mountain merely represents so much hay for his cattle or, perhaps, so much log to warm his home. Practical considerations apart, the intense pleasure that we experience upon encountering a rare and original masterpiece of art for the first time palls with familiarity and prolonged exposure. With time, we tend to lapse into a state of complacency and indifference.

Is this not the reason why, for example, the security officers in charge of the Percival David Collection in the Courtauld Institute of Art in London, which contains some of the rarest pieces of ancient Chinese ceramics dating from the Song Dynasty (960–1279) to the Qing Dynasty (1644–1911), regard these veritable treasures with a genial air of indifference, verging on a sense of boredom? The *gendarmes* in the Louvre in Paris are equally blasé about the stupendous painting collection of Italian, French, German, Dutch and Venetian old masters, including the famous *Mona Lisa* by Leonardo da Vinci, which was stolen once (but subsequently retrieved) and, on another occasion, vandalized by some demented tourist.

Likewise, when the royal necropolis of the Ming emperors outside the city of Beijing was first opened to visitors during the late 1950s or early 1960s, many Western scholars visiting the Ding Ling mausoleum of Emperor Wanli (1572–1620) and his two wives expressed astonishment that the rare and priceless tomb furniture of the emperor was left to the care of an old peasant rather than to some armed security guards. They were equally baffled that this old custodian regarded the onerous responsibility entrusted upon him with an air of nonchalance, as he puffed contentedly on his old pipe. According to a journalist writing for the *Illustrated London News*, when some of these visitors enquired whether the Chinese government was not concerned about the possibility of thefts and break-ins, the reply raised even more eyebrows. No, they said, because the Ding Ling tomb and its entire contents were the common property of the people living there!

The cluttered appearance of antique and period objects on the table top and shelves of the massive sideboard (8 ft or 240 cm high and 5 ft or 150 cm wide) shown here in the background, together with a 1950s settee and a glass case containing antique silver and other bric-à-brac, reminds one of the interiors of many antique shops in Jonker Street (now Jalan Hang Jebat), Malacca, some 25 years ago. Courtesy of Mr Peter Wee, Katong Antique House.

It is not our habit to esteem anything until we have lost it or, perhaps, until we suddenly realize that it is in danger of being lost beyond redemption. That was the case of Straits Chinese furniture. Expert cabinet-makers did not esteem it as highly as the best of traditional Chinese or Western furniture. Household furnishings and movables (constructed mostly out of tropical and semi-tropical hardwoods and sometimes decorated with fabrics and cushions) were specifically made for old Baba homes in the former Straits Settlements of Singapore, Malacca and Penang between 1840 and 1940. But they became scarce in the late 1960s and early 1970s because of a sudden surge in demand by British Armed Forces personnel and, especially, members of the foreign diplomatic corps living in Singapore and Kuala Lumpur.

This sudden demand came about when the British government decided in 1965 to close down all military bases at Butterworth in Province Wellesley, the Terendak Base in Malacca and the naval base and other military installations in Singapore. All British military personnel were to be repatriated to Britain.

Thus, by the beginning of 1969, those members of the British Armed Forces who had been stationed in Malacca for a decade or more and who had come to love the old-world charm of the Baba houses in Heeren Street (now Jalan Tun Tan Cheng Lock), Jonker Street (now Jalan Hang Jebat), Kampung Hulu and the environs around Bukit China, Tengkera and Klebang Besar, went on a shopping spree to buy up antique and period objects to take home with them. Most of these pieces came from old Baba homes, particularly those ornately carved red-and-gold cabinets, bedsteads, bridal chairs, chests-of-drawers, teakwood furniture made in the styles of 16th- to 19th-century English and European furniture, selected pieces of blackwood/rosewood furniture, as well as other bric-à-brac of Victorian and 19th-century European origins.

The sudden craze for mementoes of old Malacca and the former Straits Settlements soon awakened the interest of the members of the foreign diplomatic community in Singapore and Kuala Lumpur; before long, many antique collectors were making frequent trips to Malacca in search of Baba antiques.

The immediate effect of the sudden demand for Baba antiques in Malacca in the late 1960s was that, within a very short time, a significant number of the relics of a former era, including some of the best of Straits Chinese red-and-gold furniture and some 18th/19th-century Dutch and English furniture, were taken out of the country – much to the alarm of the authorities of the State Museum of Malacca. Some concerned people began to warn that, unless the state government took steps to regulate the export of culturally important artefacts, Malacca was in danger of losing its cultural and historical heritage.

During the halcyon days of the late 19th and early 20th centuries, it was customary for wealthy Babas in Malacca to own several houses, both in town and in the country. Their townhouses were built in the manner of traditional Guangdong shophouses though, as a matter of fact, they were used entirely for residential purposes. These were located in the Heeren Street/Jonker Street vicinity, while their country houses were located further away from the town centre – in Tengkera and Klebang Besar along the western coastal stretch. The spacious colonial-style house shown here is an example of a wealthy Baba country house located along Klebang Besar.

As it was, the dearth of historical evidence going back to the Portuguese era (1511–1641) was evident for all to see: except for some decaying tombstones and crumbling walls on St Paul's Hill and the extensively weathered gate of Fort Famosa, there was virtually nothing else left from that period. As for the legacy of the Dutch rule in Malacca (1641–1795), only a handful of buildings in the Stadthuys area, with their characteristic red walls, was all that remained. What happened to the heritage of the Portuguese and the Dutch could also happen to the Baba culture. That was what some well-meaning people feared at the time. Unfortunately, some of their worst fears have indeed come to pass.

I happened to be in Malacca making the rounds of the shops along Jonker Street in the company of some friends sometime in early 1969 when I first heard about this concern for the cultural heritage of the Straits Settlements. I was introduced to the Kutty brothers (who were both still alive then), the elder of whom ran the family business known as 'Kutty Brothers'. The younger brother operated a different establishment a little way down the same street, called 'Abdul Sharikat'. Mr Kutty of 'Kutty Brothers' was a spry and genial old man who eagerly showed us around his cramped and cluttered shop, stacked from floor to ceiling with an incredible variety of old furniture, including chairs, tables, sofas, bureaus with rolled tops, sideboards, 'tallboys' (a high chest-of-drawers divided into two sections and supported on four legs), glass cases, washstands, hatstands, cabinets, bedsteads, etc. There were many glass cases filled with delicate porcelain; there were crystal and beautiful table lamps with cut-glass containers and ruby glass shades. Mr Kutty also stocked old Minangkabau brassware in his cupboards, antique Malay embroideries and old silverwork. There was even a 1930 Baby Austin parked in front of his shop! For most of his regular customers, the cramped and cluttered confusion of Mr Kutty's shop was a delightful place to poke about on weekends.

Amidst all this jumble of old-world artefacts, Mr Kutty went about calmly and cheerfully showing his customers around, stopping every now and then to explain the origins of some of his pieces. There were several sets of exquisitely carved chests-of-drawers and a set of eight armchairs made out of teakwood and designed after the style of Victorian chairs. All these, Mr Kutty explained, had been bought up by some British army officers formerly attached to the Terendak Camp in Tanjong Kling. Since 1968, his business had picked up drastically as homeward-bound armed forces personnel and their wives went on shopping sprees to buy up those antiques which best reminded them of their stay in Malacca. Mr Kutty was in a buoyant mood as he described the contents of the various shipments of antiques which he had sent overseas, or of those he was still in the process of packing for shipment to Britain and the United States. In the same way, his brother was also doing brisk business in antique furniture as well as other bric-à-brac of Victorian and European origins.

In those days, it was still possible to obtain a very fine set of 19th-century red-and-gold wedding cabinets for 200 or 300 ringgits. But even then, Mr Kutty and his nephew, Mohideen, were already expressing concern that the supply of antique Chinese furniture found in Malacca, especially those from old Baba homes, might be depleted before long. Many of the old Peranakan families had disposed of the bulk of their heirlooms, and the younger generation of Babas were increasingly resisting the persuasion of brokers and runners to part with the contents of their ancestral homes.

Strangely though, this sudden rage for local antiques and objects of art in Malacca did not have any significant impact on the junk and antique trade in Singapore and Penang – at least not until around 1971. In Singapore, the situation was quite the opposite of that in Malacca. Here the government's policy of rapid urban redevelopment to rejuvenate old and decaying buildings at the core of the city forced many traditional Chinese merchants and traders, as well as the descendants of Baba merchants, to relinquish their home-cum-shops and move to government-built flats in the outlying satellite towns. The result of this large urban displacement was that a substantial amount of old artefacts, including furniture, fixtures, fittings and other movables such as clocks, wall mirrors, chandeliers, screens, phonographs, pictures, scrolls, altar tables, porcelain, camphorwood chests and other knick-knacks of a bygone era, had to be cleared out and disposed of – mostly for a song to the junk-pedlar.

There was, therefore, a big glut in the junk market. CCC Junk Store, formerly located in a cul-de-sac off Bukit Timah Road, was filled with all sorts of bric-à-brac, mostly at giveaway prices. The custodian of an old *gongxi,* or clan association, off Balestier Road offered to sell the entire contents of that old building, consisting of paintings, calligraphy and 57 pieces of blackwood furniture, all in good condition, with the characteristic patina of long usage and ageing. The collection ranged from an imposing opium bed to several large cupboards, at least 20 armchairs, tea tables, semi-circular side tables, mahjong tables, altar tables, a couple of scroll tables, benches and divans. And it was all going for $3000!

The situation in Penang was somewhat similar, though there was nothing in Georgetown in those days corresponding to the kind of extensive demolition that was happening in Singapore. In the late 1960s and early 1970s, Georgetown still retained much of its former colonial charm and leisurely pace of life. As for the junk stores in Rope Walk, Kimberley Street, Carnavon Street, Kota Kolam and even Penang Road, they were quite simply filled with an incredible assortment of old furniture and other bric-à-brac. There were, in particular, two shops in Kota Kolam in which the whole of the ground floor was practically filled with either whole or dismantled parts of brass and brass-and-iron beds with their characteristic posters and three-sided balustrades. A certain Mrs Saw, who ran a junk store in Rope Walk, had a houseful of typically Fujian-style blackwood furniture, most of which was decorated with inlaid mother-of-pearl designs. Along Chulia Street, at least four old silversmiths were still turning out old-fashioned silver jewellery, while the porcelain shops in Carnavon Street were filled with a large selection of late 19th- and early 20th-century wares.

In fact, the sheer quality and variety of antique furniture available in the various junk stores in Singapore, Malacca and Penang at the time far exceeded anything to be found in the combined holdings of furniture of all the museums in Singapore and Malaysia. Those of us who took the trouble to visit these junk stores probably did not realize then that we were being treated to a once-in-a-lifetime opportunity of seeing and studying at first hand the fascinating varieties of antique furniture of the former Straits Settlements era. Unfortunately no one took the trouble to investigate and to catalogue the different kinds of antique furniture then extant; this was so with the other types of Straits Chinese cultural objects, but more so with furniture because it happened to be both beautiful and useful. Before long, some of the finest pieces were bought up and sent out of the country, while the rest – the more mediocre pieces – passed into the hands of local collectors and museums.

Over a quarter of a century has passed and the supply of old and genuine Baba furniture has virtually run out, except for reproductions which are being made nowadays in increasingly larger quantities to meet the desires of a younger generation of upper-middle-class professionals for period furniture of the Straits Settlements era. As authentic old furniture becomes more expensive and difficult to procure, the new generation of collectors have to content themselves with modern reproductions. There are a number of furniture dealers who hire the services of skilled cabinet-makers in Singapore and Malacca, and possibly in Kuala Lumpur and Penang as well, to make reproductions of antique furniture fashioned out of *merbau* wood – a local variety of hardwood similar in colour and texture to rosewood of the genus of *Dalbergia*, endemic to Malaysia's tropical rain forests.

Most collectors of antique furniture in Singapore and Malaysia have quite a fair idea of what I mean by 'Straits Chinese furniture', especially if they happen to have read my earlier works on porcelain, gold- and silverwork, and beadwork and embroideries of the Baba community. As for the descendants of traditional Babas of the former Straits Settlements, many will remember having seen these pieces of furniture in the homes of their grandparents; others will recall growing up in houses where such items were a common everyday sight. The difficulty for the student of the subject, however, is to define and describe the notion of 'Straits Chinese furniture' more precisely so that it refers only to those categories of household furnishings and movables which authentically reflect the tastes, customs and traditions of the former generations of Babas and, more importantly, excludes those types of furniture which are alien to Baba culture.

~ chapter one ~

What Is Straits Chinese Furniture?

Nearly 15 years ago, my wife and I attended a talk on Straits Chinese furniture given by a young and personable Malaysian who ran a business in antique furniture in Kuala Lumpur. Having acquired an interest in the subject, I was naturally very interested to find out what our young speaker had to say about this large area of study. I was eager to know in particular how he intended to define the term 'Straits Chinese furniture'. What arguments would he give for calling some furniture 'Straits Chinese' and others not?

Every student of Straits Chinese cultural heritage knew at the time that there was very little published information available. Contemporary writings on the subject were practically non-existent, while 19th-century writers had paid scant attention to Straits Chinese cultural artefacts. While photographs dating back to 1900 provided occasional glimpses of period furniture,

Teak furniture designed in English and European styles was already used by the Baba community in the 1880s. But teak-and-gold cabinets of the kind shown here only made their appearance between 1928 and 1939 when red-and-gold namwood wedding cabinets became increasingly scarce and expensive in the wake of the mounting civil war in China. Before long, however, local Shanghainese cabinet-makers were making up for the shortage in namwood cabinets by turning out teakwood versions of the originals. These, however, incorporated an architectural façade of European inspiration and traditional Chinese art motifs. Courtesy of Mr Peter Wee, Katong Antique House.

no systematic treatment of the subject existed. It was with these considerations in mind that we awaited our guest speaker with eager anticipation. The promise that his talk was to be illustrated with colour slides whetted our appetite even more.

But to our surprise and disappointment, he began with some perfunctory remarks about who the Babas were and, without more ado, plunged into a description of ancient Chinese furniture constructed out of several species of subtropical hardwoods of the genus of *Dalbergia*. Purple sandalwood and rosewood furniture, our young speaker pointed out, was traditionally made for those who could afford it, namely, the mandarins of the Imperial Court in China, including those of the scholarly class who held public offices. Since the more wealthy Babas of the former Straits Settlements habitually furnished their homes with a similar type of blackwood/rosewood furniture featuring mother-of-pearl inlays, our young speaker tacitly assumed that Straits Chinese furniture consisted exclusively of this category of traditional household furnishings. With this, he went on to describe the virtues of *huanghuali*, *zitan* and *hongmu* (Chinese trade names for the various species of *Dalbergia*), namely their smoothness of texture, their richly figured grain, their subtle shades of colour, ranging from light, golden brown to purple and black tones, and the denseness and heaviness of the wood – properties

which were greatly appreciated by ancient Chinese cabinet-makers. He also went on to draw attention to the demanding Chinese art of joinery in which the various components of a piece of furniture were held together, not by nails and screws, but by a combination of mortises and tenons, pegs and, where necessary, bone glue. Finally, we were treated to a presentation of slides showing a representative range of cabinet designs unique to rosewood furniture.

When the talk ended, it suddenly occurred to me that either we had come to the wrong lecture, or, more likely perhaps, the title was a misnomer. It was impossible that the speaker had never stepped inside a traditional Baba home in Kuala Lumpur, Penang, Malacca or even Singapore. If he had, he could hardly have failed to notice that quite a few varieties of furniture are to be found and each of them is stylistically conspicuous in its design. These range from several types of rosewood and blackwood chairs, stools, round tables, altar tables, semi-circular tables, opium beds, mirrors, picture frames and tall flowerstands, all inlaid with elaborate patterns of mother-of-pearl, to carved namwood wedding cabinets, wedding beds, chests-of-drawers, altar tables, benches, wedding chairs, washstands, etc., painted with reddish-brown lacquer and ornamented with goldleaf carvings and engravings. Carved teakwood chairs and dining tables, wedding cupboards, sideboards, roll-top tables, armchairs, break-front cabinets and games tables were also designed after the manner of English and European furniture, including Jacobean, Queen Anne, George III, Louis XVI, Renaissance, Gothic, Chippendale, Hepplewhite and Regency styles.

Then, perhaps, he would have been less inclined to assert that Straits Chinese furniture consisted exclusively of rosewood movables of the type traditionally used by the mandarins in China, without flying in the face of facts. Which, among these bewildering varieties of furniture, could be said to express more authentically the culture of the Babas? That he did not trouble to mention and describe the different types of furniture regularly found in old Baba homes could indicate that he might not have actually studied the interior fittings and other movables of a typical Peranakan house. Otherwise he would have noticed that the traditional Babas were more catholic and adventurous in their tastes than their counterparts in China, namely the mandarins.

Another feature about the lecture which reinforced the impression that our young speaker was perhaps not too familiar with the interior furnishings of a traditional Baba home was his inclusion of slides showing such items of rosewood furniture as scroll tables, used by Chinese scholars for painting, plain rectangular bookcases with splayed legs and low tables for supporting musical instruments such as the zither. Now anyone who is sufficiently familiar with Straits Chinese culture will assure you that such items of scholarly furniture were never found in Peranakan homes because the Babas were, until the beginning of the 20th century, largely a community of merchants and traders. Painting scrolls, practising calligraphy, playing the lute or reading Confucius' analects were not the habitual pastimes of merchants and traders. Hence, such items of furniture should not be included in the category of Straits Chinese furniture.

The so-called 'Portuguese' furniture

One other example will suffice to bring out the point I am trying to establish here concerning the initial difficulty a person encounters when referring to, or writing about, Straits Chinese furniture. There appeared, about a decade ago, in one of the many glossy magazines, an article purporting to describe what the writer termed as 'Portuguese' furniture peculiar to Malacca. It was suitably illustrated with a number of fairly good photographs showing representative examples of this type of antique furniture in the collection of a lady who happened to be the wife of a distinguished and highly respected High Court judge. The reference to 'Portuguese' furniture, or even 'Portuguese-style' furniture, was clearly intriguing, since Portuguese influence in Malacca had been completely eclipsed by the coming of the Dutch in 1641 – more than 350 years ago. It would have been highly unlikely, therefore, even for the most astute of antique hunters to discover authentic Portuguese furniture dating back to the 16th century. For one thing, the hot and steamy climate of Malacca is notoriously destructive of even the hardest timber, while termites, woodworm and other vermin relentlessly prey upon wooden structures of every sort. Besides, the chequered history of Malacca from the time that Alfonso d'Albuquerque conquered the city in 1511 to about the end of the 18th century, when the British seized control of Malacca from the Dutch, was marked by frequent outbreaks of war and hostility – a fact which makes it almost certain that the bulk of relics dating back to the Portuguese era (1511–1641) would have been largely destroyed, if not by the passage of time, then by the depredations of war.

Still, I took the trouble to scan through the

photographs of the so-called 'Portuguese' furniture just in case something interesting and unique might turn up. I did not find anything unusual or remarkable in the illustrations. Instead, it occurred to me that these examples of the so-called 'Portuguese' furniture turned out to belong to a category of Straits Chinese furniture made exclusively of teakwood and which became extremely popular with the Anglicized Babas of the Straits Settlements from about 1880 to the 1930s, up to the outbreak of World War II. Teakwood furniture of this type was largely modelled on antique English/European archetypes dating between the late 16th and the 19th centuries. The difference, not apparent at first sight, lies in the types of ornamental motifs employed: the motifs occurring on such locally crafted examples of English furniture were largely taken from auspicious and religious symbols characteristic of traditional Chinese art. This combination of English/European furniture designs and ancient Chinese ornamental motifs in teakwood furniture of this type is unusual as it is peculiar to Straits Chinese cultural artefacts. Some people have named it 'Malacca-style' furniture. I prefer to call it 'Straits Chinese' furniture.

Why the writer of the article in question should have plumped for the term 'Portuguese' to describe this type of furniture was not clear to me, since it was factually incorrect and misleading. It was possible, though, that he might have been misled into believing that, since the Portuguese were the earliest European settlers in Malacca and their descendants (however mixed through centuries of intermarriages) are still living there and speak a brand of antiquated Portuguese, it might be assumed that relics of the Portuguese era in Malacca, including Portuguese furniture, were still to be found. Alternatively, it might be hypothesized that the subsequent generations of Portuguese descendants continued the tradition of cabinet-making of their forebears, but incorporated motifs of local origin into their handiwork. And since extant pieces of the so-called 'Portuguese' furniture look quaintly European and Asian in design, the hypothesis seemed to have some basis in fact.

The truth of the matter, however, is that the bulk of the so-called 'Portuguese' furniture,

Left: The English-style chair and oval table shown here have been misconstrued by certain writers and collectors in Malaysia as antique Portuguese furniture. So, too, has the mirrored sideboard with a bow-front cabinet shown in Fig. 8. In actual fact, however, these pieces of furniture are only datable to the closing decades of the 19th century and/or the opening decades of the 20th century – their antiquated appearance notwithstanding. They are definitely not dateable to the 16th or 17th century during the Portuguese era in Malacca. And what is even more pertinent, they were crafted locally out of teakwood by Chinese cabinet-makers. Courtesy of Prof and Mrs Yusoff Talib.

Above: Teakwood sideboard. Notice that the table top is of teak rather than marble, while the central portion of the lower cabinet projects outwards to form a bow-front which is elegantly reinforced by a series of radiating petals from below. This style of cabinet design has its origin in 18th-century French furniture. It is not to be mistaken for antique Portuguese furniture of the 16th or 17th century. Height: over 6 ft (180 cm). Courtesy of Mr Peter Wee, Katong Antique House.

whether found in Malacca, Singapore or Penang, was probably made by skilled Chinese cabinet-makers, many of whom came from Shanghai from about the latter part of the 19th century. We have no evidence, either direct or circumstantial, that a strong and continuous tradition of cabinet-making ever existed among the Portuguese of Malacca. As a matter of fact, no antique Portuguese furniture, whether of the 17th century or any other subsequent period, is to be seen anywhere in Malacca – not even in the Malacca State Museum. Indeed, most extant pieces of this so-called 'Portuguese' furniture in private collections came not from old Portuguese homes in Malacca, but rather from old Baba homes in Singapore, Malacca and Penang. The older generations of surviving Babas and Nonyas will readily tell you that the bulk of their antique teakwood furniture was made by *tukangs* Shanghai (Shanghainese carpenters).

Towards a definition of Straits Chinese furniture

It is clear from the foregoing accounts that the notion of what constitutes Straits Chinese furniture is by no means so clear and unambiguous that most people would have no difficulty whatever in distinguishing between, say, rosewood/blackwood furniture of the type traditionally made for the mandarin class in China and a similar type made for the Straits Chinese. Likewise, it is not easy, except to people who have taken the trouble to study antique furniture in depth, to tell the distinguishing differences between, say, an original 17th-century Restoration period chair (1660–1702), and a local reproduction made for the Straits Babas at about the turn of the 20th century. Similarly, there are not many among avid collectors of Straits Chinese furniture who are apprised of the fact that clear stylistic differences exist between the type of red-and-gold carved furniture found in traditional Baba homes in Malacca and a corresponding type of red-and-gold furniture used as ceremonial wedding furniture by the Babas of Penang. And the difficulty we have here is not simply a matter of learning to sort out the different details concerning the structure and designs of the different types of furniture in question. Rather, it is the more fundamental one of deciding, on the basis of what we have already discovered concerning the various types of furniture regularly seen in old Baba homes, how best to define the notion of Straits Chinese furniture in such a way that it embraces those types of household furnishings and movables which authentically reflect the customs and beliefs of the Babas of that era.

This broad working definition of 'Straits Chinese furniture', while obvious enough when one reflects upon it, is fundamental in any meaningful discussion of the subject. But it is precisely what I found missing in most extant articles which have been written in several of those glossy magazines on the subject. It was the lack of such a working definition which marred the two discussions we noted at the beginning of this chapter. To recapitulate, the gentleman from

Kuala Lumpur concentrated all his effort on describing the beauty and wonder of blackwood/rosewood furniture, apparently because he was so enamoured of it that he omitted to take the trouble to study carefully the interior furnishings of a traditional Baba home. Also, his inclusion of such furniture as the mandarin scholar's writing table, tables for executing scroll painting, tables for supporting the lute or the zither and unadorned rectangular cupboards with splayed legs for storing books and calligraphic instruments indicated that he might not have realized that the scholarly pursuits of traditional mandarins in China were largely alien to the predominantly merchant and trading community of the Malacca Babas. Hence, such pieces of furniture, so dear to the heart of the mandarin scholar, could not, by any stretch of the imagination, be included under the rubric of 'Straits Chinese furniture'.

As for the article on the so-called 'Portuguese' furniture, or for that matter, 'Portuguese-style' furniture, the writer may not have realized that there is, in fact, no distinctive type of furniture which may be described as 'Portuguese' in the history of European furniture, even in Portugal itself! The kind of furniture found in 16th- and even 17th-century Portugal was largely inspired by, and designed after, the types of furniture found in Spain and Italy. And as for the so-called 'Portuguese' furniture found in Malacca, such household furnishings, whether they happened to be found in the homes of present-day descendants of 16th-century Portuguese settlers or in Baba homes, were in fact the handiwork of a former generation of Shanghainese cabinet-makers who operated small family establishments between the closing decades of the 19th century and the first two or three decades of the 20th century.

If we now apply the rule-of-thumb mentioned earlier, namely that only those types of household furniture, movables and fixtures customarily found in Baba homes which embody their customs and ways of life are to be regarded as genuinely Straits Chinese in taste, then there are three distinctive types of furniture which should be

included in a definition of 'Straits Chinese furniture'. They are:

(1) **Blackwood/rosewood furniture** of the type formerly made by Chinese cabinet-makers in Guangdong, Fujian and Zhejiang provinces, and (the point is worth noting) which usually came with ornamental patterns featuring mother-of-pearl inlays.

(2) **Carved namwood (*Machilus nanmu*) furniture**, mostly from Fujian and Zhejiang provinces, which was usually patterned with bright red or reddish-brown lacquer and sported elaborate ornamental carvings depicting figures, horsemen, court scenes, landscapes and floral patterns in giltwork.

(3) **Teakwood furniture**, most of which is modelled on English/European furniture designs dating between the 16th and 19th centuries. But, as Straits Chinese teakwood furniture was made

by Chinese cabinet-makers steeped in a Chinese tradition of cabinet-making, such Anglicized or Europeanized furniture differs from its original archetypes in subtle ways, such as, for example, in having Chinese ornamental motifs rather than European ones. But more of this later.

In addition to these three principal types of furniture widely used in old Baba homes, not only in Malacca but also in Singapore and Penang, one may occasionally discover that some of the wealthier Babas had all their household furnishings designed in exclusively European styles. A good example may be seen in the house of Mr Tan Chay Yan along Klebang Besar, Malacca. The internal fixtures of this spacious home included wood panels for the walls, pannelled doors, broad wooden staircases with Gothic balustrades, wooden partitions and wooden windows with coloured glass panes. The movable items of furniture, including chairs, tables, writing bureaus, cabinets and bookcases, were all made of teak. But the design was 19th-century English Gothic. Mr Tan's house was probably built towards the closing years of the 19th century, or perhaps at the turn of the 20th century.

Another wealthy tin and rubber magnate, Mr Eu Tong Sen (he was not a Baba but a Cantonese), built a large Germanic-style house on the summit of Mount Sophia, Singapore, in 1927 and furnished his entire house with European furnishings, including large bedsteads, Italian oil paintings, stained-glass windows, marble busts, etc. The dining room was

Left: In its natural state, freshly-cut namwood (Machilus nanmu) is of a greenish-brown colour. But when the timber has been exposed to the atmosphere after a period of years, it takes on a darker shade of brown – the greenish hue having been oxidised by being exposed. The altar table shown here, with its archaic carvings of cloud-and-dragon patterns, is a typical example of namwood furniture regularly seen in old Baba homes. Courtesy of Prof and Mrs Yusoff Talib.

Above: Although namwood is a dense and somewhat heavy timber, it is not classified as a hardwood in the same sense that rosewood, blackwood, mahogany, ebony and satinwood are said to be hard. And it is not impervious to wood rot caused by termites and other types of wood-boring insects either. For this reason perhaps, traditional Chinese cabinet-makers in the southeastern provinces of China made it a rule to varnish all their namwood furniture with several coats of red and brown lacquer in addition to gilding over the carved panels, as this red-and-gold set of cabinets shows. Courtesy of Mr Peter Wee, Katong Antique House.

particularly remarkable for its high ceiling, stained-glass windows and a massive dining table with a seating capacity of 24. The chairs, designed in Cromwellian style, sported leather backs stretched down by brass-head nails. The cushioned seats were also covered with leather held down by brass nails.

Of the three categories of furniture, the first type, namely blackwood/rosewood furniture featuring ornate designs with mother-of-pearl inlays, is what one should describe as 'ceremonial furniture'. It is usually laid out in a symmetrical fashion in the front or reception room of a typical Baba home and was intended for receiving and entertaining guests on all formal and ceremonial occasions, such as Chinese New Year, weddings and birthdays.

As for the second type, the red-and-gold, sometimes referred to as 'giltwood', furniture, it should also be regarded as ceremonial furniture. This is because all the various red-and-gold furniture in Baba homes was used for wedding ceremonies. In fact, all such furniture was kept in the bridal chamber. Red-and-gold furniture was constructed almost entirely out of a species of cedarwood said to be endemic to the southeastern part of China, known as namwood. Namwood furniture is largely confined to four-poster beds (both double beds and single beds), two-tiered wedding cabinets, chests-of-drawers, dressing tables, bridal tea tables with high-backed matching chairs without armrests, washstands, footstools, etc.

The uses which the third type of Straits Chinese furniture – including chairs, tables, bureaus, sideboards, consoles, tea tables, card tables, dining tables, display cabinets, benches, bookcases, divans, etc. – were put to were much more varied than those of the other two types. Apart from the fact that their structural designs were based on English/European archetypes and made entirely out of teakwood (*Tectona grandis*), which, incidentally, is not endemic to any part of China, this Western variety of furniture was never intended to be confined to any specific part of the Baba household.

While the more conservative Babas insisted on furnishing their reception halls with only blackwood/rosewood furniture of the type imported from Fujian and Zhejiang provinces (the Penang Babas appeared to have adhered more faithfully to this custom), the more avant-garde of the Anglicized Babas who have acquired a taste for things English, such as Mr Tan Jiak Kim and Mr Tan Chay Yan of Malacca, preferred to equip their reception halls with Western-style furniture. This included heavy and ornately carved teak-and-gold console tables with polished marble or granite tops (after the fashion of Italian and French consoles of the 17th and 18th centuries), large framed mirrors with elaborate carvings, Victorian armchairs and sofas, carved pedestal tables also with marble tops, paintings or prints of original European works, glass epergnes and centrepieces, and Victorian table lamps with ruby glass shades.

Upper façade of the Heeren Street house, Malacca, said to have been originally owned by Mr Tan Jiak Kim, the grandson of another well-known Malacca personality, Mr Tan Kim Seng. Notice the louvred windows, the recessed Renaissance Italian arches and the fluted side columns with Corinthian capitals. Mr Tan Jiak Kim was a prominent municipal counsellor of Singapore during the first three decades of the present century.

The Babas, unlike their more conservative compatriots who strictly adhered to old Chinese customs, were thus much more adventurous and eclectic in their taste for furniture, and other things as well. There is a historical reason for this. The Babas were the descendants of original Chinese immigrants, some of whom had been living continuously in Malacca since the beginning of the Ming Dynasty (1368–1644). While other communities of immigrant Chinese in Southeast Asia and elsewhere believed in preserving the Sinic purity of their customs and traditions by resisting as much as possible the influences of 'barbarian' cultures, the Babas, who had long been separated from the mainstream of Chinese civilization, tended to be more liberal in their attitudes towards things foreign to Chinese culture. After all, their forefathers were among the first of early Chinese traders who married native girls and settled permanently in Malacca. The descendants of these early immigrants not only came to adopt local customs and practices, but also spoke a patois known as 'Baba Malay'. The character and temperament of the Babas, which set them apart from other communities of overseas Chinese, may be attributed to their having lived in Malacca for several centuries. Likewise, the cosmopolitan character of the city itself was largely attributed to its having been the chief trading centre of Southeast Asia for more than 200 years (from

Every visitor to the historic Heeren Street in Malacca never fails to notice the presence of this imposing Dutch/German-style house because it is the tallest and most prominent piece of architecture along this street. It is said to have belonged to a wealthy banking family and was built during the second decade of the present century.

1400 to 1614), when merchants and traders regularly met and mingled to negotiate their business transactions. Hence, the kind of culture that eventually developed was less affected by parochial national habits and prejudices. This, then, was the kind of ambience that nurtured Straits Chinese culture down the ages.

However, where the development of a distinctive style of furniture was concerned, the influences of the Arabs, the Indians, the Javanese, the Bugis, the Acehnese and the Malays on the Straits Babas appear to have been negligible, except in minor details such as the occasional adoption of floral and foliated or arabesque designs into the ornamental-work of their furniture. The Arabs, Indians and Malays had no distinctive furniture of any sort to speak of (for example, they did not customarily sit on chairs, but rather on lovely, hand-woven carpets or mats laid on the ground), while the kinds of furniture which they subsequently developed for their own uses were largely based on the styles and techniques of cabinet-work peculiar to Chinese and European traditions. For this reason, where the first and second types of Straits Chinese furniture are concerned (carved blackwood/rosewood and red-and-gold furniture), they remained essentially Chinese in style and structure.

It was the coming of the Europeans to Malacca which had a decisive impact on the development of the third type of Straits Chinese furniture. There are, however, no extant written records which describe its origins and evolution. Historians, unless they also happen to be students of art and archaeology, do not, as a rule, pay any attention to the development of the arts and crafts, mainly because these humble artefacts do not influence the course of human history for better or for worse. Still, it is possible to surmise, on the basis of circumstantial evidence, that when the Portuguese arrived in Malacca early in the 16th century, followed by the Dutch in the middle of the 17th century, and finally by the English towards the end of the 18th century, they brought with them distinctive types of European furniture peculiar to their respective cultures.

In the beginning, the European traders and settlers probably brought with them some of the various types of household furniture which they needed from their own countries. But this must have been costly and inconvenient because furniture was bulky and took up valuable space in the hold. The voyage by sailing ship from England or Holland to Malacca in those days took some six months or more, depending on the vagaries of wind and weather. The European settlers must have discovered before long that skilled Chinese artisans and cabinet-makers were available in Malacca. At the same time, the wealthier Chinese merchants and traders living there were known to have had their own distinctive style of furniture which showed excellence not only in the joinery but also in the superb qualities of the wood used.

Whether it occurred to those early European traders that getting local Chinese cabinet-makers to turn out reproductions based on their own European originals was preferable to importing them is difficult to say. In any case, judging from all available evidence, neither the Dutch nor the English (not to speak of the Portuguese whose furniture dating back to the 16th and early 17th centuries had disappeared altogether) availed themselves of the services of local Chinese cabinet-makers. This is clearly indicated by the fact that

those extant pieces of Dutch furniture dating between the 18th and 19th centuries, which are found in Malacca or the major cities in Java, were almost certainly of European workmanship, judging, that is, by the types of wood used in the construction (oak, walnut, cedar, etc.) and the types of fittings attached to them. In Indonesia, Javanese reproductions of Dutch furniture appear to have been turned out in quantity only in the 20th century.

As for the English, they were the last of European maritime nations to colonize some of the countries of Southeast Asia. In fact, the British East India Company formally laid claim to Penang in 1786, Malacca in 1795 and Singapore in 1819. There is evidence that for about 90 years after the founding of Penang, or about 60 years after Singapore became a Crown Colony (that is, until about 1875–1880), British traders and administrators in the Straits Settlements relied on imported furniture from England for all their office and household equipment and fittings. Some of these types of furniture may still be seen in private collections in Singapore. However, from about 1880 or thereabout (one can't be too dogmatic about the dating here), reproductions of antique English and European furniture, made exclusively from teakwood, began to make their appearance. As they gained acceptance and popularity, the production of this type of furniture increased and continued for the next 50 years into the 1930s, when it began to decline. By the time World War II started, production had practically ceased altogether.

The earliest reproductions of English-style furniture made by Chinese (more likely Shanghainese) cabinet-makers in Singapore, Malacca and Penang were almost certainly commissioned by the growing ranks of colonial civil servants, officers of the British Armed Forces, or perhaps wealthy merchants of British business organizations who lived in the Straits Settlements. Since the quantity of furniture required, especially in the civil service and the armed forces, was large, importing all these office and household movables from England would be costly. It occurred to some people, therefore, that having their furniture requirements met locally by Chinese cabinet-makers was more economically feasible: teakwood, an excellent hardwood from Thailand and Burma, was readily available and labour costs and delivery time could be cut substantially.

The advent of English/European styles of furniture created a vogue for such elegant interior fittings which had an air of old-world charm about them. And the Babas, who had all along greatly admired the authority and elegant dignity which characterized the lifestyles of the *orang putih* (white men), naturally found the English/European type of furniture most appealing to their taste. More than any other community of overseas Chinese, the Babas, especially those from well-to-do families, became the most enthusiastic patrons of this type of English-style furniture. They proudly installed this furniture in their parlours, dining rooms and family rooms. In the course of time, the widespread use of English-style teakwood furniture in traditional Baba homes led to its being regarded as an intrinsic part of the Straits Chinese heritage.

So much then for a general account of what Straits Chinese furniture consists of and some of the initial difficulties associated with attempts to arrive at an acceptable definition of this term. In the following chapters, I shall discuss in greater detail each of the three types of Straits Chinese furniture.

~ *chapter two* ~

Blackwood/Rosewood Furniture

Of the three principal types of furniture peculiar to traditional Straits Chinese culture, blackwood/rosewood furniture is probably the oldest. From the viewpoint of structural design and ornamentation, it is among the most conservative of Chinese furniture. Even so, none of the oldest extant pieces found in the Straits Settlements, particularly Malacca, can, in my opinion, be dated earlier than the beginning of the 19th century. There are, in fact, no marked and dated pieces of blackwood furniture extant. Incidentally, I use the term 'blackwood furniture' to include both purple sandalwood, or *zitan,* and rosewood, or various types of *huali* woods, for reasons which will be apparent shortly. Most existing pieces of blackwood furniture found in old Peranakan homes are either of late 19th or early 20th century dating, that is, if we go by circumstantial evidence based on information concerning the year when the house in question was built, or failing which, the date when the furniture was installed. This being the case, the dating of antique Chinese furniture is more often than not based on conjecture. This is because it was not customary for Chinese cabinet-makers,

unlike their European counterparts (e.g. Boulle in France and Chippendale in England), to engrave either their names or the names of their workshops and dates on the pieces of furniture made by them.

Besides, the type of blackwood furniture most widely used by Baba clients – and they preferred only one type of blackwood furniture – invariably came with decorations made up of small and variously shaped pieces of mother-of-pearl inlaid on the more prominent surfaces. I shall, for convenience, refer hereafter to this type of furniture as 'inlaid mother-of-pearl blackwood'. According to Wang Shixiang[1] and Gustav Ecke[2], elaborately carved blackwood furniture, including the inlaid mother-of-pearl type, was introduced only during the Qing Dynasty (1644–1911), particularly during the 18th century in the reign of Emperor Qianlong (1735–96). In contrast, the best of classic Chinese furniture intended for royalty, nobility and mandarin officials, which was largely made during the Ming Dynasty (1368–1644), was simple, unpretentious and of elegant design. The relations between the various structural components of a piece of furniture were functional and clearly articulated. Ornamental carvings were kept to the barest minimum, superfluous decorations being completely dispensed with. Traditional Chinese cabinet-makers were content to rely on the richly figured

Blackwood chair in Cantonese style. The distinctive feature here is that the back rails and splat are modified to resemble bent and interlacing bamboo stems showing buds at the joints. Note that the cabriole legs are also of the same design. Private collection.

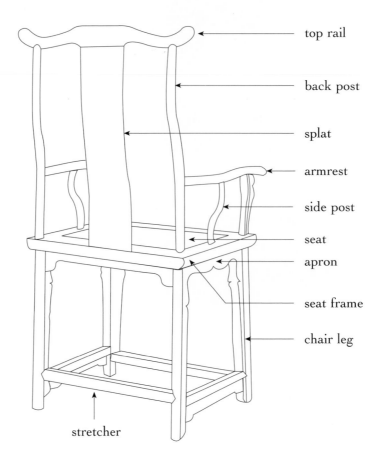

top rail

back post

splat

armrest

side post

seat

apron

seat frame

chair leg

stretcher

grain of *huanghuali* (rosewood) and *zitan* (blackwood), their warm colour tones ranging from golden honey to purple-brown with streakings of black, and above all, the sheer denseness and silky smoothness of the wood, to bring out the beauty in such furniture.

During the Ming Dynasty, and the Song Dynasty (960–1279) in particular, the homes of wealthy and titled mandarins were apparently less cluttered and crowded with furniture than they were subsequently during the Qing period. This may be inferred from paintings and woodcuts dating back to these periods showing the interiors of the imperial court and the homes of the landed gentry. Invariably, the furnishings were sparse and neatly arranged in a symmetrical and auspicious fashion. In such settings, the simple and classic beauty of Chinese blackwood furniture was shown at its best. By the Qing Dynasty, and

especially during the 18th century, at least five centuries had gone by and most types of blackwood/rosewood furniture now extant had already been invented and repeatedly copied down the ages. In a culture where the cult of originality was non-existent, and where the spirit of innovation was never actively encouraged, it was not altogether surprising that the later generations of cabinet-makers and designers made no serious attempts to improve upon the achievements of their Ming predecessors. Hence, they continued to turn out such household movables and fittings which largely retained the basic structure and designs of Ming archetypes. Modifications, whenever these were deemed necessary, were confined to matters of detail, such as the absolute size of a piece of furniture or greater emphasis on ornamentation through the use of relief carvings, inlaid-work, pierced-work, appliqué-work and marble slabs with curious streakings. Generally, blackwood furniture of the Qing period tended to be heavier and more massive in construction. Whereas the beauty of Ming furniture depended on the simplicity of its design, the functional

This is an illustration of what a typical Ming period chair crafted out of huanghuali *(the Chinese trade name for several species of* Pterocarpus*) looks like. The elegant design and structural soundness of Ming period furniture is clearly epitomised in this high-back armchair.*

articulation of its structure and the sensuous qualities of *huanghuali*, Qing period furniture relied for its appeal on a super-abundance of decorative carvings and inlaid ornamentation which would have horrified the most non-conformist of mandarins of the Ming Dynasty.

Towards the latter part of the Qing period, a newfangled method of beautifying blackwood furniture with a profusion of inlaid chips of mother-of-pearl combined, more often than not, with slabs of curiously patterned Yunnan marble, began to gain increasing popularity with the business and merchant class, particularly in Fujian Province. Blackwood furniture with inlaid mother-of-pearl decorations and Yunnan marble slabs was eye-catching, flamboyant and showy. This explains why it appealed to merchants and traders rather than to scholars and court officials steeped in a tradition of aesthetics which prescribed elegance in simplicity and understatement in matters of ornamentation. For this reason, perhaps, this type of blackwood furniture did not appear among the furnishings of the Imperial chambers in Beijing until about the turn of the 20th century, during the reigns of Guangxu, Empress Dowager Cixi and Puyi. However, in the film *The Last Emperor*, which, for the first time, filmed inside the grounds and the various chambers of the Imperial Palace and presumably used authentic stage props of the period, the young emperor, Puyi, was shown sitting on one of those huge, three-sided, low-backed couches ornately covered with inlaid mother-of-pearl decorations for his breakfast (or was it lunch?) in the company of his English tutor, Reginald Johnston. While most people may not have noticed anything unusual about the young emperor sitting on a couch of such barbarous ornateness, students familiar with the type of classic furniture traditionally used by the

aristocratic class in China must have been astonished that court furniture could have deteriorated to such poor taste in the twilight years of the Qing Dynasty.

Apart from this, most extant pieces of blackwood furniture in the Imperial Palace, which previously belonged to the Qing emperors (as seen in photographs of the interiors of what is now known as the 'Palace Museum' in Beijing) appear to have been fashioned out of several species of blackwood variously known by their trade names, *zitan* and *hongmu*. Experts are divided on whether they belong to *Pterocarpus santalinus* or *Pterocarpus indicus*, or perhaps some species of the *Dalbergia* genus of tropical and semi-tropical hardwoods. Certainly, they are among the densest, heaviest and hardest of hardwoods. They take on a fine polish, are of a very smooth texture, richly marked with figured grain and generously streaked with venations of purplish-black. Ornately carved furniture made almost exclusively out of dark – almost black – *zitan* wood was highly appreciated by the royalty of the Qing Dynasty[3].

For this reason, perhaps, Ming-style furniture of the types so magnificently illustrated in Gustav Ecke's *Chinese Domestic Furniture* and Wang Shixiang's *Classic Chinese Furniture* (including high-backed official armchairs, trestle-legged painters' table, square and rectangular tables, altar tables, low tables for supporting musical instruments, bookcases, display cases, splayed-leg cabinets, coffers, large couches with three-sided low panels, canopy beds, flowerstands, stools, etc.) appeared to have been conspicuously absent among the furnishings of the emperor's private chambers. Unlike the dark, more elaborately decorated furniture of the Qing period, Ming furniture is structurally elegant and functional, with ornamental carvings employed very sparingly. But

Most Chinese furniture buffs would probably describe this rather long and elegant blackwood (Dalbergia) table as an 'altar table' or, perhaps, as an ornamental table for standing antique Chinese porcelain vases. However, during the Ming, and even the Qing, dynasties, mandarin scholars in China regularly used such tables for scroll painting. Notice that on this table, the traditional sparsely adorned front and side aprons have been modified to form a crowded network of interlacing plum blossoms. Height: 3 ft (90 cm). Length: 5 ft (150 cm). Dating: Qing Dynasty. Private collection.

more distinctively, much of Ming furniture is made out of several varieties of rosewood, known by their Chinese trade names as *huali* or *huanghuali*. These have now been identified by many scholars as belonging to the genus of *Dalbergia*, of which several species, namely *Dalbergia hainanensis*, *Dalbergia latifolia* and *ormosia hennyi*, were commonly used for constructing Ming furniture. *Huanghuali* is different from *zitan* or *hongmu*. Its colour in antique furniture is that of golden honey or perhaps that of mature French cognac. The genuine pieces of vintage Ming have a certain translucency or glow about them, especially when the wood has been regularly polished and waxed down the ages. Beneath this lovely gloss is a wood of high density and great strength. It matures to take on an amber tone of medium to dark orange-yellow. There is evidence to show that old *huanghuali* was carefully selected from the most mature parts of the timber at the lower trunk of various species of *Dalbergia*. This is because mature timber has a deeper colour and more beautiful grain displaying wavy streakings, whorls and eyes. Certain subtropical species of *Dalbergia* from Yunnan, Thailand, Burma (Myanmar) and Vietnam emit a pleasant aroma which does not disappear with age. From very early times, the intrinsic qualities of *Dalbergia* have been greatly appreciated, so much so that traditional Chinese cabinet-makers sought to exploit the strength and sensuous beauty of *huanghuali* to create furniture of functional and expressive simplicity.

The style of Qing period blackwood furniture

But to return to Qing period blackwood furniture: apart from the preference of Manchu royalty for *zitan* furniture[4], the Qing style of furniture is characterized by an unrestrained tendency to overload it with an incredible profusion of carvings in the form of floral and foliated motifs, often intermingled with religious and auspicious symbols, including figures of immortals, *lohans*, gods and goddesses, mythical animals, insects and other mystical forms of representation. In many cases, there is not a square inch of surface which is not somehow filled with an ornamental carving of one sort or another. In Qing furniture the art of the woodcarver took on a prominence which had been unthinkable in earlier dynasties, so much so that it virtually overshadowed the skills of the cabinet-maker and the excellence of the joiner's art which was so clearly manifested in the classic furniture of the Ming Dynasty.

Following the precedence set by Qing royalty, this preference for ornately carved furniture soon became the sole criterion for assessing the value of blackwood furniture. The rationale behind this system of pricing was simply that the more carvings a piece of furniture carried, the more demanding was the skill required and the greater was the amount of labour expended in its production. That the use of excessive carvings and inlaid- and appliqué-work could ruin the essential design of a piece of furniture appeared either to have been ignored, or else dismissed out

of hand. For most people, then, the tacit assumption was that there could be no better justification for preferring the elaborate style of blackwood furniture than the fact that it enjoyed the patronage of Qing royalty. If anything, therefore, it behoved lesser mortals to emulate royalty in matters of taste!

We may take it then, that antique blackwood furniture of this style, which is datable to the 18th and 19th centuries, largely imitated the prevailing taste of the Qing court. It is true that in the eyes of conservative mandarin scholars and officials, Qing period furniture was overwrought, decadent and of poor taste. Nevertheless, during the Qing Dynasty, the arbitration of court taste did not devolve upon the traditional mandarins, but rather upon the Manchu nobility. For this reason, there is not, in any of the publications showing the interiors and interior furnishings of the emperor's private chambers in the Imperial Palace in Beijing, any sample of Ming-style or even authentic Ming period furniture to be seen. And yet many of these very chambers had been used by Ming

emperors (16 of them in fact) for 276 years, from Hongwu (1368–98) to Chongzhen (1627–44). How, it may be wondered, could the artistic legacy of such a long and illustrious dynasty vanish without a trace?

One possible explanation is that the Manchu royal house, from the ascension of Shunzhi (1644–61), was particularly concerned that the new dynasty should not in any way be associated with any object or emblem which might unwittingly serve to revive the cause or the memory of the Ming Dynasty[5]. Since furniture constituted a class of very conspicuous objects – and Ming furniture was distinctive and very Chinese in taste – it had to be done away with, if necessary, by fire. In the long history of China, the changes which attended the succession of one dynasty by another were always bloody and traumatic – the destruction of some pieces of furniture, imperial property notwithstanding, was an insignificant indication that the Mandate of Heaven had devolved upon a new order.

There was another likely cause for the almost total disappearance of Ming furniture. The

Imperial Palace which was built by Emperor Yonglo (1402–24) at the turn of the 15th century and added to by succeeding emperors, was made almost entirely from timber, except for the ceramic roof tiles and the floor. Hence, the risk of fire was ever present. According to official history, the palace was burnt down and rebuilt many times at enormous cost during its long history. Wanli (1572–1620) was said to have spent the stupendous sum of nine million silver taels repairing parts of the burnt down palace during his reign, while Tianji (1620–27) experienced three major outbreaks of fire during the six short years of his reign. The repairs were said to have amounted to six million taels. During the reign of the last of the Ming emperors, Chongzhen, the palace was captured twice and set on fire: in 1644 a young rebel, Li Zicheng, captured the palace, set fire to some of the buildings and forced the emperor to commit suicide in disgrace. In 1645 Wu Sangui and the Manchu forces defeated Li Zicheng, seized the palace and, once again, burned a large portion of the building to ashes[6].

Whatever remained of the interior furnishings peculiar to the Ming Dynasty – and a fair quantity must have survived the holocaust – must have been removed and destroyed by imperial decree, or else looted and privately sold to people who revered the memory and glory of the Mings.

The advent of the Qing Dynasty did not effectively force cabinet-makers to cease producing the Ming type of furniture, except perhaps for the Imperial Court in Beijing. Indeed, scholars and ex-officials loyal to the heritage of the Ming era continued privately to make use of a whole range of that classic type of furniture so noted for its elegance and expressive simplicity. The proof of this is borne out by the existence of many such pieces of Ming-style furniture in China, as illustrated lavishly in the works of Kates[7], Ecke[8]

and Wang Shixiang[9]. There are, among extant private collections outside China (e.g. Hong Kong, Taiwan and the Philippines), many pieces of blackwood furniture which are datable to the late 17th and 18th centuries. Thus, notwithstanding attempts by successive governments of the Qing Dynasty to erase the memory of the Mings, the tradition of woodcraft and cabinet-making unique to the Ming Dynasty continued to flourish in China.

Before we proceed to discuss Straits Chinese taste in blackwood furniture, some observations about the standard of workmanship may be noted here. Chinese mandarins, steeped in their admiration of Ming culture, were openly critical of late 18th- and 19th-century mother-of-pearl blackwood furniture which, with its emphasis on the superabundance of ornamentation, was regarded as clear evidence of decadence. Even so, the fact remains that the cabinet-makers of the Qing period, like their counterparts in the Ming Dynasty, were all trained in the same tradition of exacting craftsmanship which characterized the schools of Soochou and Hangchou during the Song Dynasty. There is no reason to suppose, therefore, that the cabinet-makers of the Qing Dynasty had lost the skill of cabinet-making and designing, joining and carving, simply because the Mandate of Heaven happened to have passed on to the Manchus.

Thus, where the skill of cabinet-making itself is concerned, Qing period products are comparable with those of the Ming Dynasty, with one major difference, namely that Qing furniture tended to emphasize ornamentation and gimmicky carvings at the expense of structural design and delight in the beauty of pure wood. Indeed, anyone who has had the opportunity of watching former generations of skilled Shanghainese cabinet-makers before World War II repair, reassemble

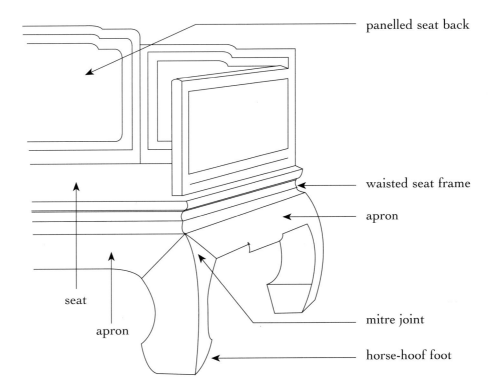

panelled seat back

waisted seat frame

apron

mitre joint

horse-hoof foot

seat

apron

Parts of a settee

and restore antique Qing period blackwood furniture would have found it hard to conceal his or her admiration for the unerring skill and precision with which the various members of a piece of furniture were cut, carved, and fitted together without the use of a single nail or screw: Chinese cabinet-makers relied entirely upon mortises and tenons for their joinery-work.

The Chinese art of joinery

This is one of the unique features of classic Chinese furniture, namely the conspicuous absence of nails, screws, dowels and pegs: all the joints are firmly secured by an ingenious variety of wood projections (tenons) of different shapes and sizes which are made to fit tightly into corresponding recesses (mortises) carved to receive them. Even glue (bone glue) was not allowed, except in unavoidable circumstances, as when a chair, stool or table is so constructed that it requires a squarish, rectangular or circular

stretcher at the base. In such instances, it is necessary for the vertical tenons to be secured to the mortises in the base stretcher by glue.

Two explanations at least may be advanced to show why the art of joinery in Chinese furniture depended on mortises and tenons and dispensed with the use of glue as far as possible. Firstly, blackwood furniture of the most classic type was constructed in such a way that it could withstand severe changes in temperature and humidity without causing unnecessary strain to the joints. Since the wood of well-seasoned *huanghuali*, *zitan* and other varieties of *Dalbergia* is extremely dense and hard, experience proved that joints secured by mortises and tenons provided the best protection against fluctuating changes of temperature and humidity. Secondly, it was customary for the Chinese to dismantle their more bulky pieces of furniture (e.g. canopy beds, huge altar tables, *kang*-type couches, tall cabinets, etc.) when moving house, or when shipping blackwood furniture across the seas to overseas buyers. The use of glue to fix the joints permanently would

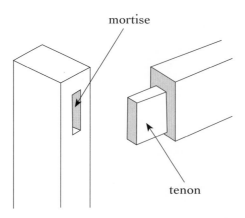

Tenon-and-mortise joint

mortise

tenon

Joinery

The method of joinery employed in all classical Chinese furniture of the Ming and Qing dynasties was based entirely on the use of tenon-and-mortise – pegs and dowels, not to mention glue and other adhesives, being avoided. However, the technique of tenon-and-mortise was not the invention of Chinese cabinet-makers. The ancient Egyptians, as far back as 1500 B.C., were already employing the art of tenon-and-mortise for fabricating their cedarwood furniture – extant photographs of chairs recovered from Thebes and the tomb of Tutankhamen clearly indicate that Egyptian cabinet-makers were already using tenons and mortises for joining the various parts of the chair together, including the use of pegs for reinforcing the joints.

Nonetheless, Chinese cabinet-makers remained unique in their strict adherence to the exclusive use of tenons and mortises in furniture joinery, as well as to the invention of some ingenious variations in the technique of tenon-and-mortise joinery, particularly the mitre joint.

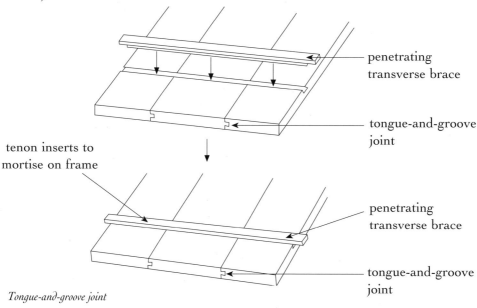

penetrating transverse brace

tongue-and-groove joint

tenon inserts to mortise on frame

penetrating transverse brace

tongue-and-groove joint

Tongue-and-groove joint

definitely be a hindrance for dismantling furniture. As for the use of pegs and dowels, so popular with 18th-century European cabinet-makers (the presence of which was regarded as a mark of authenticity), this would not do either. For one thing, pegs and dowels tended to mar the natural pattern and 'flow' of wood grain, without any compensating advantage, either for constructing or stripping down a piece of furniture.

Another characteristic invention peculiar to the Chinese art of joinery, and which is of considerable antiquity (datable to the Han Dynasty of 206 B.C.–A.D. 220), is the mitre joint. In mitre jointing, the two members of a piece of furniture, made to form a 90°-corner, are executed in such a manner that the connecting surfaces are cut at an inclination of 45°, with the interlocking structure, forming the complex of mortises and tenons, being concealed from view. This acute angular technique of effecting a joint allows the exposed surfaces of the connecting members to present a smooth and continuous plane whereby the 'flow' of the wood grain may be displayed to advantage. It also presents a balanced appearance in the structure of the furniture. By further bevelling and sculpting the surfaces of a piece of furniture, especially along the inner edges, the waist and the aprons, and by means of a complex of convex and concave planes, Chinese cabinet-makers were able to highlight the sheer qualities of pure wood. Not all mitre joints extant, however, are cut at inclinations of 45°; some are more than 45°, while others are less. In any case, the angle of a joint was entirely determined by the structure and design of a particular piece of furniture.

Since joinery in classic blackwood furniture was entirely executed by the use of mortises and tenons, a study of the various types of mortises and tenons found in such furniture, including the methods of sculpting these complex interlocking joints, provides valuable insight into the skill and quality of ancient craftsmanship. Among other things, it shows that precision cutting and joinery can be achieved without the use of modern power tools, but simply by eye and hand, aided with somewhat primitive hand-made tools. *Huanghuali* and *zitan* woods, when properly dried and well-seasoned, become exceedingly hard and dense, and hence are difficult to work with. However, they enable joiners to construct tenons and mortises of exceptional strength and complexity. If joinery posed no easy task for the joiner, the construction of an entire piece of furniture required an even greater expenditure of labour and skill of a very high order, involving the combined talents of the cabinet-maker, the joiner and the woodcarver.

Finally, a curious anomaly may be noted here: most writers who have written appreciatively about the skills and great craftsmanship which went into the making of antique blackwood furniture, especially Ming furniture, have consistently omitted to mention, describe or illustrate the kind of tools employed in fashioning these superb pieces of furniture. Most accounts simply do not include a chapter, or even a section, to show and describe the kinds of tools which Chinese cabinet-makers, joiners and woodcarvers regularly used for sawing, cutting, drilling, planing, carving, shaving and filing, nor for that

matter, the techniques by which various constituent parts of a piece of furniture are made and assembled to form the finished product.

Undoubtedly, such an account is probably more appropriate in a manual for would-be carpenters and cabinet-makers. The average intelligent reader, so it is felt, may not be interested in knowing how antique furniture is made. But equally he might, and a short account (suitably illustrated with diagrams of tools and furniture in various stages of manufacture) highlighting the more important aspects of furniture-making would go some way to providing a more in-depth appreciation of the *modus operandi* of Chinese cabinet-work. As it is, most of us have no clear idea of how classic Chinese furniture was made, our appreciation being largely confined to aesthetic contemplation of the finished product.

By contrast, many books on English and European furniture regularly include photographs, old engravings, lithographs and diagrams illustrating the incredible variety of ingenious tools which cabinet-makers used, the cluttered interiors of workshops and explanatory drawings showing how different furniture components (e.g. wood-turning, marquetry, etc.) were cut and finished.

Blackwood furniture in Straits Chinese taste

From a stylistic point of view, at least *four* different types or styles of blackwood furniture produced in China continuously from the Ming Dynasty to the end of the Qing period may be noted. First, there is the type of furniture already dealt with in the preceding section, which (by common consent of scholars and students of Chinese art) may be regarded as the classic type of Chinese furniture, namely Ming period pieces, distinguished by the sheer elegance and simplicity of their design. It was a style of furniture which virtually dispensed with ornamentation of any sort not related to its structural and functional design. Most scholars who have written about Chinese furniture invariably regard classic Ming period furniture as embodying the highest achievement of Chinese cabinet-makers, in much the same way that English writers regularly refer to Queen Anne period furniture in early 18th-century England as among the best in the English tradition of cabinet-making and woodcraft.

The second type of blackwood furniture which gained considerable popularity in the Qing Dynasty, from the reign of Emperor Qianlong up to that of Guangxu, refers to the variety of *zitan/huali* furniture which was profusely ornamented with relief carvings of floral and foliated motifs, and religious and auspicious symbols covering practically all exposed surfaces. As previously noted, this type of furniture came to be synonymous with the imperial taste of the Manchu royal house, and was endlessly emulated up to the end of the 19th century. All extant furniture and fittings in the private chambers of the Imperial Palace in Beijing belong to the Qing period style of furniture.

The third distinctive style was a logical follow-up of the second. It is characterized by a superabundance of ornamentation, including relief carvings and pierced-work which are further embellished by the application of inlaid-work consisting of thousands of scintillating pieces of mother-of-pearl chips. Nineteenth-century works of this style of furniture went even further by adding variously shaped slabs of Yunnan marble bearing unusual streakings and markings to table tops, the seats and backs of chairs, couches and canopy beds. Furniture in this style depends for its appeal not on the structural articulation of its overall design, but rather on the overwhelming

effect conveyed by the complex mass of decorative motifs dazzlingly highlighted by chips of mother-of-pearl, especially when set against a sombre, dark background of *zitan* wood. Curiously enough, the business and merchant community, known for its fondness of ostentation, found this style of furniture very much to its liking. We will discuss more of this later.

The fourth category of blackwood furniture may, for lack of a more suitable name, be termed 'Cantonese blackwood' because it was peculiar to Guangdong (Canton) and, from the second half of the 19th century, Hong Kong. The population of this area in southern China is predominantly Cantonese. Cantonese blackwood furniture may be regarded as a mixture of all the various styles noted above, except that Cantonese cabinet-makers and carvers tended to be more sparing and conservative in their use of carvings and inlaid decorations – in fact, inlaid mother-of-pearl ornamentation rarely occur in Cantonese furniture. Where relief carvings and pierced-work are employed, the motifs are usually large, bold and realistically depicted, after the fashion of Ming period carvings. The Cantonese were particularly fond of bamboos, lotuses and plantains. They also used marble slabs for the seats and backs of chairs more frequently than is perhaps desirable.

One of a pair of blackwood armchairs of the type which dispenses with the use of figured marble slabs and mother-of-pearl inlays. Instead, the rectangular pierced splats sport carvings of grapevine enclosing a circular panel with a qilin and a coin – both symbols of prosperity. The two side panels inside the armrests depict butterflies. Dating: 19th century. Author's collection.

But the most distinctive aspect of Cantonese furniture, in my opinion, was the impact of European furniture designs upon the conservative Chinese art of cabinet-making. Cantonese blackwood chairs and tables of 19th-century dating (18th century pieces being much more difficult to authenticate) show the strong influence of European designs: armchairs with shield backs, oval backs, scrolled armrests and cabriole-like legs were definitely European in taste. Cantonese cabinet-makers also borrowed the European concept of a settee with a high back and a curved top rail; they avoided padding chair seats and backs with stuffed cushions held down by brass tacks[10]. Instead, they filled the spaces on the backs of their chairs and settees either with bold relief carvings of floral and foliated motifs and/or marble slabs with curious streakings and wavy lines. Thus, with all the solid carvings of *zitan* wood and marble slabs built into its structure, Cantonese furniture became very weighty and bulky.

Of the four principal styles of blackwood furniture extant, it is the third category, featuring inlaid mother-of-pearl decorations, which was most popular with the Baba merchants and traders of Malacca, Penang and Singapore throughout the 19th century – the bulk of extant collections of mother-of-pearl furniture in the Straits Settlements is largely of 19th-century dating. This is shown by the fact that in most old Baba homes, it is this type of blackwood furniture rather than, say, the Cantonese version or the Manchu type with ornate carvings in relief or the handsome and well-proportioned Ming type, which takes pride of place.

I have never been able to elicit from present-day Babas any plausible explanation as to why their forebears preferred blackwood furniture with mother-of-pearl motifs to other designs in existence. Some to whom I posed the question simply shrugged their shoulders: for them these artefacts had existed in their houses for as long as anyone could remember and no one thought there was anything unusual about them. A couple of elderly Nonyas, however, said they believed blackwood furniture with inlaid mother-of-pearl decorations was preferred because it looked grand and imposing. Besides, only the well-to-do Babas could afford to own such furniture. While this may well be so, the evidence seems to indicate that the rage for mother-of-pearl furniture was consistent with the tradition of the Hokkiens in Fujian Province for several centuries. Thus, when the merchants and traders prospered in their maritime business, they tended to make a conspicuous display of their new-found wealth. And since the Babas are descendants of former generations of Fujian merchants and traders who settled in Malacca a long time ago, it was natural that they should emulate the attitudes and lifestyles of their forebears. Thus, they loved nothing better than to flaunt their riches, especially on all ceremonial occasions such as weddings, birthdays, Chinese New Year, mooncake festivals, anniversaries of their departed ancestors, etc. That being the case, one has only to look again at the four principal styles of blackwood furniture

In the eyes of many knowledgeable people, there is no doubt whatsoever that rosewood/blackwood furniture made to Cantonese tastes is, more often than not, characterized by simple refinement and elegant design. That Cantonese cabinet-makers, like their Ming counterparts in Zhejiang and Jiangsu provinces, celebrated the figured grain, the honey tone and sensuous beauty of pure rosewood is clearly seen in this reclining chair. Courtesy of Mr Peter Wee, Katong Antique House.

mentioned above to notice that the variety which features mother-of-pearl decorations is perhaps the most striking and showy of them all, aesthetic considerations apart.

Whether this habit of flaunting their wealth was crucial in determining their choice of blackwood furniture with ornate mother-of-pearl inlays, the fact remains that 19th-century Babas were consistently fond of showy and florid things. This is abundantly evident to anyone who takes the trouble to acquaint himself with the designs of, among other things, their ceremonial costumes, their porcelain, their embroideries and beadwork, their jewellery, their gold and silverwork, their art of cooking and, above all, the cluttered interior furnishings of their homes. The student of Baba culture will soon realize that the traditional Babas had a morbid dislike of void and vacant spaces. The art of understatement in ornamentation was utterly alien to their idea of what is beautiful and pleasing.

But then, the tastes of 19th-century Babas, both in the former Straits Settlements and in Java and Sumatra, were consistent with the prevailing fashion of the late Qing period, from the closing decades of the 18th century right through to the end of the 19th century. The Emperor Qianlong set the standard of good taste in the Imperial Court by his preference for art objects with ornate and colourful decorations. In fact, the use of mother-of-pearl inlays in blackwood furniture was first inaugurated in his reign.

Although the Straits Babas had consistently stuck to their preference for the mother-of-pearl style of blackwood furniture, their choice was largely confined to a narrow range of household furniture. This included high, rectangular altar tables, standard square altar tables, low-backed, throne-like armchairs (always in sets of three pieces consisting of two chairs and a tea table), semi-circular display tables (always in sets of two), a circular tea table with four matching stools, a pair of benches featuring side and back panels, *kang* couches (locally referred to as 'opium beds') each of which is complemented by a low table, a kind of day bed, occasionally a square mahjong table, flowerstands, picture frames and, in some rare instances, four-poster canopy beds decorated with inlaid mother-of-pearl patterns.

As a predominantly merchant and trader community, the former generations of Babas made no pretensions to scholarly tastes. For this reason, they did not equip their homes with furniture traditionally meant for the scholar-gentleman: one will not find in old Baba homes blackwood furniture of the types highlighted in Kates', Ecke's and Wang Shixiang's works, namely high-back official armchairs, round-back armchairs, scroll or painting tables, writing tables, display cases for antique objects, bookcases, low *kang* tables for resting musical instruments, cabinets with splayed legs, wine tables and coffers. This is as it should be, because, dating back to the Han Dynasty, the types of individuals who regularly embarked on voyages in search of trade, wealth and business opportunities consisted mainly of

View of the back hall of a traditional Baba home in Malacca showing the two large side partitions, which are ornamented with giltwood carvings, separating the front from the back hall. In the centre is a typical circular marble table which is supported by a stout central column standing on three short cabriole legs. Behind the table stands the ancestral altar table with its paraphernalia of religious objects and offerings.

merchants, traders, artisans, soldiers, revolutionaries, free-booters and even escaped criminals. Mandarins, landed gentry and nobility, being more conservative and less adventurous in their outlook, were averse to entertaining the prospect of sailing away in uncomfortable junks in search of some delusive objectives and maybe having to settle down in some barbarian country.

Those pieces of blackwood mother-of-pearl furniture which the Babas imported from China for their domestic use were intended mainly for furnishing the main hall, where they regularly received their guests and business associates. They were literally showroom pieces, specifically made to look grand and eye-catching. The arrangement of the furniture was also noteworthy, although it was not peculiar to the Straits Babas. In fact, it largely imitated the pattern of furniture layout for the home of every mandarin official in China from the Ming Dynasty to the end of the Qing Dynasty. Among other things, the rules – largely unstated – required that (1) the furniture must be organized in a balanced and symmetrical fashion, (2) it must always come in sets or in multiples of two, and (3) the various movables must be placed side-by-side with their backs against the wall, so that as much space as possible in the centre of the chamber is left empty. The various pieces of furniture were arranged as though the reception

hall of a mandarin's home – in our case a Baba merchant's home – were a replica, on a somewhat smaller scale, of the reception hall of some official of the Imperial Court.

Applying these guidelines to the arrangement of furniture, the interior decor of a typically traditional Baba reception hall in Malacca, Singapore and Penang is as follows: on entering the main door into the reception hall, the visitor notices at once that the centre floor space is taken up by a circular tea table with four matching stools of the same design. Next, he notices that the space along each of the two side walls, to his left and his right, is taken up by chairs and tables placed side-by-side with their backs against the wall and arranged in an identical pattern. The mode of arrangement along each side of the wall is as follows: a semi-circular display table is placed in the middle, and two sets of elaborately carved, throne-like chairs (each set consisting of two chairs and a small tea table placed between them) with matching rectangular tea tables are placed on either side of it. The space at the far end of the wall facing the main door may be left blank. A partition consisting of eight gilded wood panels decorated with carvings and lattice-work, reaching up from the floor to the ceiling (about 12 feet), may be substituted for the brick-and-cement wall. However, in those houses where the partition between the main reception hall and the family room is a brick-and-cement wall, the space in front of the wall may be taken up by a set of two altar tables, one of which is large, high and rectangular in shape, while the other is square (3 feet 6 inches by 3 feet 6 inches) and somewhat lower. This set of altar tables is

View of the interior of another Baba house, also in Malacca, showing the circular blackwood tea table with matching stools, set against a background made up of four high teak partitions, carved and lacquered in black and gold. The side door at the far end (left) gives a glimpse of the kind of blackwood furniture used in this house.

usually dedicated to some household god or goddess who happens to be revered by the householder and his family. Statues or painted portraits of the deity are usually displayed, together with all the paraphernalia of religious offerings (e.g. an oil lamp, joss sticks, candles and candlesticks, incense burners, offerings of fruit and flowers, flower vases, etc.). Finally, behind the visitor to the left and right, namely the spaces below the two front windows flanking the main door, there are two benches of a relatively unadorned design.

With that, we complete our general survey of the standard types of floor furniture in mother-of-pearl style in the main reception hall of a typical Baba house. If we now take a look at the walls in the reception hall, we discover that they, too, are adorned with paintings, pictures, hanging scrolls, mirrors and black lacquered boards with carved and gilded characters. In particular, we may notice that hanging directly above each of the two semi-circular display tables are two huge mirrors hung in such a way that they tilt slightly forward. These mirrors may be mounted in blackwood frames embellished with inlaid mother-of-pearl or, as is the case with the more Westernized Babas, they may be made entirely of Bohemian glass. In other instances, we may encounter large rectangular mirrors held in place by broad teakwood frames

which are carved and gilded with floral and foliated carvings in high relief. Some of these mirrors are 5 feet 6 inches high and 3 feet 6 inches wide, and each of them could weigh up to 100 lbs or more! On either side of these large mirrors, the wall space is taken up either by pairs of narrow, rectangular pieces of framed embroidery (never tapestries for some curious reason) or, perhaps, oil paintings by some little-known 19th-century European artist. It is, however, rare to find silk hangings of calligraphy in old Baba homes because apparently latter-day Babas could neither read nor write Chinese characters. However, black lacquered signboards ornamented with two or more carved and gilded characters are occasionally encountered.

Small blackwood picture stands with inlaid mother-of-pearl, standing about two feet high and mounted with panels of silk embroidery or bead-work, or perhaps a combination of silk embroidery and beaded designs, are usually placed upon the pair of semi-circular display tables in the reception hall.

Repertory of traditional blackwood/rosewood furniture

Chairs

The standard Straits Chinese blackwood chair is a square, throne-like piece of furniture embellished with ornate patterns of inlaid mother-of-pearl. Unlike the classic Ming chair, the chair back is low, reaching up to shoulder level, and is perpendicularly straight without any hint of raking. In fact, it is prefabricated separately to

Rail and balusters of part of a restored staircase. The landing post is newly constructed probably out of nyatoh *timber – a variety of medium-hard tropical wood found in West Malaysia. In the background is a partial view of a large blackwood opium bed decorated with elaborate inlays of mother-of-pearl. Courtesy of Mr Peter Wee, Katong Antique House.*

form a rectangular frame which is then tenoned into the back edge of the seat at the two extremities. In prefabricated construction of this sort, the traditional components of the chair back, such as the uprights, the top rail and the central splat, disappear. Instead, the uprights, for example, now appear as the stiles of a modified rectangular frame rather than as continuous components of the rear legs, fitted to the corners of the seat frame at mid-level, with stretchers at the base.

As for the top rail, it now appears not as a distinct and separate horizontal bar, but as a modified horizontal component of the back frame mitred to the stiles. The most common type of top rail or cresting panel, regularly seen in the Straits Chinese style of blackwood chair, is that of the double hump thus:

In the case of classic Ming chairs, however, the top rail is a crossbar shaped like a yoke – the central portion of the top rail being somewhat flat or horizontal, while the two extremities curve gently upwards thus:

As for the so-called '*lohan* chairs', the top rail is a curved and rounded bar, so constructed that it is tenoned into both the front and back posts, as well as the curved back splat, to form a circular railing.

All high-back Ming chairs traditionally feature a curved splat centrally located between the back posts and secured in position by the top rail and the seat frame. This is meant to support a person's back when he is seated on a chair. It is an essential component of the chair back.

But by the time of the Qing Dynasty, the designs of chairs had undergone some radical changes – for the worse, in my opinion. In particular, the armrests and chair back were now constructed not as integrated components in the structural design of the chair, but as self-contained units, separately made and fitted to create a chair of a rather box-like structure. Thus, instead of the traditional chair back featuring the normal splat curved in a concave fashion to counterbalance the rake of the back posts, a typical Qing period chair features a frame-like chair back with a built-in circular or rectangular casing enclosing a slab of grey Yunnan marble, usually marked with curious streakings simulating a landscape of sorts. Carvings of floral and foliated and/or other auspicious symbols fill up the remaining spaces between the circular panel and the inner frame of the chair back. In those instances where marble slabs are not employed, a different kind of splat-substitute, such as a rectangular, vase-shaped or flower-basket panel cramped with carvings, is used. The carvings are invariably executed by a combination of pierced-work and mother-of-pearl inlays.

The armrests, normally constructed with the help of the front and side posts, are now substituted by two rectangular frames, considerably smaller than the chair back frame, featuring carved motifs. These side frames are tenoned into the seat frame at the base and the chair back frame to ensure a rigid and firmer attachment.

As indicated previously, the chair seat in all Qing period blackwood furniture is not, as with that of a typically European chair, constructed of a seat railing which is supported at the corners by four legs and below by a network of webbings

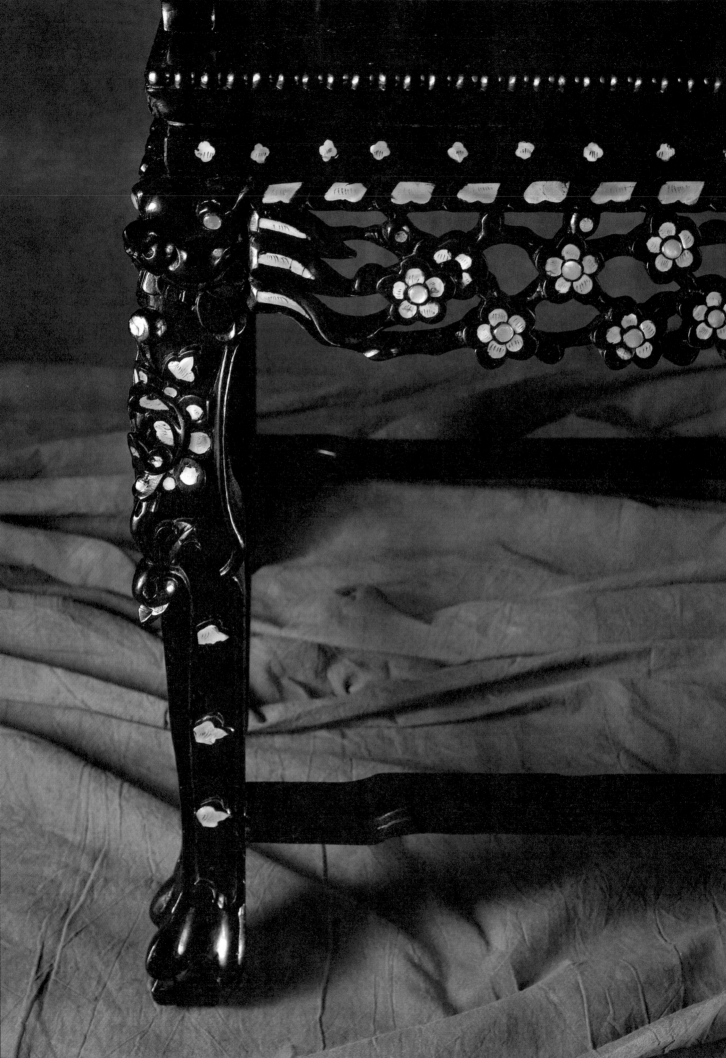

over which a stuffed seat is upholstered. Stuffed furniture was, in any case, non-existent in China. Rather, the chair seat in Chinese blackwood furniture was made up of a complex of two separately constructed, horizontal frames, super-imposed upon each other. The top rectangular frame is the seat frame proper. It encloses a slab of wood to form the seat. Alternatively, the seat is made up of a mat of woven bamboo strips. Sandwiched into the bottom of the seat frame is a slightly smaller rectangular frame wth rounded sides known as the 'apron'. The function of the apron is to strengthen and reinforce the seat frame above, as well as to connect it to the stretchers below. As with all other types of classic blackwood furniture, the joinery for the seat frame, the aprons and the stretchers is effected by mortises and tenons.

In harmony with the square and box-like structure of the chair, the legs have square cross-sections and rounded edges. They are mounted in a straight and perpendicular manner without the slightest hint of splaying that one notices in the high-back armchairs of the Ming Dynasty.

Left: A close-up of the cabriole front leg of the blackwood chair featured above showing the gargoyle mask and mother-of-pearl inlays. True to its traditional square form, the knees of the front legs are much less pronounced. Courtesy of Mr Peter Wee, Katong Antique House.

Above: This detailed picture of one of the two blackwood chairs shown on pages 40–41 shows more explicitly the overall structure of a typical Hokkien/Baba chair. Apart from the clear and elegant articulation of the various structures, the most notable feature is that the front legs are cabrioled to end in claw-and-ball feet, while the knees are carved to resemble gargoyle faces. Usually the Hokkien/Baba type of chair has straight legs. Courtesy of Mr Peter Wee, Katong Antique House.

Among the more highly decorated types of blackwood chairs, the upper extremities or 'knees' of the front legs are carved with gargoyle-like *taotien* masks which are highlighted by chips of inlaid mother-of-pearl. Four base stretchers, mounted between five and six centimetres above the ground, serve to reinforce the strength and rigidity of the legs. Incidentally, the bar over the front stretcher was meant to be a footrest. For some reason or other, it was never customary for a Chinese to sit on a chair with his feet (even when wearing shoes) resting on the floor, partly because chairs were never placed on floors which have been fully carpeted from wall to wall. Chinese winters, especially in the north and the west, were severely cold and the uncarpeted part of the floor was much too cold for one to rest one's feet. Hence, chairs had to be so constructed that a horizontal bar placed directly over the front stretcher serves as a footrest. In antique chairs this bar always shows signs of wear and abrasion. In consequence, the chair seat of a traditional blackwood chair (even without a cushion or upholstery of any sort) is higher than that of an average European chair. In fact, the average height of the chair seat in such Chinese chairs is about 19^1/$_2$ inches (49 centimetres), while that of an average European chair is just over 17 inches (42.5 centimetres).

The traditional Chinese cabinet-maker was not unique in designing his chairs to include four base stretchers; European chairs up to the 17th century regularly sported similar base stretchers. The only unusual feature of Chinese chairs is that the front stretcher, reinforced by a thin horizontal bar, doubles up as a footrest, whereas in pre-

18th-century European chairs the base stretchers merely served as carpentry devices for reinforcing the strength and rigidity of the legs. So ingrained was the conservatism of Chinese cabinet-makers that even when they were commissioned by wealthy Straits Chinese merchants during the 19th century to build chairs for use in tropical conditions, they did not, except perhaps among Cantonese cabinet-makers, modify the overall height of the chair seat for these square and throne-like chairs.

Incidentally, blackwood chairs with mother-of-pearl inlays are not the only type of antique furniture extant throughout Malaysia and other parts of Southeast Asia where Chinese communities have flourished. Successful merchants and traders belonging to other dialect groups (e.g. the Hakkas, the Hainanese, the Teochews and the Cantonese) also commissioned blackwood chairs, among other items of blackwood furniture, for their homes and business establishments. The difference between the Babas and the more conservative Chinese merchants and traders was that the latter preferred their type of blackwood furniture to be *without* mother-of-pearl inlays. The decorations in their type of blackwood furniture consisted largely of relief and open-work carvings. In the Cantonese variety, the carvings are sparingly executed. And from an aesthetic point of view, blackwood chairs without mother-of-pearl inlays undoubtedly look a lot more pleasing, as they display the highly-figured grain of *zitan* and *huanghuali* more effectively.

Stools

Historically speaking, the stool was one of the oldest and commonest items of household furniture in China. It was, and still is, more universally used in China than in any other country in the world. For a thousand years at least, stools, rather than chairs, featured conspicuously in homes, shops, tea houses, street stalls, restaurants, farms, schools, workshops, monasteries, temples, theatres and even the various households of the Imperial Court. By contrast, the chair, by which is meant a large, throne-like piece of furniture with a high raked back, with or without armrests, was a latecomer. From the Song Dynasty to the Ming Dynasty, it was used mainly as a ceremonial piece of furniture reserved for officials and nobility[11]. The stool, however, was made in large quantities. Even today, in many parts of China and Southeast Asia, it remains the commonest piece of furniture for sitting on while performing a whole variety of daily chores, from eating, feeding, drinking, cooking, washing and sewing to darning socks and weaving silk.

So widespread was the use of the humble stool throughout China (as illustrated in many ancient paintings, some dating back to the 10th century) that most people hardly notice it at all. However, the more astute students of antique Chinese furniture who have observed how universally used the stool was, and still is, throughout China have been led to believe – rather erroneously in fact – that until fairly recently, there were no chairs and that the Chinese either sat on the floor like all nomadic tribes in Central Asia or perhaps on low stools. P. S. Fry[12], the English authority on antique (Western) furniture also writes: "In 1600 the Chinese were still sitting on the ground or on low stools for meals or to drink tea from bowls on low tables. Seventeenth-century tables and stools had curved scroll legs, or straight legs turned inwards towards the bottom." The statement is as misleading as it is erroneous.

It was not customary for the Chinese in China or elsewhere, even for the poorest of peasants, to sit on the ground, unless the floor was suitably covered with grass mats, wooden planks or, better still, woollen carpets. This was because the floor, especially in autumn and winter, was much too cold to sit on. Unlike nomadic tribes in Central Asia, the floor of most Chinese homes was uncovered and uncarpeted. Woollen carpets were expensive luxuries which only the nobles, mandarin officials and wealthy merchants could afford. If the Chinese were shown sitting on the ground, it was usually in the interiors of the court or the homes of some wealthy officials who could afford to carpet the floor. Musicians were normally shown either sitting on the carpeted floor or on low stools. As for the majority of peasants, they either squatted or sat on low, homemade stools constructed out of bamboo strips or wood obtained from locally-grown trees.

Neither was it true that the Chinese began to sit on chairs only from 1600 onwards. What is true, however, is that most extant blackwood chairs are unmarked and undated. Nevertheless, the Ming Dynasty lasted 276 years from its inception in 1368 to its eventual demise in 1644. Hence, if a chair were, on stylistic and other circumstantial evidence, dated to the Ming Dynasty, it could be as early as 1400 or as late as 1600. In fact, if we are to believe the evidence presented by those rare and authenticated scroll paintings still extant (and there is no reason why we should not), the Chinese have been sitting on chairs *and* stools as far back as the Five Dynasties (907–960) which succeeded the Tang Dynasty (618–906). For example, a painting by Gu Hongzhong dated to the 10th century, entitled *The Night Revels of Han Xizai*, which is in the collection of the Palace Museum in Beijing, shows an elderly personage dressed in white and sporting a tall, tapered black cap, sitting on a high-back chair without armrests listening to a group of

female musicians performing with flutes. Judging by the posture of these musicians one can surmise that they were sitting on low stools. This is confirmed by the outlines of the barrel stool on which the male musician sat. Another painting, entitled *Concert at the Palace*, by Zhou Wenju, displayed at the Art Institute of Chicago, is also dated to the Five Dynasties. In it, another elderly personage, dressed in white but sporting a different sort of black cap, is shown sitting at the corner of an enormous *kang* bed (or platform) listening to an orchestral performance by female musicians. What is interesting about this painting is that the lady-in-waiting is shown sitting on a round, cushioned seat stool supported by four inward curving legs. Finally, there is a vertical scroll in Tofuku-ji, Kyoto, which shows a portrait of Wu Zhun, the Zen master, sitting on a large, solidly built blackwood armchair with a high and curving back and cabriole-like legs curving outwards at the feet. The painting is dated to 1238. There is no doubt, then, that stools as well as chairs of a very highly developed design were already used in China by the 10th century, except that in the case of chairs, only high-ranking people were privileged to sit on them.

But be that as it may, the popularity and ubiquity of the stool as an item of furniture in Chinese society throughout the ages is definitely not reflected in Straits Chinese culture. Except for the circular tea table with its four matching stools (usually with square or circular seats supported on four legs) placed in the centre of the main reception hall of a traditional Baba home, the stool hardly features anywhere else in the house. The exception is perhaps in the kitchen, where one finds a few low stools made out of local woods and designed in native style, namely a flat, horizontal slab of unpainted wood supported at both ends by two smaller rectangular slabs of wood, vertically nailed into position.

The Babas did not care much for stools, which they probably regarded as menial and plebeian, and thus more befitting of peasants and labourers. They much preferred chairs, especially that variety of high-back teakwood chairs with armrests, fashioned by local carpenters after the designs of antique English/European chairs, which appeared to be more dignified and more comfortable to sit on. (This will be discussed in more detail in chapter four.) For this reason, it was not customary for the Babas to sit on stools when eating, drinking, conversing, sewing, embroidering or performing any of the daily household chores. As for the circular tea table with its set of four matching stools placed in the centre of the reception hall, this set of furniture was intended more as a formality than as a functional item of the furnishing. Neither guests nor members of the family regularly sat on the stools around the table for socializing; on the contrary, guests were usually ushered to sit on the square-back, throne-like armchairs placed against the side walls of the reception hall.

In any case, stools made according to traditional Straits Chinese taste were normally embellished with inlaid motifs of mother-of-pearl. However, the Babas seemed to have avoided stools of the more conservative design, namely drum- or barrel-shaped stools supported by four or six inward-curving legs fixed to a circular base stretcher. Generally, they preferred stools with square, circular or, in some cases, fan-shaped seats tenoned to seat railings, each of which is supported by four square-cut legs terminating with hoofed or claw-and-ball feet.

Settees and couches

In antique blackwood furniture made according to Straits Chinese taste, the settee is a long wooden bench with a high back and side panels serving as armrests. The high-back bench was perhaps not an original design of Chinese furniture and may have been inspired by European settees, some of which could have been imported to Guangdong during the 18th or 19th century. Nonetheless, the Chinese had, as far back as the 10th century, during the era of the Five Dynasties, invented a huge *kang* bed rather like the size of present-day king-sized beds without the thick mattress. This featured upright panels on three sides of the bed, clearly seen in the two scroll paintings by Gu Hongzhong and Zhou Wenju mentioned earlier.

The traditional Chinese version of a settee is a long and narrow rectangular bench sporting three rather low side panels, perhaps no more than 10 inches (25.5 centimetres) high. The high-back settee, in which the back panel is constructed in three separate rectangular panels, with the central panel taller than the two flanking ones, was either a European idea or a later development of the Qing period.

In Straits Chinese homes, two types of settee-benches are to be found: some blackwood benches with inlays of mother-of-pearl have low side panels or railings, while others have shoulder-high back panels and lower side panels. The high-back settees with mother-of-pearl inlays tend to be somewhat more garish and overwrought because of the sheer quantity of mother-of-pearl chips required to fill the wood panels. Such settees were found more frequently in the homes of Penang Babas than those in Malacca or perhaps Singapore. This is to be expected because the Penang Babas appeared to have been more conservatively Chinese or Hokkien in their tastes. Georgetown was more predominantly Chinese than Malacca, which had a long history of Minangkabau, Portuguese, Dutch and English influences on its Baba culture.

A typical Straits Chinese settee is constructed on the design of the square, throne-like blackwood armchair we described earlier. In fact, it is just an elongated version of the low-back armchair – its length being equivalent to that of three such chairs joined together side-by-side. The seat, as discussed, is not a simple seat frame held together by outward curving aprons, supported at the corners by four legs and superimposed by the seat frame. It is a complex of three flat frames surmounted one on top of another: the topmost seat frame encloses a floating panel which is supported by a number of transverse braces underneath. The seat frame is then tenoned at the corners into a slightly smaller, waisted frame in which the outsides project concave surfaces – thus the waist-like effect. The two frames thus fitted together are finally attached (again by tenons and mortises) into the seat railing which is made up of four outward curving aprons held together at the corners by the four legs.

The four legs are not exactly straight and perpendicular because there is a certain bulge and curve on the outer surfaces from the shoulders to the feet, while the edges are all rounded somewhat. Chinese cabinet-makers seemed to have had an aversion to sharp and clear-cut edges. The feet are mostly hoofed and curve inwards. Incidentally, the legs of all blackwood chairs are carved and sculptured out of solid blocks of wood; it was considered unworthy of a craftsman to attach separate ear-pieces to the shoulders of cabriole legs, as was regularly done in European chairs of the 18th and 19th centuries.

A typical Straits Chinese settee is just over 5 feet (150 centimetres) long, over 2 feet (60 centimetres) wide and from 2 feet 6 inches (75 centimetres) to 3 feet 6 inches (105 centimetres) high. It is smaller than similarly designed couches of the early Qing and Ming periods. An example of a low-back, three side-panelled couch of this design, illustrated in plate 22 of Ecke's work, measures 7 feet 6 inches (200 centimetres) long, 3 feet (90 centimetres) wide and 2 feet 8 inches (80 centimetres) high. Except for the Cantonese type of settee, which was apparently influenced by European settees, all traditional Chinese settees are much too large and too deep to fit the human body comfortably. It is not possible to sit on a Straits Chinese settee and lean backwards because the depth of the seat is slightly over two feet (60 centimetres). Some writers have speculated that Chinese blackwood chairs, or settees for that matter, were deliberately made big and deep enough to accommodate a variety of cushions (these were usually stuffed with dried grass fibres) and fitted with armrests. Photographs of the various types of thrones and chairs in the Imperial Palace in Beijing clearly show that they come with padded seats and backs, and some even have cushions to serve as armrests. Straits Chinese blackwood chairs and settees are, however, rarely padded with seat and back cushions. This is only done during wedding ceremonies when chairs intended for the bride and groom are draped with red embroidered covers held in position by seat cushions.

Traditional settees and couches are constructed without stretchers and the strong and solidly carved legs are left freestanding. However, dispensing with stretchers meant that the aprons had to be sufficiently broad and thick to withstand the strain caused by outward-sheering forces when pressure is applied upon the seat. One has only to examine the aprons of most extant couches and settees to appreciate the strength and thickness of these component structures.

In passing, it ought to be mentioned that the most elegant of the high-back blackwood settees are not those made to Straits Chinese taste, but those made in the Cantonese style. The Cantonese settees are less squarish and rigid-looking. This may be attributed to the fact that traditional Cantonese cabinet-makers, like their Ming predecessors to a large extent, preferred to carve and sculpt most of the component parts of a piece of furniture into rounded (oval, in fact) members. Very often they were carved to simulate bamboo stems, complete with notches and buds. They also showed a pronounced inclination for the curved line and avoided, whenever possible, anything that was straight or angular – the only exception being the seat frame which, in a settee or a chair, requires a rectangular structure. Front legs were sculpted whole out of solid blocks of blackwood to give that characteristic cabriole or elongated S-shaped profile, but they did not always terminate in hoofed or claw-and-ball feet. Some cabriole legs were simply rounded and tapered at the base. Rear legs were similarly rounded and constructed in one whole all the way from the ground to the top where the back posts are joined to the top rail. In order not to give a straight and rigid profile to the seat back, the two uprights were carved to fan outwards and upwards where they are met and joined at

Of the various types of blackwood benches and settees found in old Chinese homes in Singapore, Malacca and Penang, the most elegant and comfortable ones are those made in what I have described as the 'Cantonese style'. Cantonese settees like the one shown here have two important features which make for bodily comfort: (1) the seat is low enough (17–19 inches or 41–45 cm) to enable the average sitter to rest his feet on the floor; and (2) the chair back, while curving backwards somewhat, is high enough to provide for lumbar and shoulder support as well as accommodating the natural bend of the spinal column. By contrast, the Straits Chinese variety of blackwood settee (i.e., those with mother-of-pearl inlays) are much less comfortable as they have straight backs (high enough for lumbar support only) and high seats (up to 23 inches or 55 cm high) which cause the sitter's legs to dangle above the floor. Courtesy of Mr Peter Wee, Katong Antique House.

the top by a one-piece top rail, suitably carved and curved to match their contours. Armrests were likewise curved and slightly recessed to fit the contours of the arms. In all cases where rounded (or oval) components were used, they were invariably carved and sculpted by hand and eye – never turned by lathe. Turning was considered unworthy of a true craftsman.

There is one other feature peculiar to the Cantonese settee: it is probably the only type of chair or bench-like furniture in the Chinese tradition of cabinet-work on which a person can sit comfortably, leaning backwards and resting his feet flat on the ground. This innovation in furniture design and construction probably had its origins in Guangdong where, during the 18th and the 19th centuries, Cantonese cabinet-makers made their first acquaintance with European furniture. It did not take these skilled and experienced cabinet-makers long to realize that the designs and dimensions of European chairs, for example, had much to do with the question of how best to fit an average human body snugly and comfortably into a chair. Once they understood and appreciated the logic of European chair designs, they set about to modify and redesign the traditional structure of the Chinese chair. Thus the unmistakable influence of European designs in Cantonese blackwood

furniture. But notice that the Cantonese cabinet-maker, for all his shrewd observations and concealed admiration for the skill of his European counterpart, did not attempt to go the whole way in imitating European furniture designs. He adapted only those features (e.g. modifications in dimensions and changes in structural design to incorporate more curved and rounded component parts) which made for comfort and innovation in design, but kept uncompromisingly to the Chinese technique of furniture construction, wood-carving and joinery.

Opium beds

The so-called 'opium bed' in Straits Chinese household furniture looks very much like an enlarged version of the three-panelled, low-back settee-bench described above. Historically speaking, however, the large *kang* couch or opium bed probably came first. In fact, the *kang*, as a raised platform made of bricks or hardened mud, warmed by heating from beneath when the weather became inclemently cold, was the most ancient and ubiquitous of Chinese household furniture. Every peasant home had a raised platform of this sort. Its subsequent development as a separate and movable piece of furniture, in the shape of a raised wooden platform enclosed on three sides by high panels, was probably perfected by the end of the Tang Dynasty. In fact, by the time of the Five Dynasties huge *kang* beds constructed out of some type of blackwood (*zitan* or *hongmu*) were already in regular use in the Imperial Court and the homes of high-ranking ministers. Thus, in Gu Hongzhong's painting, *The Night Revels of Han Xizai*, referred to earlier, an elderly personage is seen sitting in a huge *kang* bed attended by four court ladies. And judging by the distribution of the figures, there was space enough for one or two more people! Likewise, in Zhou Wenju's horizontal scroll entitled *Concert at the Palace*, a high-ranking person is shown sitting at the edge of a high-back *kang* couch listening to an orchestral performance by court musicians. Zhou's painting is also dated to the Five Dynasties[13].

The dimensions of these early *kang* beds are not, of course, given, but taking a cue from the sizes of extant *kang* beds of the Ming and the Qing periods, we may guess that they must at least have measured sevenfeet (210 centimetres) long, five feet (150 centimetres) wide, with the longest of them measuring up to 10 feet (300 centimetres) long and six feet (180 centimetres) wide. *Kang* beds illustrated in Ecke's and Wang's works average around seven feet (210 centimetres) long and five feet (150 centimetres) wide.

The Straits Chinese version of the *kang* couch is somewhat smaller; it is about 5 feet 6 inches (165 centimetres) long, 4 feet 6 inches (135 centimetres) wide and 3 feet 6 inches (105 centimetres) high. The structure of these couches is practically identical to that of the settee-bench, but for its greater depth. It has the same three-panelled enclosure, the seat back being composed of three smaller panels of which the centre piece is taller and broader than the two flanking ones. All the frontal surfaces, including the seat, are either completely covered with complex patterns of inlaid mother-of-pearl, or else a combination of round, square or rectangular marble slabs and ornamented with mother-of-pearl inlays. Traditionally, the opium bed always came with a low *kang* table at three feet (90 centimetres) long, two feet (60 centimetres) wide and one foot (30 centimetres) high. This table is placed transversely at the centre of the bed. Opium beds have thick and solid legs. These are carved in one piece out of solid blocks of wood. They bulge outwards at the shoulder and curve inwards towards the base, where they terminate in huge claw-and-ball feet.

Some allusions to the history of opium-smoking and its connection with the opium bed are relevant here. To people familiar with the traditional lores of the Straits Babas, opium beds were actually used by wealthy merchants and traders in days gone by for opium smoking. Opium was in fact available in the Straits Settlements in those days, although it was not meant for local public consumption, but for export to China. Even before the founding of Singapore in 1819, special licences were granted, upon payment of fees, to certain farmers in Malacca and Penang to operate opium farms, while those merchants and traders who could afford to pay considerably higher licence fees were allowed to operate opium shops. The business in opium was so lucrative that one year after the founding of Singapore, in 1820, Colonel Farquhar, Resident in Singapore, was prevailed upon by the local mercantile community to grant licences for the cultivation of opium and the setting up of opium shops in the colony. Sir Stamford Raffles, who came to learn about this while he was in Bencoolen, objected to Singapore being used as an opium supply base, but his objections went unheeded. The mercantile community insisted that free trade based on the principle of *laissez-faire* be adhered to with a minimum of government interference.

Opium then was available from local farms in Singapore, Malacca and Penang. But opium smoking was by no means a widespread habit, partly because local consumption was prohibited by law, and partly because considerable social odium was heaped upon the indiscriminating use of this highly addictive and debilitating drug. To the small coterie of people who could afford opium, it was believed that, taken in moderation, especially as a kind of post-prandial treat, opium helped to lessen nervous tension by inducing a state of relaxation. The Chinese in China had a long history of opium smoking: the hill tribes who live in the southwestern provinces of Yunnan and Guangxi, where the opium-poppy plant (*Papaver somniferum*) grows, have intimate knowledge of both the beneficial and harmful effects of opium. But opium smoking in China was, for a long time, confined to a small section of the aristocratic and mandarin class. For the vast majority of the population, opium was something very exotic, expensive and hard to come by. The authorities in China were, of course, well apprised of its dangerous effects on the health of the people and of the other social evils attendant upon opium addiction. For this reason, the sale and trafficking of opium in China was publicly proscribed, so much so that opium addiction never became a

serious problem.

But towards the end of the Qing Dynasty, between 1830 and 1860, opium addiction in China, especially in Guangdong, suddenly became a matter of grave public concern as more and more people fell victim to this debilitating drug. Investigations by government authorities showed that the immediate cause of widespread opium addiction among the people was the availability of an enormous quantity of cheap Bengal opium which was dumped in Guangdong by many of the European nations trading with China. British, Dutch, French, Spanish, Portuguese and German ships carried enormous quantities of Indian opium to Guangdong in exchange for Chinese tea, silk, porcelain and silver currency, despite official protests from the Chinese authorities against the opium trade. European traders maintained they had a right to engage in free trade with any country, including China, and they were prepared to assert their rights by force of arms if necessary. China had no choice but to go to war to assert her sovereignty. But she lost ignominiously to the superior arms of Britain and other European countries and was forced to sue for peace. The humiliation which she suffered subsequently at the hands of the various European powers, including the ceding of Hong Kong island, the opening up of Guangdong, Xiamen and Shanghai to ships from the West, as well as the payment of huge war damages amounting to millions of silver taels, did not in any way convince most mandarins and intellectuals in China that those Western powers were therefore legally and morally justified in enforcing the sale of opium upon a helpless China. They noted that the Western claim to free

trade did not apply to the trafficking of opium in their own countries. If anything, therefore, the odium against opium trafficking grew rather than diminished in China. The opium trade is still regarded by many historians as one of the darkest episodes in the history of Western relations with China[14].

Tea tables

Of the four or five different types of blackwood tables which the former generations of Straits Babas regularly furnished their homes with, none were of course ever intended for scholarly pursuits after the manner of the Chinese scholar-gentleman. Hence, there were no lute tables, tables for painting and calligraphy, games (e.g. go and sixes) tables, tables for displaying rare and antique porcelain or wine tables. As a predominantly mercantile community of merchants, traders and planters, the wealthy Babas had neither the time nor the inclination for such scholarly pursuits as playing the lute or zither, reading books, composing poems, practising calligraphy or painting. Nor, perhaps, would a life spent largely in the competitive world of business transactions leave much time and leisure for cultivating the fine arts of wine-tasting and sophisticated literary and philosophic discussions. Classic tables of these types, which are lavishly illustrated in books on antique Chinese furniture, are naturally absent in old Baba homes.

Straits Chinese blackwood tables were meant to be either functional or ceremonial, and among these blackwood tables were tea tables (only two types, namely the ceremonial circular type and the small square or rectangular version placed between two chairs), altar tables (in two styles, square and rectangular) and semi-circular ornamental tables.

The circular table with its complement of four matching stools, placed in the centre of the reception hall, was meant to,be largely ornamental and ceremonial in function. The Babas themselves, especially the more Westernized among them, rarely sat around the table to sip tea while receiving friends and guests in their homes. Rather, they sat on armchairs laid out along both sides of the hall, sipping tea and conversing with their guests. In old Baba homes where heavy blackwood furniture was entirely replaced by teakwood furniture, the centrepiece consisted of a circular teakwood table with a marble top, supported at the centre by a solidly carved pillar or, in some cases, by a central pillar surrounded by four smaller ones, with four short, outward curving legs at the base. Four teakwood armchairs with cane seats (and sometimes with cane backs as well), made after the fashion of antique English-European chairs, usually complement it. These chairs were far more comfortable and, thus, more

frequently used for tea and small-talk sessions.

The design of the circular blackwood table is conventional: the table top consists, in most cases, of a circular frame between $2^{1}/_{2}$–3 inches (6.25–7.5 centimetres) broad encasing a slab of figured marble, which is supported by one or two transverse braces at the bottom. The table top is then tenoned into a slightly smaller, waisted frame with its characteristic concave mouldings. The two top frames are in turn fitted onto the top circular apron railing by tenons and mortises at the junctures where the four legs are joined or positioned. It should be noted though that the waisted frame is not always constructed as a separate entity in itself. In some instances, it is integral to the same piece of wood constituting the apron frame. Immediately below the aprons are four ornamental stretchers carved in pierced- or open-work. The legs are freestanding, ending either in horse-hoofed feet or claw-and-ball feet. Small chips of variously shaped mother-of-pearl with white and yellowish lustre are inlaid into the principal obverse surfaces on the table. Most of these tables are just over three feet (90 centimetres) high.

While it was customary with the traditional Babas to furnish their reception halls with circular blackwood tea tables, this type of table was by no means universal in China, certainly not during the Ming Dynasty when square tables were very common and round ones hardly encountered. In fact, mandarin scholars of conservative tastes would most certainly have preferred square tea tables with matching square stools. In J. C.

Ferguson's *Survey of Chinese Art*[15], there is a photograph of a typical reception room in a scholar's house showing such a square tea table.

Semi-circular tables

Semi-circular tables (usually a pair of them placed diametrically opposite each other across the reception hall) were meant to be largely ornamental. The Babas used them as stands for a pair of rectangular table screens about 2 feet (60 centimetres) high and about 1 foot 2 inches (35 centimetres) wide. The screens were usually framed with embroidery, tapestry or bead-and-embroidered panels depicting phoenixes, peonies, quails, mandarin ducks, antelopes and butterflies – auspicious symbols of wedded bliss, longevity and fecundity. Rarely were such tables used with a pair of antique porcelain vases or jars, as in the homes of the more conservative Chinese.

The Cantonese and other dialect groups seem to have preferred semi-circular tables with what look like pie-crust mouldings on the table tops, while others opted for trapezoidal types of side tables. But the traditional Babas apparently adhered to the plain semi-circular table with mother-of-pearl decorations. The table itself is of conventional design and construction. It is about three feet (90 centimetres) at its greatest length, 14–15 inches (35–37.5 centimetres) at its widest and 30 inches (75 centimetres) high. The straight legs end in hoofed feet and are strengthened by three curved frontal stretchers and one back stretcher mounted between the legs at about three inches (7.5 centimetres) above the ground. The only unusual feature about the semi-circular table is that it is always accompanied by a matching base support shaped exactly in the pattern of the semi-circular table top. The base support is about five inches (12.5 centimetres) high, and its top panel is characterized by lattice-work. The table stands on the base support or pedestal, but the feet are not tenoned into the base frame. The function of the base support is purely ornamental: it serves to raise the height of the semi-circular table without making its legs appear unduly long and spindly. The maximum height of the semi-circular table, when mounted upon its base support, is about three feet (90 centimetres).

Altar tables

In many old Baba homes that I have visited in Singapore and Malacca, two sets of altar tables, with their complement of ancestral tablets, statues, paintings of household gods and other objects of worship, may be found, one in the main reception hall and the other at the far end of the family room. I have also noticed that the majority of these altar tables, whether found in homes or antique shops, are constructed mainly out of namwood (known as *nanmu* in Chinese, or *Machilus nanmu,* its Latin equivalent) and not out of any extant species of *Dalbergia* or rosewood/blackwood. Blackwood altar tables with mother-of-pearl inlays were rare, apparently because they cost much more than namwood altar tables. Nonetheless, it was still possible up to about 10 years ago to encounter occasional mother-of-pearl altar tables in Singapore and Georgetown, Penang. Going by rule-of-thumb observations, it appears that some of the finest examples of mother-of-pearl blackwood furniture came from old homes in Penang. The largest and most impressive pair of altar tables that I have seen in all these years is to be found in the Buddhist Association in Georgetown. Each of these is a massive and heavily constructed table, no less than 14 feet (420 centimetres) long, three feet (90 centimetres) wide and at least four feet (120 centimetres) high. All the component parts must have been separately crafted, carved and inlaid with mother-of-pearl in China (Shanghai or Xiamen) and subsequently shipped to Penang, where they were then assembled locally. They were simply too heavy and bulky to be packed in one piece inside a crate. Altar tables, whether in Baba or Chinese homes, always came in a two-piece set: a high, rectangular table with upturned ends and a standard square table somewhat lower in height. The larger of the two tables, namely the high altar table, is a structure which reminds one of the Greek letter *pi* or π, with the stretched horizontal line resting upon two widely parted vertical lines. It consists of an elongated rectangular table top five to six feet (150–180 centimetres) long, about 1 foot 6 inches (45 centimetres) wide and 3 feet 6 inches (105 centimetres) to four feet (120 centimetres) high. The two ends of the table top have upturned flanges which, in some cases, are carved to look like the ends of a scroll.

The table top is usually constructed out of several slabs of wood laid side-by-side and attached together by tongue-and-groove joints, reinforced by transverse braces below. These slabs of wood, especially blackwood, are thick and heavy – average thickness being 2–2$^{1}/2$ inches (5–6 centimetres). While most high altar tables are stretched rectangular with flat, straight fronts, many pieces have bow fronts which are further accentuated by the outward curving of the carved apron panels fitted below the table top. But whether the front happens to be flat or bow-like, the carved apron panels are invariably made to protrude and curve outwards to project an appearance of strength and solidity – which is what they are.

Many high altar tables are constructed without a distinct waist frame underneath the table top. Instead, a broad frieze running the entire perimeter of the altar table, decorated with carvings in relief and open-work on the front and side under panel, is substituted for the standard apron under frame. Incidentally, the broad carved panels which form the frieze were never intended to be purely decorative in function. They also serve as upper stretchers for holding and strengthening the legs in position.

The front and side panels of the under frame are rarely cut to form plain, rectangular bars. Very often the lower edges are shaped in broad, serpentine curves narrowing at the extremities, or perhaps, in a series of wave-like curves. In those altar tables featuring straight, square legs, the front and back legs are usually strengthened at the lower ends by transverse braces. But the front legs (for aesthetic considerations) are never connected by stretchers. A long stretcher, whether straight or bow-like, connecting the two front legs at the lower ends would be unnecessarily distracting. In altar tables where the legs are perpendicularly straight, the feet are invariably hoofed and no carved *taotien* masks appear at the top ends of the legs. But in those instances where the legs are sculpted cabriole-fashion, the knees always feature carved *taotien* masks, while the feet are of the claw-and-ball type.

Square tables

As for the square altar table, the design tends to be conservative and conventional: it measures about three feet (90 centimetres) by three feet (90 centimetres) and is about 30 inches (75 centimetres) high. The table top may or may not come with a corresponding square slab of figured

marble encased within the top frame and supported by transverse braces underneath. But where marble slabs are absent, the surface is entirely embellished with floral and foliated patterns of mother-of-pearl. A large surface of this sort, when covered completely with mother-of-pearl patterns, can be extremely dazzling, especially when set against the dark and figured grain of blackwood. Most square tables are constructed with narrow aprons supported at the corners by four straight and square-cut legs ending in hoofed feet. Where the aprons are thin and narrow, the sides are ornamented by the addition of four broad and ornately carved panels spanning the width between the legs and fitted immediately below the aprons. Apart from serving as ornamental panels, they also act as stretchers for securing the legs more firmly together. Occasionally carved spandrels are added to the upper ends of the legs, but even without these accessories the square mother-of-pearl table is already overwrought.

The square table is customarily placed immediately in front of the high altar table and its function was, as it still is today, to serve as an additional receptacle upon which food, incense, altar lamps, joss stick holders and other paraphernalia of worship can be placed. On such red-letter days as All Souls' Day (*Qing Ming*) or the anniversary of the particular ancestor revered by the family, a splendidly embroidered altar cloth in red silk may be hung over the front of the square table.

Mother-of-pearl

Mother-of-pearl, as its name suggests, is obtained from the lustrous part, or nacre, of several species of pearl oyster (*Pinctada*). It is also obtained from the inner layers of the giant green turban shell (*Turbinidae*) found in the shallow seas in many parts of Southeast Asia. In the days before the mass production of plastics, great quantities of the giant green turban shell used to be harvested to extract its lustrous nacre for making buttons. Even now, the shells of pearl oysters are still collected in the shallow seas around many of the islands east of Java and in the Philippines, not so much for the rare, baroque pearls they happen to contain as for the mother-of-pearl with its attractive accretions of bluish-green and yellow nacre. In the Philippines especially, several species of shells with mother-of-pearl nacre are used for making ornamental forks and spoons, inlays for boxes and other objects of virtue, small tables, fruit bowls, lampshades, etc. Buttons fashioned out of mother-of-pearl are still obtainable in haberdasheries, but they cost three or four times more than plastic buttons.

Seafaring Chinese merchants and traders who had traded with the countries of Southeast Asia since the Han Dynasty knew about the trade in mother-of-pearl. Down the ages, Chinese traders have imported enormous quantities of pearls of every type and description (including the rare black pearl) from the countries of Southeast Asia. Empress Dowager Cixi was said to have been so obsessed with the legendary and aesthetic properties of pearls that she instructed that when she died her corpse was to be magnificently clad in seven layers of ceremonial clothing and placed into a huge coffin filled with tens of thousands of pearls!

The vogue for mother-of-pearl inlays on blackwood furniture was said to have been popularized by the Qing emperor, Qianlong during the 18th century. Blackwood furniture with inlays of mother-of-pearl must have been expensive right from the beginning. This is because working with mother-of-pearl was such a nuisance. Very often the raw shells with their outer encrustations have to be treated with nitric acid solutions of various strengths to get at the lustrous nacre within. And having done that, the nacre must be cut into thin sheets between one and two millimetres thick. Nacre, it is true, is not a very hard substance. It is between $3^1/2$ and four on the Mohs scale of hardness (diamond, the hardest known substance, is rated 10 on the Mohs scale) but it is hard enough to require a fine fretsaw or a small hacksaw fitted with a sharp blade to do the cutting.

In working with mother-of-pearl inlays, the wood-carver must first trace out the decorative patterns on the various surfaces of a piece of furniture. Then he has to use a variety of small gouges to excavate shallow depressions about two millimetres deep within the various decorative patterns intended for mother-of-pearl chips. When this task is completed (and it is no small task when the artefact to be embellished is a huge altar table or one of these giant *kang* couches), he will have to begin cutting a large quantity of small mother-of-pearl chips which will correspondingly fit into the pre-cut patterns originally executed on the various surfaces of the piece of furniture. Finally, he applies a variety of black bone glue into each of these shallow depressions. The glue is allowed to stand for a while before the wood-carver inserts appropriate pieces of mother-of-pearl into position. To ensure more effective bonding, a bit of garlic is added to the glue.

Blackwood and rosewood belonging to various species of *Dalbergia*, when properly dried and matured, are very hard and close-grained. Cutting, carving and sculpting the various components of a piece of furniture and fitting them together by mortises and tenons is already a skilled and demanding job. But when you have to add mother-of-pearl inlays to form complex patterns on the surfaces of an otherwise completed piece of furniture, the labour and skill required is considerably increased. And so, too, is the cost of producing mother-of-pearl furniture. However, there are many people who prefer the classic blackwood furniture to be *without* the florid distractions of mother-of-pearl inlays. For one thing, they detract from the beauty of classic designs; for another, they spoil the intrinsic lustre and loveliness of pure wood so well manifested in *huanghuali* and *zitan*.

One last observation concerning mother-of-pearl furniture: during the early 1970s – from about 1972 to the eve of the full evacuation of the American armed forces from South Vietnam following the fall of Saigon to the victorious North Vietnamese army in March 1975 – a flood of inlaid mother-of-pearl furniture of outlandish 18th- and 19th-century French designs suddenly descended upon many antique furniture shops in Singapore. Most dealers intimated that these quaint, Western-influenced pieces of oriental furniture came from Saigon. Some even said their supplies came from the former imperial city of Hue and that such furniture was once the property of former wealthy Vietnamese families. There was evidence to show that many of these pieces of furniture were probably looted from abandoned homes of wealthy Vietnamese and subsequently smuggled out of Saigon into Hong Kong and Singapore. Whatever the truth of the matter was, these pieces of furniture were extremely elegant and comfortable, especially when compared with the staid and more squarish pieces of blackwood furniture found in old Baba homes. The wood was of a lighter shade than that of Chinese blackwood furniture, but it was hard, heavy, lustrous and satin-smooth. Obviously, it must have belonged to one of several species of *Dalbergia* endemic to Vietnam. Indeed, according to Chinese records, Chinese traders had been importing several varieties of *huali* and *zitan* from Vietnam (formerly known as Annam or French Indochina) from as far back as the 14th and 15th centuries.

But the most remarkable feature of antique Vietnamese rosewood/blackwood furniture in French designs is the quality and artistry of the mother-of-pearl patterns inlaid upon it. Vietnamese mother-of-pearl chips are exceedingly beautiful; they shimmer with the iridescence of pink, orange, blue, green and yellow. The species of pearl oyster used for extracting this type of mother-of-pearl was probably different from those used by the Chinese (which were a more whitish and opaque kind of mother-of-pearl) and they must have come from the coastal waters of Vietnam. But what really made Vietnamese inlaid mother-of-pearl furniture so distinctive and remarkable was the outstanding quality of the inlaid patterns themselves. Whether the patterns happen to depict phoenixes, dragons, carps, magpies, quails and antelopes or peonies, magnolia, bamboos, lotuses and plum blossoms, the mother-of-pearl chips, already beautifully endowed with rainbow hues, were cut and shaped with such precision, realism and refinement that Chinese mother-of-pearl patterns appeared crude and shoddy by comparison – an example of an original Chinese invention being refined and perfected by China's neighbours.

~ chapter three ~

Namwood Red-and-Gold Furniture

Red-and-gold furniture, the second variety of Straits Chinese furniture, is sometimes referred to as 'giltwood' furniture. This term is all right, except that, where antique Chinese giltwood furniture is concerned, it was not customary to cover the entire wood surface of a piece of furniture with gilding of thin pieces of gold leaf, after the manner of French and Italian furniture of the Rococo era (i.e. the first half of the 18th century). Chinese cabinet-makers were much more sparing in the use of gilding: only those parts of a piece of furniture in which bas-relief and open-work carvings occur were gilded. The remaining plain and unadorned surfaces were simply painted over with either red, brown or black lacquer, or else a combination of those. This method of judiciously confining the gilding only to the more prominent surfaces of a piece of furniture (e.g. the carved panels and decorated border) is perhaps aesthetically more appealing, as it enables the ornamented and gilded portions of, say, a cabinet, a console table or even a chair, to stand out against a contrasting background of

There is a monumental quality about the appearance of this red-and-gold cabinet. But it is barely 2 ft (60 cm) wide and just over 4 ft (120 cm) high! Too small to serve as a wardrobe, it was probably used for storing jewellery and other ceremonial accessories of the bridal trousseau. The craftsmanship is of a high order, but, regrettably, the cupboard has been stripped clean of all traces of original patina. There are many such 'new' antiques in Singapore. Dating: late 19th century. Private collection.

sombre red, black or brown. When the carvings are executed sparingly and not, as with the overwrought Penang variety, in an overwhelming fashion, red-and-gold furniture has a quiet glimmer and old-world charm about it. For this reason, the term 'red-and-gold' is, therefore, more appropriate than 'giltwood', with its connotation of lavish and excessive gilding characteristic of European Rococo furniture.

However, 'red-and-gold' must not be construed too literally, giving the impression that this variety of Straits Chinese furniture is exclusively rendered in red and gold. As a matter of fact, while red and gold are the principal colours, with connotations of auspiciousness, black as well as brown lacquers are also used for the margins of framed panels, the aprons, the spandrels and the inner parts of open-work carvings. Sometimes the background of an entire piece of carving is painted with black or brown lacquer and gilding of thin gold foils is then applied over its surface. Altar tables, in particular, often come in black and gold or brown and gold. But certain items of furniture, such as the four-poster bridal bed, the bridal table, bridal high-back chairs, stools, the two-tiered wedding cupboard, the dressing mirror, the washstand and the chest-of-drawers, are so finished that red and gold stand out as the principal colours. Carved screens (some are almost 12 feet or 360 centimetres high),

partitioning the front reception hall from the family living room, are usually rendered in brown and gold in most old Baba homes in Malacca. In Singapore, however, many of these screens are painted in red, brown and black, with gilding being applied only to the carved panels. For the purpose of this book, the term 'red-and-gold' is therefore used somewhat loosely to refer to a variety of Chinese giltwood furniture which, during the 18th and 19th centuries, was extensively crafted in the southeastern provinces of Guangdong, Fujian and Zhejiang, both for domestic use as well as for export to overseas Chinese communities (especially the Hokkiens) in Malaya and Indonesia.

Namwood

The bulk of extant pieces of Straits Chinese red-and-gold furniture is made out of namwood which, according to Kates[16], is a species of cedar peculiar to China known as *Machilus nanmu*. Namwood is a medium hardwood which is heavy, dense and durable. Its grain is coarser and less dense than that of *huanghuali* (*Dalbergia*) and *zitan* (*Pterocarpus*), and it does not have the silky smoothness or lustre of rosewood and blackwood. Nor, for that matter, does it display the complex figured grains so highly prized in cabinet woods. Nonetheless it is heavy, sturdy and easy to carve on, and, being native to China, was much less expensive than *huanghuali* and *zitan*. According

Pintu pagar, or the outer gate, of a typical Baba home in Malacca. Until 25 years ago, practically every Baba house along the former Heeren and Jonker streets (now renamed Jalan Tun Tan Cheng Lock and Jalan Hang Jebat respectively) had a set of such handsome gates at the main entrance to the house. But from about 1970 onwards, most of these lovely ornamental gates had largely disappeared, and spotting them in Malacca today is a rare and pleasant experience.

This particular set of gates is carved and gilded on both the obverse and reverse sides. It is just over 5 ft (150 cm) high and 5 ft (150 cm) wide and it is probably made of namwood. All the Malaccan types of pintu pagar have no upward tapering pediments. Dating: turn of the century. Courtesy of C. K. Tan Gallery.

to Soame Jenyns, namwood was also prized as a coffin wood which, during the Ming Dynasty, was reserved only for royalty. Thus, the huge coffin of Emperor Wanli (1572–1620) was made entirely out of namwood.

Namwood is a yellowish-brown wood which darkens with age and exposure to the atmosphere. The heartwood has a curious greyish-green tinge, but when exposed to air for a long time, it turns brown. However, in the namwood of old furniture aged 100 years or more, the core still retains its greenish colour, and this can be shown by sawing through the wood and noting the colour of the sawdust. Whether it is through inadequate drying or seasoning processes, antique namwood furniture shows extensive evidence of shrinkage, so much so that it is not uncommon to find that the tenons in floating panels, carved panels and parallel planks have become loose and detachable after an interval of, say, 80 to 100 years. In particular, if one examines the planks inside the drawers and the backs of old red-and-gold cabinets, one usually notices that they are no longer tightly sealed together, but that slits have formed between the planks. The wood itself does not split along the grain, nor does it warp. But shrinkage is very evident – even in the warm and humid climate of the tropics.

Namwood is surprisingly durable when it is well protected by several layers of lacquer and when it is not subjected to damp and wet conditions. The proof is that there are many extant pieces of carved, red-and-gold furniture which are close to a century old, or older, and still in a very fine state of preservation. Until several years ago, my wife used to own a two-tiered set of red-and-gold wedding cupboards with ornate gilded carvings, standing at least seven feet (210 centimetres) high, and which were then authenticated at 105 years old. Except for a few chips and bumps along the lower aprons, a couple of loose panels and some shrunken panels in the back, there was no sign of any wood rot at all. And this in spite of the fact that namwood is not immune to dry rot and attacks by termites and other forms of wood-boring insects. Generally, antique namwood furniture shows evidence of some decay, especially in the legs of chairs, cabinets and tables. This is largely due to the fact that the undersides of the feet, whether hoofed or modelled into gargoyle-like carvings, are not protected with lacquer but left exposed. The rot, however, is not extensive and can be easily filled up with one of several brands of plastic wood available.

Unlike blackwood and rosewood furniture, where transparent lacquer is applied to bring out the intrinsic qualities of lustre, satin smoothness and the figured grains of the timber, namwood is, almost without exception, entirely painted over with several layers of opaque red, brown or black lacquer, as the case may be, to conceal the wood beneath. This is done partly with a view to protecting the wood and partly with a view to creating a new variety of furniture (and fixtures) for serving certain ceremonial and symbolic purposes. Thus, red-and-gold namwood furniture in traditional Straits Chinese culture was intended for wedding ceremonies only, while red-and-gold, black-and-gold and brown-and-gold altar tables, and carved and gilded screens, pillars, beams and rafters were used to beautify as well as to add a touch of splendour to the decorations in temples, palaces and the palatial homes of wealthy mandarins.

Teakwood

Not all extant pieces of red-and-gold furniture and fixtures found in old Baba and Chinese homes in Malaya were exclusively made out of namwood, which, in any case, had to be imported from China. In Singapore and Malacca, for example, it was not uncommon that some of the larger pieces of carving, such as wall screens (between 10 and 12 feet or 300 and 360 centimetres high), beam panels, brackets, railings and balusters of staircases and doors in Baba homes, Chinese medicine shops, Chinese associations and temples were found to have been carved out of teakwood (*Tectona grandis*) or, in some cases, out of one or several varieties of hardwood of the families of *Dipterocarpaceae* and *Leguminosae*, such as *balau*, *chengal*, *kekatong*, *rengas* and *merbau*.

This fact was, of course, known to the older generations of Babas and Chinese merchants who commissioned the installation of these ornate and gilded carvings. But since most of these fixtures were carved and gilded at least 70 or 80 years ago, most people had forgotten or were simply ignorant of what type of timber had gone into the making of these antiquated carvings. It was only when repairs and restoration work had to be carried out, and the old lacquer and giltwork had to be scraped and stripped to reveal the wood beneath that cabinet-makers and wood-carvers discovered that teak and some varieties of local hardwoods were used instead of namwood.

Teakwood is native to India, Burma (Myanmar) and Thailand, and from about 1880 to 1939, teak became the most popular cabinet wood for making a variety of Sino-English or Sino-European furniture in Malaya and Singapore. The Babas were the most enthusiastic patrons of this type of furniture. But more of this will be dealt with in chapter four. Although documentary evidence is scanty and hard to come by, there is evidence to indicate that by the end of the Qing Dynasty, namwood had become quite scarce in China. By contrast, teakwood was readily available and much less expensive as it was imported in large quantities from Burma and Thailand for making furniture and other carved fixtures in the homes of the wealthy Chinese. As a medium-hard wood, teak is resistant to wood rot and easy to carve on. Hence, it was extensively used for carved red-and-gold fixtures which, in days gone by, were executed by craftsmen and carvers sent out from Xiamen and Shanghai to Singapore, Malacca and Penang to work on various projects, lasting from several months to a year or more.

Juwood

It is true that the bulk of antique red-and-gold furniture in most old Baba homes is made of namwood, and some of these pieces of namwood furniture may date back to the beginning of the 19th century, even though authenticated evidence is hard to come by. But namwood was not the only type of timber used for making red-and-gold furniture and carved panels. The Chinese had been using another type of wood known as juwood, or *nanyu*, a species of southern elm belonging to the genus of *Ulmus*, for several hundred years. The species of Chinese elm from which juwood is obtained is said to have come from Jiangsu and Zhejiang. It is a light-coloured wood, somewhat resembling old pine, has

beautiful grain and is lighter and less dense than namwood. Until seven or eight years ago, carved red-and-gold, black-and-gold and brown-and-gold furniture made out of juwood was practically unknown in Singapore, Malacca and Penang. Namwood was the standard type of timber employed in such furniture and carvings. Then, in about 1980 or 1981, several antique dealers in Singapore went to Hong Kong and from there established contacts with suppliers of antique furniture in Guangdong, Shantou and Xiamen, from whom they managed to obtain large quantities of red-and-gold juwood furniture. Some they sold in Hong Kong and the rest was shipped out to Singapore. Dealers who had previously dealt with red-and-gold namwood furniture obtained from local sources such as old homes, shophouses, medicine shops, Chinese associations and temples (many of which were dated to the late 19th century) did not, at first, realize that the supplies of antique red-and-gold furniture they had imported from China were made of a different wood. But since many of these pieces of furniture were defective and had to be repaired and restored, skilled carpenters and carvers were set to work on them. When they began taking them apart to repair loose joints and broken components, and followed up by scraping and stripping away the old lacquer, they soon discovered that the wood beneath was different

from namwood: it was light-coloured, somewhat yellowish with a very slight tinge of brown. Superficially, it felt and looked like one of the several varieties of pine wood. But it was not pine. It was juwood, a variety of southern elm. For those who swear by namwood, however, juwood was no better than pine because in colour, grain and weight it could have passed off as some variety of soft pine. Nevertheless, they noted that the craftsmen who executed these pieces of furniture had put considerable skill and effort into the carvings, which in most cases, were of superior quality.

Gilding

Until the recent importation of red-and-gold juwood furniture and carved fixtures from South China, most extant examples of red-and-gold, black-and-gold and brown-and-gold furniture executed in traditional Chinese taste, and dating back to the 19th century, were made out of namwood. The method of embellishing wooden furniture (and also lacquerware, pottery and metal objects) with a thin covering of gold leaf is an ancient one in China, going as far back as the Zhou Dynasty (c. 11th century–221 B.C.). The ancient Egyptians were, however, among the earliest people to practise the art of gilding

Close-up of high-relief gilded carvings.

furniture, stone and metal objects, jewellery and royal mummy cases; the tomb furniture of Pharoah Tutankhamen (3300 years old) provides some of the finest examples of the Egyptian art of gilding.

The application of thin foils of leaf gold to carved furniture is a skill which few amateurs can acquire by simply reading about it. It is a manual skill which is not easily communicable by words and has to be mastered only through practice, observation and lots of patience. There are many ways of going about it. Nevertheless some general observations about the art of gilding may be useful in enabling the student of giltwood furniture to understand the basic procedures involved.

In the traditional European method of gilding, the surface of a piece of furniture which is to be decorated with leaf gold (e.g. the places where the principal carvings – in bas-relief or open-work – appear) has to be primed by rubbing a mixture of gesso (plaster of Paris) and size (sealing glue or varnish) to cover up the pores, cracks and other imperfections and to enable the details of the carved-work to stand out clearly. It is then allowed to dry thoroughly. Next, the primed surface is rubbed down until the exposed surfaces are smoothened and the details clearly revealed. When the rubbing process has been completed, a sticky and adhesive size or varnish is applied to the surface and allowed to stand until semi-dry (i.e. just sticky enough to adhere to the tips of the fingers). Gold leaf may now be applied to the carved surfaces.

In the traditional Chinese method of gilding, the priming of the carved surfaces is done without the application of gesso or chalk. This can easily be seen by gently scraping away a small portion of the gilding with a penknife and noting that the surface immediately beneath has no chalky substances of any sort. Instead, scrapings of red lacquer appear. In the Chinese method of gilding, the priming process is effected first by rubbing the carved designs with very fine sandpaper to remove all those raw sharp edges and coarseness on the wood. When this has been completed, the carvings are thoroughly dusted and a type of dark red lacquer painted over them and allowed to stand until semi-dry. Thin foils of gold leaf are then applied over the carved surfaces.

Many years ago, when I had the opportunity of watching Chinese craftsmen apply gold leaf on large panels of carvings, I noticed that the gilding process was simultaneously carried out by two people laying down small rectangular pieces of gold leaf over the surface very rapidly. The way it was done, lifting the covering flap containing the gold leaf with one hand and with a quick but deft movement of the other hand, inverting the foil straight on to the carvings, struck me as a very simple and easy process. Easy, that is, until I tried to repeat the procedure myself! I then discovered that either the piece of gold leaf did not come off clean and whole from the tissue coverings, or when it did, it flew off in the wrong direction and was easily torn to shreds by clumsy fingers trying to guide it back. The more I fumbled with these delicate pieces of gold foil, the more frustrating the process became. If I was careless and breathed directly onto the piece of exposed gold foil, it either flew out of the wrapping or it curled and broke into tiny shimmering shreds. It was all very disheartening and I wasted countless pieces of precious gold leaf without obtaining any satisfactory result. Obviously gilding is a skilled job which amateurs cannot successfully dabble in.

Twenty years ago, it was possible to obtain a packet of gold leaf containing 100 sheets, measuring $1^3/4$ inches by $1^1/2$ inches (4.3

centimetres by 3.7 centimetres) for about S$10 from any Chinese medicine shop. Even so it was considered expensive.

Gold leaf, believe it or not, is a quarter of a million of an inch thick! Its thickness is, in fact, calculated at $^1/280,000$th of an inch. So delicate indeed is a piece of gold leaf that it is almost translucent when seen against a light. The methods by which gold leaf is beaten to this degree of thinness are partly traditional, involving hand-beating with the aid of various types of wooden hammer, and partly by modern processes of squeezing gold ingots by electrically driven rollers into long ribbons of about $^1/1000$th of an inch thick. Where modern machinery is not available, as in most cottage industries in Asia, the entire process of making gold leaf is carried out by hammering a piece of alloyed gold ingot, again and again, over several days, until a ribbon of gold of the requisite thinness is obtained[17].

While gold is highly malleable, it is not readily workable when pure. However, when pure gold is smelted together with a small quantity of silver or copper in a crucible, the resultant alloy becomes much easier to work with. An ingot measuring 2 inches by $1^1/8$ inches by $^1/8$ inch can be rolled into a ribbon 240 inches (600 centimetres) long and $^1/1000$th of an inch thick. From this stage of thickness (or rather thinness), gold leaf can be further cut into square pieces and hammered steadily by sheathing it between heavy paper and other suitable padding until it is semi-transparent in thinness. In this way, a small piece of gold ingot can yield thousands of sheets of gold leaf. In many parts of China, India, Burma, Thailand and Laos, gold leaf is still being made in the villages by this ancient method of hand-beating gold ingots with wooden hammers of various shapes and weights. Some gold-beaters still prefer to work with pure gold ingots. Labour costs are still low in some parts of Asia, but gold leaf remains an expensive item in the gilding of furniture and other objects of great value.

Gold leaf which has been applied to carvings can be burnished to a high gloss by gentle rubbing with a fine cotton pad. Loose ends of gold leaf are simply brushed away with a camel brush. In European methods of gilding it is customary to press loose sheets of gold leaf into position by pouncing the surface with a fine cotton pad. Chinese craftsmen, however, do not resort to pouncing, but blow directly onto the gilded surface to secure any loose sheet of gold leaf into position. Gentle dabbing with a fine brush also helps. Once gold leaf has been firmly adhered to the priming of lacquer and/or gesso and size, and allowed to dry out thoroughly, it will preserve its gilded state indefinitely, provided it does not come into contact with corrosive acids or mercury compounds: the gilded furniture from the tomb of Tutankhamen maintained its pristine qualities even after a lapse of over 3000 years! And many extant pieces of red-and-gold furniture in old Baba homes in Singapore, Malacca and Penang are still in a very fine state of preservation. But over the last 30 years or so, as Georgetown, Malacca and Singapore became more urbanized and industrialized, heavy emissions of exhaust fumes from motorcycles, cars, trucks and buses have caused the atmosphere to become more acidic and corrosive, and thus inimical to giltwork in the long run. Still, when all is said and done, gold remains the most durable of precious metals.

Finally, gilding must be distinguished from metallic gold paints which are widely used nowadays for painting or spraying on furniture, mirror frames and other types of wood surface. The base from which these paints are made is metallic powder, especially copper. Metallic gold paints are inexpensive and easy to apply. But

Cabinets with barred or traceried windows fitted with glass panes of various geometric patterns, such as the one shown here, are said to have originated in England during the 17th century when cabinet-makers were unable to procure glass panes in large sheets. So they were forced to improvise by constructing variously shaped mouldings to accommodate the smaller types of glass panes then available. But the ornamental value of traceried doors or windows was soon appreciated. Namwood cabinets of the type shown here were used both as wardrobes and as display cabinets for antique china and silverware. Courtesy of Mr Peter Wee, Katong Antique House.

they do not have the lustre of gold and they tarnish very quickly because the copper base tends to oxidize upon contact with oxygen present in the atmosphere, thus giving gold paints a characteristic dull and greenish-yellow colour. Gilding, by contrast, lasts for centuries.

Design and workmanship

As with blackwood and rosewood furniture constructed out of *huanghuali* and *zitan*, red-and-gold namwood furniture was entirely fitted together by joints secured with mortises and tenons. No nails, screws or glues were ever used; yet the joinery was so good that those extant pieces of red-and-gold namwood furniture in old Baba homes (which had not been moved or dragged about frequently, or otherwise left in dark and damp places) remained largely intact and well preserved, even after 100 years or more, except for some slight shrinkage here and there in the wood panels.

In so far as design and workmanship are concerned, red-and-gold namwood furniture was constructed according to the same tradition of cabinet-making and joinery which characterized *huanghuali* and *zitan* furniture. The basic design of most extant pieces of namwood furniture is typical of classic Chinese furniture: it is conservative and functional in form, solidly constructed, box-like and rectangular in structure. The principal components of any piece of furniture, such as the seat frame, table top, legs, uprights, aprons, railings and stretchers, whether they happen to be plainly constructed or ornately carved, are always boldly conceived, substantial in proportions and firmly fitted together. Solid craftsmanship was as much a fundamental feature of namwood furniture as it was with blackwood furniture. On the whole, extant pieces of 19th century red-and-gold namwood furniture are more bulky and heavily constructed than many extant pieces of *huanghuali* and *zitan* furniture of the Ming Dynasty.

For all its colours and the exuberant splendour of its carvings, red-and-gold furniture is perhaps more archaic in some fundamental respects than blackwood furniture of the classic Ming period. For example, if one looks carefully at the carvings of those complicated cloud scrolls and what look like dragons with foliated tails on the aprons, stretchers and spandrels, as well as those *taotien* masks at the corners and at the bases of chair and bench legs, one is immediately reminded of those complex relief motifs on the Shang, Zhou and Warring States bronzes, as well as paintings on silk, lacquer and wood recovered from early Han period tombs. The resemblance between the archaic quality of those carved scrolls in red-and-gold namwood furniture and the motifs of ancient bronzes and paintings is so clearly apparent one cannot help concluding that while the Shang, Zhou and Han cultures may have been buried and forgotten long ago, their influence was still vividly felt and manifested in the decorative motifs of red-and-gold furniture made in the southeastern provinces of China. An interesting speculation comes to mind: did the remaining survivors of the Shang, Zhou and Han periods, whose civilizations grew and flourished in the Yellow river basin in the north and northwest, move south and southeast to Zhejiang, Fujian and Guangdong to perpetuate their cultures among the 'southern barbarians'?

Students of antique Chinese furniture may have noticed this peculiar archaic quality about the decorative motifs of red-and-gold namwood furniture, but so far no one seems to have drawn attention to the singular resemblance between the carved motifs of namwood furniture and the relief motifs on the Shang, Zhou and Warring States bronzes and jades. Nor has anyone pointed out that the scrolled carvings on the apron panels of namwood furniture resemble the serpentine motifs on Han period artefacts[18]. This may be attributed to the fact that while most people regard Ming and early Qing *huanghuali* and *zitan* furniture as the paradigm of all that was excellent in Chinese cabinet-work, no one took the trouble to look at red-and-gold namwood furniture from southeastern China, and which in any case, was never used either by the fastidious mandarin aristocrats or by the royal court in Beijing. Nonetheless, the fact remains that in this neglected corner of China, its most ancient art lived on in the domestic furniture of the southern Chinese.

But to return to the comparison between classic blackwood furniture and red-and-gold namwood furniture: whereas blackwood furniture of the Ming and early Qing periods was largely simple, functional and unadorned in its design – carvings and ornamentation being kept to an absolute minimum – namwood red-and-gold furniture was showy, richly coloured and resplendent with carved and gilded panels and border trimmings which gleam with the splendour of gold set against contrasting backgrounds of red, black and brown lacquers. And as if gilding was not impressive enough, Chinese craftsmen even had chips of mother-of-pearl inlaid into the borders enclosing the carved and gilded panels!

But for all its splendid gildings and intricate carvings, namwood furniture remains basically conservative in its structure and method of construction. Among the more traditionally designed pieces of red-and-gold furniture (e.g. two-tiered wedding cabinets, chests-of-drawers and settees) found in well-to-do Baba homes in Singapore and Malacca, the carved and gilded panels are invariably neatly confined within floating rectangular panels, while the framework components are left bare and unadorned.

One notices that in these pieces a certain restraint was imposed upon the amount of gilding allowed. Even with the Penang variety of red-and-gold furniture, which is overly decorated, with gilded carvings being worked into practically every square inch of all the frontal surfaces, the main structure of its design remains clear and uncomplicated. For one thing, there are no eccentric baroque distortions or superfluous attachments to spoil the overall symmetry of a piece of namwood furniture because Chinese carvers had the good sense to keep all their ornamentation confined within bounds prescribed by the structural design of a piece of furniture. For another, while one may deprecate the excessive gilding and ornate carvings of the Penang variety of red-and-gold namwood furniture on the ground that it smacks of poor taste, one cannot, however, fault it for poor craftsmanship or inferior cabinet-work. Besides, apologists of the Penang variety of red-and-gold furniture could calmly retort by quoting the old adage *degustibus non est disputandum* (in matters of taste there can be no dispute).

But, be that as it may, gold leaf has always been a rare and expensive commodity, and the art of gilding is one which requires considerable skill and patience. The purpose of gilding is to give an object a certain touch of luxury. When judiciously applied, gilding enhances the value and splendour of red-and-gold furniture. However, when a piece of furniture is sloshed all over with gold leaf until it is dazzlingly brilliant, the sense of luxury and preciousness is lost, and the piece of furniture in question ends up as a vulgar object of mere ornamentation.

Dating based on ornamentation

While we are still on the subject of ornamentation in furniture, we may note here that there is a tacit belief among students of antique Chinese furniture that those household movables which happen to be decorated with complex and elaborate carvings may be said to be of more recent dating (i.e. of the Qing Dynasty) than those which happen to be functional and unadorned in their designs. As a general rule, there is, of course, evidence to support such an assumption. Scholars who have studied all the available evidence on the subject have observed that Chinese furniture predating the Qing Dynasty (that is to say, furniture dating from the Ming Dynasty to as far back as, say, the Song Dynasty) was starkly unadorned in its structure and design.

And while there are no extant pieces of antique furniture which can, with certainty, be dated back either to the Yuan (1271–1368) or the Song dynasty (960–1279), paintings do exist of the interiors of domestic households and the courts of high officials dating to the Yuan and Song periods which depict the kinds of furniture used in China in those days. The types of furniture, when one scrutinizes the pictures carefully, turn out to be surprisingly similar in structure and design to authenticated furniture of the Ming Dynasty. The institution of complete ornamentation in furniture, as well as in other objects of art, really began with the reign of Emperor Qianlong (1735–96), when all official

artefacts made for the emperor's household and his court were decorated with elaborate ornamentation.

Lately, some dissenting people have questioned whether the uncritical acceptance of this method of dating Chinese furniture is justifiable. They maintain that there are, in fact, extant pieces of Ming furniture which come with elaborate ornamentation. Conversely, they say, there are authentic pieces of Qing period furniture which are quite without any ornamentation at all. The writers do not tell us how they arrive at this conclusion. The point about this controversy is that it is difficult to be too dogmatic on this issue because, for one thing, the precise dating of any piece of antique Chinese furniture is very often a matter of conjecture, based largely on circumstantial evidence and rarely on direct evidence. For another, the cult of originality has never been a strong point in the Chinese system of values. Quite the contrary. As a conservative people true to the Confucian precept of honouring the teachings of their ancestors, the Chinese have always tried to preserve their ancient beliefs and practices intact – sometimes for centuries on end.

Thus, when it comes to the tradition of cabinet-making in China, it is entirely in keeping with their conservative tradition to have blackwood furniture of 19th-century dating, but made to 16th- or perhaps 17th-century design. This is what I have noticed from my own observations in the past. Several years ago, when I was in Malacca on an information-gathering trip, Mr Kee Tak Lip of Keris Woodwork and K and S Antiques showed me several bench-like seats, one of which was made of namwood and painted in a reddish-brown lacquer, and which, on stylistic considerations alone, could have been given a Ming period dating. Mr Kee, however, was quite positive that the several benches in his workshop were all of 19th century dating. And since Mr Kee bought his antique benches from some old homes in Malacca – and there are virtually no residential houses left in Malacca which are over 150 years old or so – the possibility of a Ming dating was remote.

If, for the sake of argument, we now apply this criterion of dating based principally upon the presence or absence of ornate carvings, we are, of course, led to infer that red-and-gold namwood furniture cannot be earlier than, say, 1750. Where the majority of extant pieces are concerned, however, all the information we have indicates that namwood furniture in the former Straits Settlements may be dated to between 1800 and 1920. This conclusion is based mainly on circumstantial evidence relating to the probable revival of the Baba community in Malacca after the ceding of Malacca by the Dutch to the British soon after the Napoleonic Wars in Europe; the founding of Penang by Francis Light in 1786; and the founding of Singapore by Stamford Raffles in 1819. As a reminder, we may note that very few, if any, examples of extant red-and-gold namwood furniture are either marked or dated after the manner of traditional Chinese paintings, porcelain, bronze, silver or lacquer-work; unless an artefact was especially commissioned by some institution (e.g. temples, Chinese clan associations, chambers of commerce), it was not customary for Chinese cabinet-makers to affix their names or their shop names, together with dates and/or the reign names of emperors, to their handiwork.

Types of carvings

Four types of carvings are employed in most examples of red-and-gold furniture: engraving, bas-relief, high-relief, and open-work or pierced-work. Carvings executed by the method of affixing appliqué attachments together are very seldom used. Chinese carvers believed in genuine sculpture, that is, a piece of carving must be shaped out of one solid block of wood: piecemeal carvings joined together by glue or nails are simply rejected as counterfeit sculpture. Engravings and bas-reliefs are generally used for border designs to depict arabesque motifs, or else on panels of less expensive types of red-and-gold furniture. Bas-relief carvings, as the name suggests, are shallow carvings which are slightly raised above the matrix of the base wood. The labour (though not the skill) expended in executing bas-relief work is less than if the carvings are executed in the round, as in high-relief carvings. All things being equal, if the price of a piece of antique furniture was determined by the amount of skilled labour expended, rather than by the desire of the antique dealer to reap a larger profit, red-and-gold furniture with bas-relief carvings ought to cost less than those pieces which are executed with high-relief and open-work (or cut-through) carvings. On the whole, this seems to be the common guideline which most dealers go by when pricing a piece of antique furniture, even though it is a well-known fact that labour – even skilled labour at that – has always been cheap in China. However that may be, bas-relief carvings need not be regarded as inferior to high-relief carvings because the quality of craftsmanship invested in the execution of a piece of furniture is determined not so much by the amount of labour invested as by the combined skill and artistry of the cabinet-maker and the wood-carver.

High-relief carvings which do not involve cutting through the base wood may look deceptively simple, but are in fact difficult to execute because the carvings have to be cut deep enough to create an impression of three-dimensional solidity. And when this is achieved with the kind of craftsmanship which endows the

various motifs with a sense of liveliness and realism, a panel with high-relief carvings can be an object of fascinating beauty. The trouble with high-relief carvings, from the standpoint of the carver, is that when small and complex motifs must be accurately cut and shaped in the round on a panel of wood no thicker than, say, 1.5 centimetres, it is difficult to avoid puncturing through the base wood and creating unsightly holes. He must, therefore, wield his carving instruments with circumspection at all times. Equally difficult to execute are the designs of the carvings, which may consist of a complex of architectural structures, mountainous landscapes, trees and flowering plants, human figures and animals, done in such a manner that the backdrop against which these motifs stand out appears flat and even. Anyone who is familiar with the types of decorations which appear on the carved panels of red-and-gold furniture will appreciate that, more often than not, the carvings are complex, crowded and full of intricate details. Obviously, the complexity of these carvings can only pile on the difficulties for the wood-carver.

A favourite design for bas-relief carving are the symbols of the Eight Precious Things (Ba Bao).

For this reason, most of the carved panels in red-and-gold namwood furniture which feature high-relief carvings are executed by the technique of pierced- or open-work. In this method of carving, the craftsman does not need to worry about preserving the underlying background of the carved panel intact. Instead, he simply cuts through all the superfluous and empty spaces between the relief motifs, leaving holes and empty spaces between the carvings. Any resultant roughness and raw edges caused by chisels and gouges can be smoothed out by fine wood files and sandpapers. However, pierced- and open-work carvings of this sort tend to leave a perforated effect upon a carved piece of wood panel, except that this is more than compensated for by a greater sense of depth and concreteness which the carvings now assume. In particular, the play of light and shadow enhances the sculptural qualities of the ornamental motifs as never before.

However, the drawback of a carved and gilded panel perforated with holes is that it affords no protection against dust, dampness and insects, especially when it is built into the structure of a door in a cabinet, the frontal panel of a drawer or the lid of a chest. Obviously, these holes must be blocked up to protect the interior of these closets and the recesses of case furniture. Chinese cabinet-makers long ago solved the problem by simply attaching a thin slab of wood, cut-to-measure, to the back of the perforated panel. This covering slab was secured by groove-and-tongue attachments.

The meanings and themes of the carvings

Unlike the Rococo decorations in 18th-century European art and architecture, the motifs which occur again and again in traditional Chinese arts and crafts (e.g. wood-carvings, bronze vessels, silverwork, jade, lacquerware, porcelain, etc.) are never purely decorative in content and in purpose. Chinese art has its roots in a civilization of considerable antiquity, and one of the characteristics of the arts of an ancient civilization, whether it be Mesopotamian, Egyptian or Chinese, is that art was largely made in the service of religion and superstition. It should come as no surprise, therefore, that the carvings on all red-and-gold furniture which still show traces of Shang and Zhou cultures are imbued with religious and symbolic meanings. And since it was also ceremonial in function – red-and-gold furniture being made exclusively for wedding ceremonies in traditional Baba culture – the themes of the various panels of wood-carvings had to be propitious for that occasion.

Thus, peonies (especially the splendid hybrid varieties made famous by their association with Yang Guifei, the famous beauty and concubine of Minghuang, the third emperor of the Tang Dynasty) and phoenixes (the legendary bird of good omen and symbol of the empress) are frequently depicted in the carved panels. Next come such motifs as the stag or antelope (symbol of longevity), a pair of mandarin ducks and two butterflies (symbols of conjugal fidelity), quails and fishes (symbols of fertility and abundance), a pair of bats and a pair of magpies (symbols of happiness and luck) – all of which are said to be auspicious of a wedded life. The very act of having these auspicious symbols carved and depicted in the furniture used by the newly wedded Baba-Nonya couple might be interpreted as an expression of hope that their wedded lives would somehow be attended by all the good things which these motifs symbolize.

Likewise, the Four Liberal Accomplishments are represented by a lyre wrapped in an embroidered case, a chess- or go-board with round boxes for the black and white chips, a pair of books and a pair of scrolls. These four accomplishments are described as *qin*, *qi*, *shu* and *hua*, namely music, chess, writing and painting. The symbols of Eight Precious Things (*Ba Bao*) are frequently represented in engravings and bas-relief. They are: (1) *zhu*, the pearl symbol which is said to grant every wish, (2) *qian*, or cash, represented by a copper coin with a square hole symbolizing wealth, (3) a lozenge representing *hua* or painting, (4) an open lozenge, a symbol of victory, (5) *qing*, the musical stone, (6) *shu*, a pair of books, symbolizing scholarly accomplishment, (7) *jue*, a pair of horn-like objects symbolizing good health, and (8) *ai yeh*, the artemisia leaf, a plant of good omen. All these symbols are represented with decorative ribbons. The symbols and/or the figure representations of the Eight Taoist Immortals appear frequently in red-and-gold carvings. The Eight Immortals are Zhongli Quan, Lu Dongbin, Li Tieguai, Cao Guojiu, Lan Caihe, Zhang Guolao, Han Xiangzi and He Xiangu.

Occasionally, the *ba ji xiang* or the emblems of the Eight Happy Auguries in Buddhism are represented. These are (1) a parasol, the symbol

of nobility in the moral sense of the word, (2) a pair of goldfish, symbolic of the union of happiness and utility, (3) a vase, purportedly believed to contain 'the elixir of heaven', (4) a lotus flower, the Buddhist symbol of purity, (5) a conch shell, the Buddhist symbol of victory, (6) the endless knot, the symbol of the Buddhist path, (7) the canopy, the symbol of victory over the religions of the world and (8) the wheel of *chakra*, the symbol of Buddhist teachings that lead the disciple to nirvana.

The Babas, like their counterparts in China, took a liberal view of religion, and traditionally Confucianism, Taoism and Buddhism were regarded as the 'Three Friends', that is to say, the three religions which have become part and parcel of Chinese culture.

Many other symbols are also incorporated into the ornamental carvings in red-and-gold furniture. These include the dragon, the symbol of imperial power and authority as well as the male symbol, and the flowers of the four seasons, namely peonies (for spring), lotuses (for summer), chrysanthemums (for autumn) and *prunus* or plum blossoms (for winter). Occasionally, a carved panel usually intended for an altar table, a 'spirit house' or ancestral tablet is represented with the symbols of the Eight Trigrams, or *ba gua*, and/or that of the *yin-yang* circle representing the duality of nature.

But motifs and symbols of good omen and of religious significance apart, red-and-gold namwood furniture is interesting for another reason: some of the most outstanding of these carved and gilded panels depict the figures of foot-soldiers, archers and cavalry-men engaged in pitched battles set against some rugged landscapes or architectural settings, while others are of court and domestic scenes showing richly garbed individuals engaged in various sorts of activities. The themes of many of these complex figured and landscape carvings are said to be dramatic representations of famous and memorable episodes drawn from historical, literary and operatic sources. These include *The Romance of the Three Kingdoms*, *Romance of the Warring States*, *The Water Margin*, *The Dream of the Red Chamber*, *Liang Shanbai and Zhu Yingtai*, *The Monkey God Stories* or *Tales from the Western Lands* (a dramatization of Tang Sanzhuang's voyage to India via Central Asia to collect Buddhist manuscripts), *Madam White Snake* and other stories and legends. These stories are often based on the lives of such famous and notorious personalities in Chinese history as Empress Wu Hou, Emperor Minghuang's mistress and famous beauty Yang Guifei, the first emperor of China, Shih Huangdi, the military exploits and political machinations of Cao Cao, and so on.

The Babas and Nonyas were not particularly

Ceremonial footstools for a traditional Baba wedding. The use of these charming articles of furniture was not, however, exclusive to the Baba community in days gone by, as these objects also featured regularly in the wedding ceremonies of former generations of Chinese nobility and Malay royalty. Nonetheless, the nuptial stools of the Babas have a distinctive character of their own: the design and structure of these stools are, in fact, an admixture of traditional Chinese carvings (e.g. pomegranates, peaches, peonies, phoenixes, lion masks and feet) and Malay art forms (e.g. the padded covering of beadwork for the stool seat and the ogival design of the seat). It is this blending of ancient Chinese and Malay art forms which makes Straits Chinese heritage unique. Author's collection.

noted for their interest in Chinese operas which, in days gone by, were staged in Malaya and Singapore by travelling operatic troupes from China in such dialects as Hokkien, Hakka, Cantonese, Teochew and Hainanese. None of these dialects was understood by those Babas brought up to speak only Baba Malay. It is true that the more cultured Baba-Nonyas read and were familiar with such classics as *The Dream of the Red Chamber, The Romance of the Three Kingdoms, The Water Margin, The Monkey God Stories* and *Madam White Snake* in Baba Malay. From the end of the 19th century to about the 1930s, a number of Peranakan Chinese writers who were competent in Chinese and Malay were actively engaged in translating Chinese classics into Baba Malay. Of these, the most famous was probably Mr Chan Kim Boon, who translated *The Romance of the Three Kingdoms* into 30 paperback volumes, each measuring $6^{1}/_{2}$ inches (17 centimetres) by four inches (10 centimetres), under the title *Chrita Dulu-kala Nama-nya Sam Kok atau Tiga Negri Berprang*. He also translated *The Monkey God Stories* under the title *Chrita (Sey Yew) Pasal Kau Chey Thian* and *The Water Margin* under the title *Chrita Dulu-kala di triak Song Kang atau 108 Prompak* in 10 volumes.

But operas based on memorable episodes from these classics were rarely performed in the Baba patois, and the majority of latter-day Babas were not conversant with Chinese dialects or else were unfamiliar with the classic operas. Those who took an avid interest in Chinese operas, those who had read the classics in Baba Malay and those who regularly attended operatic performances by travelling Chinese *wayang*

troupes had to be quite proficient in one of the more popular dialects. But they belonged to a small minority. Yet, here you have, prominently carved in these gilded panels of red-and-gold furniture, famous scenes and episodes taken from the classic operas and romances. If one infers from the evidence of these carved panels that the Baba-Nonyas were avid fans of Chinese operas, one would be mistaken.

Now the mere presence of art motifs having symbolic, dramatic and religious significance in red-and-gold furniture is not, in itself, something extraordinary. Much of folk art in China (and elsewhere) was customarily ornamented with epic scenes and memorable episodes taken from fables, legends and romances. Nor are such decorations confined to furniture; they are also found on porcelain, lacquerware, folk paintings, silverware and embroideries. However, with royalty and the aristocratic mandarin class, decorative ornaments, following the traditions of the court tastes of the Song Dynasty, had to be restrained, formalized and understated – more hinted at than explicit. Where furniture was concerned, the functional and elegant simplicity of Ming period blackwood furniture, as illustrated in standard texts, was regarded as the paradigm of upper-class taste. By contrast, Straits Chinese furniture, especially the red-and-gold variety, was more reflective of folk arts and crafts, not surprisingly so because the traditional Babas and their seafaring forebears who came to Southeast Asia were merchants and traders. Hence, the red-and-gold variety of Straits Chinese furniture does not feature in standard texts on classic Chinese furniture.

Repertory of namwood furniture

Chairs

There is virtually only one type of red-and-gold namwood chair extant and this is the pair of high-back wedding chairs without armrests meant for the bride and groom during wedding ceremonies. There is another type of namwood chair which is low-back, squarish and throne-like, and comes with armrests. It is similar in design to blackwood chairs of the type with mother-of-pearl inlays, except that it is sparsely ornamented, with simple carvings of cloud scrolls being confined to the frontal and side aprons immediately below the seat frame, and on the narrow splat centrally placed between the uprights. All the component parts of this type of chair are square-cut, apparently to emphasize the symmetry between the structure and design. Chairs of this type are, however, simply painted over with several coats of dark brown lacquer without any trace of gilding at all. And until the coming of that variety of English/European style furniture made out of teakwood, families of more modest means regularly furnished their reception halls with namwood chairs of this sort with matching tea tables, instead of the more expensive blackwood chairs with mother-of-pearl inlays.

The pair of red-and-gold wedding chairs is constructed virtually on the same design as the variety of namwood chairs noted above, except for structural modifications, namely that (1) they have no armrests, (2) the narrow central splats as well as the uprights are extended upwards almost to the level of the sitter's head, (3) the uprights, instead of being symmetrical with the square-cut back and front legs, are rounded and slightly raked at the top, and (4) the cresting or top railing, instead of being a straight or bent crossbar, is either yoke-shaped, or else carved into the form of two gilded dragons facing each other in pursuit of the legendary flaming pearl. The splat is usually engraved with a gilded stork or some other auspicious animal inside a square or circular medallion in the centre. The other ornamented parts of the chair are the frontal and side aprons, carved with simple cloud scrolls and outlined in gilt. Four square stretchers are located at the lower ends of the chair legs which terminate in hoofed feet.

The wedding chair is high as chairs go, being just about four feet (120 centimetres) from the ground to the top rail. The bride and groom, when formally seated on these chairs, had to have their feet supported by two oval-shaped stools elaborately carved and padded with beaded cushions. It was also customary to drape the pair of wedding chairs with long, rectangular panels of red flannel material which has decorations of dragons and *qilins* embroidered in gold thread.

The wedding footstools

The wedding footstools are rarely seen nowadays. They were infrequently encountered even 25 years ago when I first began to take an active interest in the cultural heritage of the Babas. This may be attributed to the fact that only one set of wedding footstools was usually passed down the family line over a period of several generations. And since they were used only at weddings and were carefully stored away at all other times, these ceremonial footstools tended to be better

preserved then the general run of household furniture which was daily sat upon, dragged about and subjected to bumps and scratches, temperature and humidity changes, and attacks by damp and wood-burrowing insects. My wife obtained, quite by chance, such a pair of wedding footstools from Malacca more than 10 years ago, probably an old family heirloom used over many generations, judging by the frayed and faded velvet of the beaded panels and the patina on the reddish-brown lacquer.

The standard red-and-gold namwood footstool is of oval shape, between 10 and 10$^{1/2}$ inches (25 and 26.5 centimetres) long, and 7$^{1/2}$ and 8 inches (19 and 20 centimetres) wide. Its height, including the slight bulge of the padded and beaded cushion, is between 6 and 6$^{1/2}$ inches (15 and 16 centimetres). The four cabriole-like legs are carved and gilded with gargoyle or *taotien* masks at the top and some floral scrolls at the foot. The aprons are carved with floral and cloud scrolls in bas-relief gilding. The stool seat is covered with an oval padding of cotton wool and over this an oval panel of red or brown velvet embroidered with auspicious wedding motifs of rocaille beads is mounted with brass tacks. For such a small piece of furniture, the components are surprisingly thick and solidly cut, joined together by mortises and tenons.

Tables

There are at least two different types of red-and-gold carved tables used in traditional Baba wedding ceremonies. The first type consists of altar tables, for example, the two-tiered high altar table, known as the *sam kai* table, usually filled with decorations and appropriate offerings to Tiangong, the God or King of Heaven, and a variation of this based on the square red-and-gold or black-and-gold namwood table. The second type consists of ornately carved and gilded rectangular bridal tables, which formed part of the furniture in the bridal chamber. One of the tables was used by the bride and groom when they ate together as part of the wedding ceremony lasting 12 days. The other was used by the bride as a dressing table on which was placed a carved and gilded dressing mirror mounted on a small, low mini-chest with two or more built-in drawers.

Sam kai altar tables

The most important of these ceremonial tables is the *sam kai* altar table. According to traditional Baba custom, this is the most important object in the wedding ceremony. It is erected to the God or King of Heaven, before whom the indispensable rite of the *chioh thau*, or *chiu thau* (as it was called in Malacca), the initiation into adulthood ceremony, was performed. The Hokkien word *chioh* or *chiu* means 'to mount' or 'to go up', and *thau* means 'head'. So literally translated, *chioh thau* or *chiu thau* means 'to go up to the head' or, in literal terms, 'to attain adulthood' (through mental or intellectual maturity).

Thus, when the Sang-ke-m, or Mistress of Ceremonies, combs the bride's hair at the *chioh thau* rites, she also utters simultaneously that the bride is no longer a girl but has become a woman. This ceremony is carried out in the main reception hall of the bride's parents' home at an early hour

of the morning in the space between the *sam kai* altar and the altar of the domestic god. While this is going on in the bride's home a similar ceremony is held in the groom's house. The groom, however, does not undergo any hair-combing rites. Instead, he is presented by the Pak Chindek, the Master of Ceremonies, with a number of objects, each of which is symbolic of his transition from childhood to adulthood and of the responsibilities of an adult and a husband-to-be. These are the *Book of Fate*, or *Reference*, a small pair of scales, a Chinese ruler, a pair of scissors, a razor, a small mirror and 10 yards of red silk thread. With the assistance of the Pak Chindek, a little boy, known as the Ku Yia, then steps forward and performs a number of prescribed gestures in front of the groom using each of these objects. For a more detailed discussion of the *chioh thau* ceremony, the reader is referred to Ruth Ho's *Rainbow Round My Shoulder* (Eastern Universities Press, Singapore, 1975) and Cheo Kim Ban's *A Baba Wedding* (also Eastern Universities Press, Singapore, 1983).

The *sam kai* altar table comes in two tiers. The bottom table, about two feet (60 centimetres) high, is actually a pedestal on which the main table, about three feet (90 centimetres) high, stands. There are four square mortises at the corners of the top frame of the bottom table, into which corresponding tenons, carved under the feet of the upper table, may be fitted. The mortises and tenons which secure the upper altar table to the base support are not tightly fitted but detachable. The frontal and side aprons of the base support table are usually carved with

auspicious motifs, such as *qilins*, antelopes, dragons, peonies, plum blossoms, figures representing the Three Abundances, etc. These are in high-relief and gilded. The legs (rather short in this case) are cabriole-like with masks of *taotien* at the top corners, and floral and cloud scrolls at the bottom. As these legs are required to support the combined weight of the base table and the upper table, they are thick-set and stoutly constructed. The top of the base support is not a plain, flat surface constructed out of parallel slabs of wood laid side-by-side and secured by tongue-and-groove joints; rather, it consists of a shaped piece of panel executed in lattice-work, grooved into the frame. In *sam kai* wedding ceremonies, burnt incense is placed on the floor beneath so that the smoke of aromatic woods may permeate through the lattices.

The main table is rectangular and just over three feet (90 centimetres) long, 1 foot 6 inches (45 centimetres) wide and about three feet (90 centimetres) high. The front and side aprons are decorated either with cut-through or open-work carvings and gilded. Alternatively, the gilded carvings may be executed in high-relief. The more elaborately designed tables have vertical spandrels on either side of the front legs and one side of the back legs.

Although altar tables and bridal tables are almost identical in structure and design, they may be distinguished thus: bridal tables for serving food feature a latticed shelf close to the base which is tenoned into the table legs at the four corners. Altar tables generally feature a base

support. Base stretchers are confined to the sides between the front and back legs only and, for this purpose, Chinese cabinet-makers devised broad rectangular panels with floral scrolls in open-work to serve as stretchers. This technique of strengthening table legs was neither new nor peculiar to red-and-gold namwood furniture, but was already used in blackwood tables with modified trestle legs dating back to the Ming Dynasty. Since no stretchers span the gap between the front legs, the carved and gilded frieze must serve the double functions of a decorative panel and a brace. Hence, the friezes which stretch across the two sides are made to ensure that the legs are firmly secured in position. All uncarved and unadorned surfaces on such altar tables are painted over with opaque red lacquer.

Sam kai tables which come complete with their base supports are very rarely seen nowadays, and only a few families in Singapore and Malacca still preserve them as treasured heirlooms. It is of course possible to improvise a *sam kai* table by building a low platform made out of several planks supported by a pair of trestles and suitably draped over with a red silk cloth. A red-and-gold carved altar table can then be placed over this platform.

Among the paraphernalia on a traditional *sam kai* table decked out for a wedding celebration is an elaborate and impressively embroidered piece of altar cloth draped over the front (and sometimes the back as well). The Babas referred to it as the *tok wee*. The *tok wee*, or altar cloth, is a square red panel, either of silk or flannel, three feet (90 centimetres) by three feet (90 centimetres), embroidered with such auspicious motifs as the

dragon, a pair of phoenixes, a pair of mandarin ducks, a pair of quails, a pair of magpies, antelopes and peony blossoms in coloured silk and gold thread, or in some cases, entirely in gold thread. Altar cloths of this type were highly prized by former generations of Nonyas. Two very fine examples of altar cloths are illustrated in figures 49 and 78 of *Straits Chinese Beadwork and Embroidery* (Times Books International, Singapore, 1987).

The *sam kai* altar table might have been an indispensable piece of ceremonial furniture for the *chioh thau* or *chiu thau* ritual of the more conservative Babas of Singapore and Malacca. But it was apparently dispensed with in Peranakan communities elsewhere in Southeast Asia, for example in Penang, Medan, Jakarta and Semarang. The late Madam Queeny Chang, in recalling her own marriage at the age of 16 in Medan sometime during World War I, mentioned that she was formally 'dressed in a traditional Chinese wedding costume' which her mother had specially bought in Penang. Madam Chang did not explicitly mention that she wore a white *baju chioh thau*, but only that she wore 'pyjamas' (the colour was not specified) as the innermost garment. Madam Kooi, the Mistress of Ceremonies, then tied an embroidered green skirt over the pyjamas followed by a large 'red satin jacket with very wide sleeves'. Finally came a sleeveless black jacket which was equally elaborately embroidered. We may presume that Queeny Chang's 'pyjamas' were a white *baju chioh thau*.

There was no mention of the *sam kai* altar table with its appropriate paraphernalia. She merely said she was led into the hall where her family's ancestral shrine was located. She was made to kneel in front of it while Madam Kooi intoned the traditional words to the effect that she was no longer a child but a grown woman. And that was all there was to the *chioh thau* ceremony.

The term *sam kai* is probably derived from the Cantonese word *sam kak*, meaning three tiers. Figuratively speaking, the *sam kai* table may be said to have three tiers, namely the base table or support, the altar table proper, and a six-sided carved and lacquered wooden box known as the *chanab*, placed on top of the altar table. The term *chanab* is probably a corruption of the Hokkien word *chai hup* meaning 'vegetable box', and this is almost literally true because the offerings which stand on top of the *chanab* (as well as on the altar table itself) and which are intended for Tiangong, the King or God of Heaven, consist entirely of fruit and vegetables. These include bowls of glutinous rice dumplings, sugar cane, oranges, slices of raw papaya soaked in sugar water, pineapples and either red dates or plums. Apparently, the King of Heaven is believed to be a vegetarian with a

preference for tropical fruit!

The *chanab* is a handsome and impressive piece of decorative art and comes in two different shapes: rectangular and hexagonal. The Baba communities in Malacca, Singapore and Penang traditionally used the hexagonal, boat-shaped *chanab* for many of their religious offerings on red-letter days.

The chanab comes in two parts: first, a hexagonal, carved and gilded three-tiered structure, with elaborate giltwood carvings executed in open-work, and second, a cover, similarly shaped, which is painted in shiny, black lacquer against which scenes of figures in court settings are rendered in gilt. The *chanab* itself is a three-tiered structure, with a top tray-like slab with carved and gilded railings. This is fitted to, and overhangs, the hexagonal structure immediately below, which is entirely gilded and carved in open-work. It is the most prominent part of the *chanab*, and may be said to constitute its core structure. This core structure, in turn, sits on a plain black slab with mouldings on the edges, six carved and gilded aprons below, and six S-shaped legs located at the corners of the hexagon. The entire structure of the *chanab* rests on the backs of six miniature *qilins* which are mounted over a plain black, hexagonal slab that serves as a stretcher.

Chanabs used by the Hokkien community in China are not all constructed with a hexagonal design. I have several *chanabs* which were brought out of Shantou, China, during the late 1960s and they are rectangular in shape. The largest of these is 18 inches (45 centimetres) long, 4¹/2 inches (11.2 centimetres) wide and up to 20 inches (50

Left and above: In Baba Malay, the word chanab *is a corruption of either two Hokkien terms, namely,* chai hup *('vegetable box') or* cha hup *('wooden box'). It does not matter, however, which of the two words is the original etymon because the* chanab *is literally a wooden box (usually hexagonal or rectangular), as well as a receptacle on which preserved fruit and vegetable offerings are placed. As an essential item of the ceremonial objects used in a traditional Baba wedding, the* chanab *was usually placed on top of the* sam kai *altar table dedicated to Tiangong or the God of Heaven. From an aesthetic point of view, the* chanab *is an exquisite example of carvings in miniature, skilfully executed down to the smallest detail and lavishly gilded to add splendour to the altar table. Author's collection.*

centimetres) tall. They, too, come in three tiers, but apparently they were not common to Baba homes in Malacca and Penang.

All extant antique *chanabs* were apparently made out of some variety of pinewood. It is yellowish in colour, light, relatively soft and easy to work with. But because they are largely protected by several coats of black lacquer and gilded and, in days gone by, were carefully stored away when not in use, many antique *chanabs* are still in a very fine state of preservation.

Bridal tables

Of bridal tables, there are two kinds which bear close resemblance in size and design to the standard *sam kai* altar table (minus the base support): the food table at which the bride and groom customarily shared their meals together during the 12 days of nuptial ceremonies, and the dressing table. Like the *sam kai* altar table, all bridal tables are painted over with several coats of opaque red lacquer, except on those panels which are ornamented with gilded carvings executed in high- or bas-relief work. However, the main difference between the design of the altar table and that of the bridal table, as mentioned, is that in the latter there is a latticed panel which is bounded in by four base stretchers located at the lower ends of the table legs. This panel is absent in altar tables where the braces are confined to the gaps between the front and back legs, and they are often constructed in the form of carved panels. Generally, altar tables either have freestanding legs or, as in the case of the *sam kai* table, are supported by a base stand with a latticed panel grooved into the top frame.

Thus, except for the inclusion of the latticed panel located at the lower ends of the table legs, the bridal table (as well as the dressing table) is very similar in most other respects to the red-and-gold altar tables peculiar to the Baba culture. It is pertinent to note here that when the bride and the groom sit down to partake their meals ceremonially, they do not sit facing each other, but rather side-by-side. This is because tradition required that the two bridal chairs be placed at the sides of the red-and-gold table facing frontally. Now this seating arrangement was observed not only in wedding ceremonies, but on all other formal occasions, according to Chinese custom. Thus, when the bride's father- and mother-in-law are seated to receive tea from her, they sit on ceremonial chairs placed side-by-side with a matching table in between. Similarly, when a mandarin official receives his guest-of-honour at his home, he usually motions his guest to a chair which is placed adjacent to his right. To the Chinese, this form of seating arrangement is regarded as the most courteous way of treating one's guests or senior members of one's family. By contrast, they regard a seating arrangement which requires the host and guest to sit face-to-face as rude and confrontational.

As for the dressing table, it is virtually identical to the food table except for one slight variation: the space normally taken up by the carved and gilded frieze is modified, in the case of the dressing table, to incorporate two or three drawers, as the case may be, and the front panels on each of these drawers are decorated with carvings of either figures in court scenes or purely floral motifs, namely peonies. There are no other structural modifications besides this. The addition of drawers to the dressing table is a useful and necessary modification, for it enables the bride to store away her cosmetics, perfumes, jewellery and accessories, such as combs, brushes, hair pins and clips, when they are not in use.

The dressing table normally comes with an ornately designed dressing mirror mounted on what looks like a miniature table with a single drawer. The dressing mirror itself is mounted on double or triple wooden frames lacquered red and carved with elaborate floral motifs in bas-relief and splendidly gilded. The mirror is of modest dimensions – about 11 inches (28.5 centimetres) long and 8½ inches (21.5 centimetres) wide. Much of the available built-in space of the miniature table is taken up by the shallow drawer which is apparently meant for storing the bride's jewellery.

Ancestor and deity tables

Apart from the *sam kai* altar table, the Babas regularly made use of another set of tables of a different design to make offerings to their most revered ancestor and their particular household deity. This type of table, usually rendered in either black and gold or brown and gold rather than red and gold, comes in a set of two, one of which is longer and higher than the other. The larger of the two tables is rectangular in shape, measuring at least 5 feet (150 centimetres) long, 1 foot 6 inches (45 centimetres) wide and slightly over 4 feet (120 centimetres) high. Most of them have a straight front, but there are also many extant pieces which have bow-fronts. Coupled with the high altar table is a smaller and lower square table which normally measures three feet (90 centimetres) long, three feet (90 centimetres) wide and three feet (90 centimetres) high. The carved aprons and spandrels depicting archaic scrolls, reminiscent of the Shang, Zhou and Warring States bronze sacrificial vessels, are executed in pierced- or open-work and outlined in gilt. The tables are mostly painted in opaque brown lacquer, but there are some extant pieces which are painted in shiny black lacquer.

Normally, two sets of this type of namwood altar table are set up in a traditional Peranakan home – the *sam kai* table being stored away, to be used only for special occasions, such as a wedding or when the Babas make offerings to Tiangong on the ninth day of the Chinese New Year. The first set of altar tables, dedicated to the household deity (this deity could be Quan Yin, Guan Di, the Monkey God or any one of the numerous gods and goddesses in the Chinese pantheon of deities), is usually placed at the far end of the main reception hall facing the entrance to the house. The second set of altar tables is dedicated to the family's most revered ancestor. (I have noticed that the most revered ancestor of many Baba families in Malacca turned out to be some matriarch.) It is usually placed at the far end of the family room.

Tables of this type have a rather antiquated appearance, largely because the decorative carvings of complex cloud scrolls on the aprons and the vertical spandrels of the legs are all derived from motifs found on ancient bronze vessels dating back some 4000 years or more. In actual fact, most of these altar tables in old Baba homes are not old by the Chinese standard of antiquity: going by circumstantial evidence based on family records, the oldest of these namwood tables may be estimated at around 150 years at the most.

All these altar tables have straight, square legs which end with formalized scrolled carvings at the feet. As a rule, square tables have freestanding legs without stretchers – the bracing being effected by the broad, carved aprons connecting the legs at the four corners. The larger and higher rectangular table usually comes with bracings connecting the front and back legs; some even have base stretchers into which the front and back legs are tenoned. The ornamental carvings on the aprons and the spandrels appear only on the front and the sides. The rear side, which faces the wall, is left unadorned.

Settees

Long namwood benches with high backs[19], elaborately ornamented with carved panels rendered in red and gold, or simply painted over with a sombre brown lacquer, may still be seen in some old Baba homes in Malacca. Like all traditional Chinese chairs, benches and couches, namwood settees are never padded with cushions or any other form of fabric covering to provide for comfort. And as a rule, Chinese chairs, benches and settees are never comfortable to sit on. The primary function of these pieces of furniture, like that of all other types of furniture in traditional Chinese homes, was ceremonial. In the case of red-and-gold namwood furniture, it was definitely intended to add a touch of splendour and luxury to wedding ceremonies.

The basic design of namwood settees, like that of blackwood furniture, is essentially rectangular and box-like in form. Such settees have straight backs and straight side panels: there are no distinct and recognizable armrests to speak of. The back and side panels are surmounted by three sets of low railings secured by struts at the corners. The back and sides feature built-in floating panels (usually three for the back and one each for the sides) which are carved and gilded. The side panels are sometimes carved on both the obverse and reverse faces. The seat is thick and of heavy construction, and it is securely tenoned into the enormous seat frame reinforced directly below by correspondingly stout aprons and the legs at the four corners. In namwood red-and-gold furniture, the pattern of those carved and massive legs is based on a variation of the cloud scroll motifs which dominate the design of the aprons. More often than not the upper corners of those massive legs are carved to depict *taotien* masks.

Some red-and-gold namwood settees are so designed that they incorporate a number of utility drawers (usually four) built directly into the frieze which spans the entire length of the settee. The front panels of each of these drawers is decorated with gilded carvings depicting figures in domestic scenes. However, the inclusion of drawers beneath the seat frame requires that the internal structure of the settee below the seat frame be modified somewhat. This is effected by cutting rectangular openings into the thick bar of timber which constitutes the frieze at regular intervals to receive the drawers. At the same time a framework, complete with rails and braces, must be constructed behind the frieze to support the drawers and to enable them to slide in and out at will. When this is completed, the entire upper structure, including the massive seat frame and the upright back and side panels, is tenoned into the supporting under-frame. This is supported by two massive carved legs in front and two plain, square-cut legs behind, braced together by a carved and gilded frieze in front and at the sides, and a plain stretcher at the back. Needless to say, red-and-gold settees of this type are heavy and of a massive structure.

Settees without such utility drawers are perhaps more elegant and less encumbered since their legs are longer and less stumpy in design, and thus more proportionate in relation to the other components of the settee. Many such settees are simply painted with dark brown lacquer without any evidence of gilding at all.

Opium beds

The term 'opium bed' is somewhat misleading. It is not exactly a bed in the sense of a traditional tester or alcove bed, complete with mattresses, pillows, bolsters and coverings of curtains – a couch, that is, in which one sleeps at night. From a structural point of view, an opium bed is nothing more than a broad and massive settee fitted with a high backboard and two low sideboards. It was never used for sleeping in, but only for smoking opium.

In fact, there are quite a number of extant red-and-gold opium beds in which the basic structure consists of two settee-sized benches laid front-to-back and secured together by three side railings made up of three carved and low back panels tenoned into the seat frame at the corners. These back and side panels are also detachable. Opium beds, when constructed in this manner, have *six*, or rather, *eight* legs, as compared with *four* legs in the case of standard opium beds which are made in one piece. This impression of a six-legged couch is largely due to the fact that when the opium bed is assembled, the front legs of one bench are loosely coalesced with the back legs of the other bench to form a sort of compound leg at the sides.

Apart from the facility with which opium beds of this design can be dismantled, especially when moving house, this method of construction allows for a more capacious couch without imposing additional stress and strain upon the seat frame and aprons, which are constructed out of solid beams of timber, each about six feet (180 centimetres) long and $2^1/2$–3 inches (5–7.5 centimetres) in thickness. If we go by the evidence, the supply of namwood in China was fast being depleted by the closing decades of the 19th century, so much so that cabinet-makers had to economize on the use of long solid beams of timber in the construction of furniture, except in those cases where the use of larger beams was absolutely necessary. Thus the fabrication of opium beds (especially of namwood) by the combination of two separate benches was an innovation in cabinet-making necessitated by the apparent shortage of *Machilus nanmu* in China.

In all other respects, the design of the red-and-gold opium bed is very similar to that of the settee, except that it is on a bigger scale. The carvings on the back and side panels, as well as on the aprons, consist of traditional motifs which are regarded as propitious for weddings. They are usually executed in bas-relief or high-relief and open-work, and painted with a red undercoat of lacquer and gilded to produce a rich and splendid effect. Some types of namwood opium bed are rendered in black and gold, and the back and side panels are carved to look like half-opened horizontal scrolls, within which a narrative painting, that is, an episode from some literary or historical legend, is depicted. The paintings are also executed in gilt against a jet-black background.

Because of its sheer size and weight, an opium bed had to be supported by massive seat rails and stout cabriole legs to take the strain imposed upon it. The aprons, which are fitted directly below the front seat rail, and the massive legs are usually ornamented with dense and complex carvings rendered in parcel gilt. In fact, ornamental carvings became so prominent in the structure of the opium bed that it is difficult not to go away with the impression that the art of the cabinet-

maker had become sub-ordinate to that of the wood-carver. Namwood does not possess the figured grain, the satin-smoothness and the lustrous sheen and colour of *huanghuali* and *zitan* wood. Hence, it has to be carved, gilded and painted over to compensate for what it lacks in terms of such intrinsic qualities.

The wedding bed

It should be obvious by now that the designs of all extant pieces of antique Chinese furniture are derived from the basic structure of a box, be it square or rectangular. The differences between one type of furniture and another, from a functional point of view, consist of modifications of one sort or another being made to the basic design of the box. Thus, a settee is a rectangular platform standing on four legs situated at the corners and walled in above by three low-back panels, while an opium bed is simply a square settee – that is, the normal rectangular settee modified to provide for greater depth. Likewise, the red-and-gold wedding bed – and there is only one type of wooden wedding bed – is simply a combination of two settee-type benches placed front to back, mounted over with three low-back panels and four tall, square posts held together by bracings at the top and tenoned into the corners of the seat frame below.

These are the components which make up the basic structure of the wedding bed. But most extant examples of wedding beds have a canopy above them; another set of plain, square posts complete with top bracings are tenoned immediately inside the four outermost posts and

Left: Four-poster canopy wedding bed of the red-and-gold type. Traditional Chinese beds are always walled in by three low panels featuring carvings or paintings, about 15 inches (36 cm) high. This peculiarity is a carry-over from the days when the k'ang or raised wooden platform was built into an alcove. When tester beds of this type came to be used in the Straits Settlements, it was customary to cover the entire bed from top to bottom with a fine cotton netting to keep out mosquitoes. Namwood. Dating: early 20th century. Courtesy of Prof and Mrs Yusoff Talib.

Overleaf: Another view of the wedding bed showing the designs on the canopy. Some Straits Chinese wedding beds have very ornate frontal aprons and elaborate canopy carvings, and practically every wedding bed has a shelf of drawers either in the front aprons or just below the canopy at the far end of the bed. Courtesy of Prof and Mrs Yusoff Talib.

it is upon this inner square frame that the lattice-work canopy rests.

Everything else remains the same as the opium bed, including the massive frontal and side aprons, the solid scrolled legs and the three low-back side panels. The other additional feature, apart from the two sets of tall, square posts with their top stretchers and canopy, are the two broad strips of carved and gilded panelling mounted across the upper extremities of the frontal posts.

As with settees, the space located immediately below the seat frame of the frontal part of the four-poster wedding bed is sometimes constructed to accommodate four utility drawers. But in those beds where utility drawers are dispensed with, the frontal panel immediately below the seat frame is modified into a fairly broad panel which is filled with densely carved motifs executed in relief-work and gilded. The frontal apron is positioned immediately below this modified panel of the seat frame. The scrolled carvings at the two ends of the aprons spill into those of the huge scrolled legs, such that the legs and the aprons appear as if they were carved from a single massive piece of timber.

Most of us nowadays sleep in beds which are largely modelled on the standard Western design. Basically, this consists of a low bedstead six feet (180 centimetres) long, five feet (150 centimetres) wide and slightly less than two feet (60 centimetres) high, including the spring and foam rubber mattress of about seven inches (17.5 centimetres) thick. Except for the high headboard, beds of this type have no side panels or railings of any sort so that access into the bed and out of it is free and easy at all times.

Traditional Chinese beds, however, are constructed without any distinct headboards or, for that matter, footboards, as in the case of half-tester beds of European design. Instead, the bedstead is walled in on three sides by low boards of equal height, without the slightest indication as to where the head-end of the bed might be located. Since all Chinese beds are four-poster beds with canopies, the side which is not walled in by a low board is the entrance to the bed. Nonetheless, the moment one climbs into bed, it is not clear, from the manner in which the bed is constructed, which side of it is the inner or head-end. Only the positioning of the pillows indicates how one should lay down to rest.

The origins of the three-sided tester bed in China are somewhat obscure. But among the 'male chauvinist' Babas, there is a story, largely spurious, about the original purpose of the three low boards in Straits Chinese wedding beds. It goes thus: in old Baba tradition, it was customary to place the wedding bed with the rear end (i.e. the side opposite the entrance to the bed) against a wall at the far end of the bridal chamber, so that

access to the wedding bed was only by way of the frontal side. It was also decreed by tradition that the bride should sleep in the inner side of the bed, while her husband slept on the outer side. Thus, with the wall on one side, her husband on the other side and her head-end and foot-end fenced in by two boards (not to mention the curtains and mosquito net), it was virtually impossible, so they say tongue-in-cheek, for any unhappy or unwilling bride to avoid her conjugal obligations by climbing out of the bed and running away on her wedding night! It must not be forgotten that, in days gone by, marriages were contracted by proxy with the approval of parents, rather than by mutual consent between the bride and groom. Hence, the chances of a mismatch were high indeed and many a bride must have thought of fleeing the bridal bed on her wedding night, if given half the chance.

But even so, the theory that the three-sided structure of the traditional wedding bed was meant to act as a preventive barrier to would-be runaway brides is more of a popular myth than a fact. A determined and unwilling bride would hardly be deterred by the low barriers (no more than 15 inches or 37.5 centimetres high) provided by the two side panels at the head- and foot-ends. Rather, the three side boards of the wedding bed may, in my opinion, be regarded as cultural relics to remind us of a bygone era when beds were customarily built into alcoves specifically constructed for this purpose. All alcoves are, of course, walled in (literally) on three sides and, up to the end of the 19th century, Chinese royalty still slept in alcove beds. Empress Dowager Cixi regularly slept in one in her summer palace, Le Shoutang, or 'Palace of Joy and Longevity', at the shore of Kunming Lake just outside Beijing.

Judging by extant photographs of the interior of Cixi's bedroom in the summer palace, her bed was a narrow one, a sort of single bed rather than the broad standard double bed. The entrance to the bed was decorated with an upper panel of ornate carvings of floral and foliated motifs executed on what looks like a variety of *zitan* blackwood. Curtains of yellow damask silk (yellow was the imperial colour of the Qing Dynasty) which covered the entrance to her alcove bed were drawn apart and secured to the sides. Another interesting feature is that the space immediately below the couch was taken up by several built-in drawers – a practice which the Babas retained in their movable wedding beds.

In those extant examples of Straits Chinese wedding beds where the frontal panel below the seat frame is either wholly taken up by a carved and gilded panel or apron, a separate set of utility drawers in two or three tiers, built to span the entire length of the bed, is constructed separately and installed into the upper side stretchers situated at the rear side of the bed.

When in use, such as during a traditional wedding celebration, the wedding bed is fully decked from the canopy to the couch with rich and expensive drapings of embroidered silk in red, pink, green and yellow. These drapes are ornately embroidered with auspicious wedding motifs hand-sewn with a combination of gold and coloured silk threads. Pillow and bolster cases are also embroidered with appropriate patterns of peonies, magpies, mandarin ducks, quails and phoenixes, and the pillow and bolster ends are sewn with silvergilt plaques of various shapes. So too are bedspreads and rectangular panels hung above the entrance to the bed. No wonder traditional weddings were such expensive affairs.

Wedding cabinets

The red-and-gold wedding cabinet is a two-tiered set of upright rectangular cases stacked one on top of the other. Wedding cabinets come in several sizes, of which the smallest is barely four feet (120 centimetres) high while the largest is almost seven feet (210 centimetres) high. The top cabinet is usually taller (just over four feet or 120 centimetres high) and somewhat slimmer than the lower or base cabinet (about three feet or 90 centimetres tall) on which it stands. Each of the two cabinets stands on a low, waisted platform which is supported at the corners by four short and curving legs braced together by aprons, three of which – the frontal and side aprons – are carved and gilded. The legs are barely six inches (15 centimetres) tall, but each of them features two carved *taotien* masks at the knee and the foot.

When it came to the process of beautifying wedding cabinets (as well as other types of utility cabinets), there was apparently some kind of tacit understanding between the cabinet-maker and the wood-carver that the latter was to ensure that all his ornamental carvings be kept strictly within the limits imposed by the basic design of the cupboard. For this reason, Chinese cabinet-makers and wood-carvers, unlike their counterparts in 18th-century Europe, made no attempt to alter the basic structure of a cabinet in order to give it an architectural façade by, among other things, including such features as pediments, cornices, architraves, fluted columns with elaborate capitals, arches, sculpted statues and ormolu attachments. Apparently, it never occurred to the practical-minded Chinese cabinet-maker and carver to modify the façade of a cupboard to make it resemble the entrance to, say, a Chinese temple, a mandarin's mansion, some ceremonial gateway like the Tiananmen Gate in Beijing or, perhaps, the entrance to the Throne Room in the Imperial Palace, namely 'The Hall of Supreme Harmony'. For them a cabinet was simply a cabinet and it must always be made to look like one. Hence, architectural ornaments, while interesting and fanciful in themselves, were considered inappropriate for the basic design of such a utilitarian piece of furniture as a cupboard.

Thus, the design on the front of the upper cabinet, which is taken up by two doors, consists quite simply of four rectangular panels (two for each door) of which the two lower ones may be said to contain the principal carved panels. As a rule, the carvings on these panels are densely packed together, usually with figures and horses set against a background of mountainous landscapes or else, some rich architectural setting. If the themes happen to be drawn from some memorable and dramatic episodes in the great classics (e.g. *The Romance of the Three Kingdoms* or *The Water Margin*), more likely than not, figures of cavalry men, archers and foot-soldiers engaged in ferocious combat will be depicted on these gilded panels. On the other hand, if the themes are derived from those classics in which romantic meetings, partings, etc., are portrayed (e.g. *The Dream of the Red Chamber* or *Liang Shanbai and Zhu Yingtai*), then richly garbed figures set against some splendid architectural settings and engaged in homely activities, such as playing musical instruments, contemplating a flight of geese, playing checkers or feasting and drinking, would be adequate to recapitulate those happier moments in the lives of the hero and the heroine of these epic dramas.

The quality of the decorative carvings differs from one set of cabinets to another. But among the higher priced examples of such wedding cupboards, the workmanship is of a distinctive quality which sets them apart from that of the run-of-the-mill type of cabinets. The best of red-and-gold carvings are traditionally said to have been done by skilled wood-carvers from the town of Ningpo, southeast of HangZhou. But it is not at all easy to tell, simply by looking at the carvings on extant pieces of red-and-gold wedding cupboards, which are of Ningpo craftsmanship and which are of Xiamen or Shantou workmanship because Chinese furniture was rarely marked to indicate its provenance and year of manufacture.

This two-tiered set of red-and-gold wedding cabinets is a splendid example of the kind of fine craftsmanship which Zhejiang and Fujian cabinet-makers excelled in. The ornate carvings are so crammed with details of horsemen and warriors engaged in combat (an indication that the theme is drawn from one of the many episodes of that classic novel, The Romance of the Three Kingdoms) and floral motifs that it takes quite some time for the viewer to get accustomed to the dazzling effect of the overall design. Dating: late 19th century. Height: over 6 ft (180 cm). Width: over 3 ft (100 cm). Private collection.

This is the upper cabinet of the traditional, two-tiered red-and-gold wedding cabinet which used to come with the bridal trousseau of the more well-to-do members of the Baba community. A special feature of this cabinet is in the figure carvings of the two lower panels: instead of the usual cut-through carvings seen in most extant examples of wedding cabinets, the various motifs in these two panels are carved in the round. But the cabinet-maker took great care to ensure that the original matrix of the wood was retained to serve as a background. This meant, of course, that he had to be careful that his chisels did not accidentally pierce through the wood and spoil his work. Namwood. Courtesy of Mr Peter Lee Liat Seng.

This is the lower section of the wedding cabinet. Notice that the design of the carvings (mainly of figures, qilins and flower vases) on this cabinet shares the same elegant refinement which is due largely to the clarity and expressive quality of decorative motifs. Courtesy of Mr Peter Lee Liat Seng.

The two upper panels of the standard wedding cupboard are more simply ornamented. Carvings in narrow strips of lattice-work are preferred for adorning the borders, while the background panels are embellished with large sprays of peony blossoms, shallowly carved in bas-relief and gilded. Alternatively, the two upper panels are partitioned into eight smaller frames (four for each panel) to make them resemble window panes. Inserted into these rectangular frames are small, thin panels, each of which is carved and gilded with an emblem of the Eight Taoist Immortals.

A curious feature of red-and-gold cabinets is that the doors do not swing on metal (brass especially) hinges, but rather on large pegs which are loosely tenoned into mortises located at the top and bottom frames beside the frontal posts. These doors can easily be dismantled simply by lifting the base and sliding the base peg sideways via built-in grooves. Likewise, the doors can be installed, again by first inserting the upper peg into its mortise followed by manipulating the base peg into the groove and then sliding the door towards the side posts.

The construction of the drawers is more perfunctory: they are simply made to fit into the rectangular gaps cut into the upper section of the lower cabinet. There are no special rails and braces for gliding the drawers in and out by the standard method of tongue-and-groove construction.

The lower cabinet is shorter and slightly broader all round than the top cabinet – the marginal increase in dimensions being necessitated by the fact that the base cupboard has to accommodate the slightly larger base frame of the upper cabinet. Sometimes the upper cabinet is mounted over the top of the lower cupboard and secured in position by the use of tenons and mortises (loosely fitted) located at the corners. But there are instances where the upper cabinet is simply stacked upon the lower cupboard without any joints – the sheer weight of the upper cupboard being eto make it rest firmly in position.

The pattern of the ornamental design on the façade of the base cabinet is standard with most red-and-gold cupboards: the upper portion is largely taken up by two centrally located drawers with frontal panels of elaborate gilded carvings, with the corner spaces on either side filled up by two small panels of carvings. Immediately below the two drawers are two smaller doors reaching down to the base frame. These doors, which also swing on rounded tenons loosely fitted into mortises, are ornamented with carved and gilded panels as well. Two narrow strips of rectangular panelling (also carved and gilded) fill up the remaining corner spaces. As with the upper cupboard, the lower cupboard is supported on a low base frame with short curving legs at the corners and carved aprons as bracings.

Incidentally, wedding cupboards of this type were specifically used for storing the bride's collection of ceremonial dresses as well as clothing for daily use. However, the interior structure of an antique Chinese cupboard – a couple of shelves and several drawers – makes no provision for dresses and other types of garments which are meant to be hung or draped on hangers and hooked to a metal or wooden rod located on the interior ceiling of the cabinet. This absence of a railing for hanging garments that one finds in standard European wardrobes is not, however, due to an oversight by Chinese cabinet-makers because the interior structure of all Chinese cupboards is similar. Rather, the peculiarity may be attributed to the manner with which the traditional Chinese stored their clothing: in Chinese custom, clothes were never draped on hangers and then hooked onto a rod specially constructed for this purpose. This is a European custom. For this reason, all European wardrobes had to be constructed in one piece to provide sufficient interior space and height for hanging garments. The Chinese, on the other hand, always made it a habit to fold their clothing into neat squares and stack them in a pile. Obviously this made for easier storage by economizing on the use of space inside the cupboard.

Break-front cabinets

There is a variety of two-tiered brown-and-gold cupboard which is very similar to the rectangular, case-like design of traditional red-and-gold wedding cabinets, but which differs from them in some significant features. It is, for example, wider (twice as wide) than the standard wedding cupboard and it sports a break-front which is so clearly reminiscent of bookcases made by English cabinet-makers throughout the 18th and 19th centuries. However, the background and unornamented areas are always painted in dark brown rather than red lacquer, while the gilded carvings (all executed in pierced- or open-work) are depicted as formalized floral and foliated scrolls.

Superficially, these cupboards might pass off as another variety of red-and-gold furniture of South China provenance. But the exceptional width of these cabinets and the break-front structure were obviously foreign to the traditional Chinese style of cabinet construction. Therefore, only those who know the difference between the style of English break-front bookcases and those which were regularly made by Chinese cabinet-makers for mandarin scholars would be able to recognize the influence of English furniture design on this type of Baba cupboard.

Another feature of these cabinets which distinguishes them from standard red-and-gold furniture is the fact that the carved and gilded ornamentation (all executed in cut-through or open-work) is invariably depicted as formalized floral and foliated scrolls rather than as naturalistic representations of figures shown in rich architectural and/or landscape settings that one regularly sees in antique red-and-gold cupboards. As is well known to students of Chinese art, Chinese artists rarely depict natural flowering plants in a completely conventional manner which is reminiscent of Islamic arabesque designs[20]. Hence, the formalized representations of floral and foliated carvings on these break-front cabinets suggest that they might have been executed by skilled Malay or Javanese carvers, with the cabinet-work being done by locally-domiciled Chinese craftsmen. It follows from this that these cabinets could not have been made in Fujian or Zhejiang, but rather in Malacca or Johor, by local cabinet-makers using a combination of English furniture design and abstract floral motifs inspired by Islamic traditions.

Thus far, I have not had the opportunity of seeing cupboards of this type stripped bare to reveal their original wood core. But all the available evidence indicates that break-front cabinets are not made of namwood, but more likely teak (*Tectona grandis*) or some variety of heavy hardwood endemic to Peninsular Malaysia, namely *merbau* (*Instia palembanica*), *balau* (*Shorea spp*) and perhaps *chengal* (*Neobalanocarpus heimu*). Not only are such cabinets large and bulky – they are about seven feet (210 centimetres) tall and about six feet (180 centimetres) wide – but they are heavy because of the nature of the hardwoods employed.

There is no evidence that break-front cabinets were ever used as substitutes for red-and-gold wedding cupboards of the type we have discussed earlier. Certainly, they did not form part of the essential furniture of a traditional bridal chamber in old Baba homes. Besides, wedding furniture was always lacquered red, while break-front cabinets always came in brown. More likely than not, they were meant to be display cabinets for storing a type of polychrome enamelware type which the Babas greatly treasured and which I have elsewhere described as Straits Chinese porcelain.

Miscellaneous items

Among other items of red-and-gold furniture which are traditionally included in the bridal chamber of a Baba home are an ornately carved and gilded washstand and a low chest-of-drawers.

In its simplest form, the **washstand** consists of a square or hexagonal wooden rack with two high back posts secured at the top by an overhanging rail and measuring about 5 feet 6 inches (165 centimetres) tall. The framework for

supporting the porcelain basin can either be square or hexagonal in form and the height from the top of the basin to the ground is roughly 2 feet 6 inches (75 centimetres). The older versions of washstands made out of *huanghuali* and dating back to the Ming Dynasty are so structurally simple that they do not include provisions for a mirror. But by the time washstands were made out of namwood to Baba specifications in the 19th century, they had undergone some modifications. Instead of plain wooden posts for the framework, carvings were added and gilded to give them a splendid appearance. A mirror enclosed by carved frames was installed into the upper part of the back posts and a small drawer was constructed below the mirror for combs, hairpins and cosmetics. As for the plain yoke-like top rail, this was now replaced by an ornately carved panel and all unadorned structures were painted in bright red lacquer. But even washstands in red-and-gold namwood are rather hard to come by these days as many such pieces went to overseas buyers who found them quaintly attractive and more easily portable than wedding cupboards and settees.

The **chest-of-drawers** (they usually come in a set of two) may also be included in the list of rare furniture of the red-and-gold variety. But I rather think that chests-of-drawers have always been scarce because their inclusion in the traditional bridal trousseau was optional and not obligatory: the more well-to-do Baba families might have insisted on having them, but the less well-off ones did not. For this reason, chests-of-drawers are not found in many old Baba homes.

As a piece of cabinet-work, there is nothing particularly remarkable about them: they consist essentially of a rectangular case about three feet (90 centimetres) long, 13 inches (35 centimetres) broad and 1 foot 6 inches (45 centimetres) high,

with three shallow drawers in two tiers built into the case – two on top and one large drawer below. The base frame is supported by four stumpy scrolled legs secured by carved and gilded aprons on the front and sides, and a plain stretcher behind. The frontal panels of these drawers are, as usual, carved with scenes showing figures in architectural settings and the entire panel is then gilded. The carvings are executed in high-relief pierced-work and the background is covered with a thin panel of wood painted red. The borders have small chips of mother-of-pearl embedded into a matrix of greenish gesso.

Other red-and-gold items of furniture include two pairs of large, wooden candlestands and a square lantern which houses the perpetual light on the ancestral altar table. The **candlestands** (they are taken out for use on such red-letter days as wedding ceremonies, the anniversary of the ancestor revered in the family altar and the sixth day of Chinese New Year) are rather large as candlestands go, being about three feet (90 centimetres) high, and are placed on the floor rather than on the altar table. Basically, the candlestand consists of a round post tenoned into a large, circular base which is supported by three short ornamental legs usually carved and gilded in the shape of fishes, dragons or *qilins*. Rising from the base plate to about the middle of the post are three spandrel-like carvings in the round,

depicting either dragons, *qilins*, carps or simply archaic scrolls after the manner of Shang and Zhou bronze vessels. These carvings are separately crafted and tenoned into the base and the side of the post. The top of these candlestands is carved and modelled after the form of a lotus or a peony blossom. A large iron spike sunk into the top receptacle allows one of those huge red candles to be firmly planted onto the candlestand.

The **square lantern**, which is regularly found on altar tables dedicated to a family's most revered ancestor, was meant to hold and to protect the oil lamp, which was always kept burning. The light from this lamp was used to light candles and joss sticks, and even to burn offerings of joss papers. It is a square frame about 16 inches (40 centimetres) high and measuring $8^1/2$ inches (21 centimetres) per side. A band of carved and gilded panels of about two inches (five centimetres) broad adorns the top and lower ends of the lantern. The rest of the space is taken up by transparent sheets of glass panelling, thus enabling the lamp to cast a dim but perpetual light upon the altar. One of the four glass panels is separately mounted on thin wooden frames and then attached to the lantern by small brass hinges. This panel serves as a door which gives access into the lantern, as for example, when the oil in the lamp runs low and has to be topped up, or else when joss sticks and candles have to be lighted.

chapter four

English-style Teakwood Furniture

The third and, in the opinion of most admirers and devotees of Baba cultural artefacts, the most representative of Straits Chinese furniture is neither that variety of blackwood furniture with mother-of-pearl inlays dealt with in chapter two, nor for that matter, the red-and-gold type of furniture which we discussed in chapter three. This is because these two categories of furniture were designed and constructed according to purely Chinese taste. However, the Babas are not, by common consent, regarded as typical representatives of the Han Chinese and their culture. Rather they are a community of overseas Chinese whose long sojourn in this part of Southeast Asia (just over 600 years, if we date the coming of early Chinese traders to Malacca and Semarang in Java, for example, from the beginning of the Ming Dynasty in 1368) has resulted in the development of a kind of hybrid culture which retained the main precepts of Confucianism while assimilating useful customs and practices of the native races of what are now Malaysia and Indonesia. Thus, when it came to the question of defining Straits Chinese material culture, it was felt that only those objects

peculiar to Baba homes which happened to exhibit a blend of cultural influences of the Han Chinese and those of other races and nations with whom the Babas had established contacts, and which had, over a period of time, become assimilated into Baba culture may, logically speaking, be regarded as authentic to Straits Chinese culture.

Now it so happens that the type of household movables in old Baba homes which meets this particular criterion of authenticity is that variety of furniture exclusively made of teakwood (*Tectona grandis*) and which is largely designed after the fashion of some 17th–19th-century English furniture. Thus, unless one looks very carefully, the designs of many of these extant pieces of furniture quaintly resemble those of Restoration, Georgian, Queen Anne, Hepplewhite, Chippendale and perhaps Regency period works. The method of construction, with its emphasis on the use of nails, screws and brackets for joinery, instead of mortises and tenons as in classic Chinese furniture, was clearly based on the English/European tradition of cabinet-work. But even more interesting is the fact that the ornamental motifs carved on these pieces of furniture (e.g. dragons' heads on chair handles and *qilins*, gargoyle-like masks, magpies, phoenixes, antelopes, carps, bats, peonies and plum blossoms on consoles, cupboards, sideboards, mirrors and dressers) are largely borrowed from traditional

The function of this unusual-looking table is not exactly clear. It could have been used as a corner table, but then why have it constructed in the shape of a double square, joined in this manner? Notice, too, that the six bamboo legs are freestanding. Height: about 3 ft (90 cm). Courtesy of Prof and Mrs Yusoff Talib.

Chinese art and religious symbols. Whereas antique English furniture was made out of oak, beech, walnut, ash, yew, elm and mahogany, Straits Chinese furniture of this type was, over a period of at least 50 years, consistently made out of teakwood. The teak tree, incidentally, is also endemic to India, Burma (Myanmar), Thailand and other parts of Southeast Asia. And to cap it all, this type of English-style furniture was mainly crafted by Chinese cabinet-makers, many of whom were skilled Shanghainese craftsmen schooled in the Chinese method of cabinet-work.

These, then, are the hybrid characteristics of the third type of furniture which, in the eyes of devotees and admirers of Baba cultural heritage, provide the defining features of Straits Chinese furniture. Whereas blackwood and red-and-gold namwood pieces of furniture are unmistakably Chinese in design and method of construction, the provenance of those pieces of furniture sporting English/European designs and Chinese ornamental motifs that are found in Baba homes is more difficult to identify. However, the cross-cultural characteristics of these pieces of teakwood

This splendid wedding cabinet, possibly the finest of the teak-and-gold variety of cabinets that I have seen in many years, does give the impression that it is of European origin because the overall structural design is indeed European in inspiration. However, a closer inspection will soon reveal that the decorative motifs of the giltwood carvings on the door panels, the drawers and the pediment panel are all Chinese in origin, namely bats and flower baskets, phoenixes and peonies and formalized floral scrolls. Courtesy of Mr Johnson Tan, C. K. Tan Gallery.

furniture have given rise to a variety of different names, such as 'Malacca furniture', 'colonial furniture', 'Dutch furniture', 'Portuguese furniture', 'Baba furniture' or, as I have preferred, 'Straits Chinese furniture'. To people who are not familiar with local jargon, these names are, of course, misleading and confusing. But to those who have seen and handled such pieces of antique teakwood furniture, with their quaint mixture of English/European and Chinese characteristics, there is no mistaking what type of furniture is being referred to by this plethora of names.

From a historical point of view, this variety of teakwood furniture, built to Baba taste, is the most recent of antique furniture in Baba culture – blackwood furniture with mother-of-pearl inlays and red-and-gold namwood furniture having been used by the Peranakan community from a much earlier period of their history, say, early in the 18th century. Exact dates are, however, difficult to pin down because there are no specific documents on the subject. But tradition has it that teakwood furniture of this type began to be made locally for British colonial officials and their families serving in Singapore, Malacca and Penang sometime towards the closing decades of the 19th century – in the 1870s or thereabouts.

When British officials of the East India Company first went to India (Calcutta, Bombay and Delhi), it was customary for them to ship out samples of essential furniture for their personal use. As time went on, however, they discovered that it was more convenient and less expensive to commission skilled native craftsmen using local varieties of timber to construct much of their household furniture based on original English designs. That was how Anglo-Indian furniture came to be made. Likewise, the early British officials sent out to administer the colonies of Penang, Malacca and Singapore, from 1800 onwards, emulated their counterparts in India by taking with them such pieces of furniture as were useful for their personal needs, and this practice was followed for many decades. Then, as in India, it was found that locally-domiciled Shanghainese artisans and craftsmen could, with some practice and experience, adapt traditional Chinese methods of cabinet-making to turn out good reproductions of existing samples of British furniture using teakwood imported from Burma and Thailand.

The early reproductions of original English furniture were probably made by Shanghainese cabinet-makers operating small carpenter shops with the help of several skilled assistants. Under normal circumstances, these skilled craftsmen made their living through a wide variety of small contract jobs to cater to the needs of the widest section of the community in which they happened to have set up their establishments. Their clientele included owners of grocery shops, coffee shops, eating houses, restaurants, hardware shops, hotels and medicine shops, as well as jewellers, butchers, money-lenders, business associations and private homes. Most of these contracts consisted of making repairs, doing renovations and supplying pieces of furniture which included work tables, meeting tables, shelves, built-in drawers and cabinets, coffers, benches, chairs, counters, etc. They also constructed lintels, doors, window-frames, wall-partitions, ornamental railings, bannisters, etc. Somewhere along the way, the quality of their craftsmanship must have caught the attention of some British officials, who

probably recalled that some of their treasured pieces of old English furniture brought over from England many years ago were now in dire need of repair, some new upholstery and a new coat of varnish. They showed some of these rickety pieces of furniture to these carpenters and asked, probably with some reservations, if the latter could repair them. It must have surprised those early British officials when these Shanghainese craftsmen examined, say, their rickety chairs and worm-eaten walnut writing tables and immediately agreed to undertake the necessary repairs. And they must have been equally pleased when two or three weeks later, a teenage Chinese boy, wearing a large coolie hat and pedalling a three-wheeled cart, arrived at their doorstep with their newly repaired and varnished pieces of furniture completely restored to their former splendour.

The craftsmanship of these Shanghainese cabinet-makers (in those days they were regularly referred to as 'carpenters') must have greatly impressed some early British residents in Singapore, Malacca and Penang. Soon, word must have got round to other British residents and, before long, more and more clients began bringing their old and wobbly pieces of English furniture to these Shanghainese carpenters for repairs, varnishing and upholstering. A time came when it occurred to some of the more enthusiastic clients to try out the skills of Chinese cabinet-makers by asking them to make reproductions of English originals of, say, Chippendale or Regency period chairs, writing tables, dining tables and sideboards, for their own use. That the results must have been equally satisfactory is attested by the fact that some of these reproductions not only exist, but became quite popular with other British residents in Singapore, Malacca and Penang. Indeed, even the more snobbish and exclusive

department stores in Singapore, such as Robinson & Co. (which was established in 1854 by Philip Robinson and James Gaborian Spicer) and John Little & Co. (which was founded in 1842 by John Martin Little and Cursetjee Frommurzee), began to employ skilled Shanghainese cabinet-makers on a regular basis to turn out various types of English furniture made out of teakwood for British clients[21]. And this, it must be remembered, was despite the fact that Robinsons and John Little (in those days, that is) prided themselves on being major importers and traders of quality products from Britain, including English furniture. The fact that locally made teakwood furniture in European styles crafted by Shanghainese cabinet-makers was considered good enough to be exhibited side-by-side with imported English furniture in Robinsons and John Little was clear evidence of the esteem with which it was held by British residents.

The earliest reproductions of original pieces of English furniture based, initially, on actual models and subsequently upon drawings, sketches and illustrations giving detailed dimensions of the various structures must, in all likelihood, have been faithful copies of the actual artefacts – from the overall design down to the method of joinery and ornamental details. For, from the standpoint of their clients, the ability to turn out exact reproductions was the acid test determining the standard of Chinese cabinet-work and, in particular, the skill of Shanghainese cabinet-makers to adapt to European methods of construction. This they passed with flying colours, and their products came to be accepted by upper-class residents of the Straits Settlements, namely British colonial officials, top civil servants, business executives and estate managers. It was only a matter of time before they became bolder and more innovative in their designs and methods of construction.

Thus far, our story about the early beginnings of English-style Straits Chinese furniture makes no mention of the role played by the Babas in the development of a distinctive style of Anglo-Chinese furniture which eventually came to be associated with the culture of that community. This is not particularly surprising because the introduction of English-style teakwood furniture in Singapore, Malacca and Penang was, as noted

The purist is bound to be exasperated by the structure and design of Straits Chinese teak furniture because it is so eclectic as to defy classification in terms of English period furniture. For example, the cresting panel and splat of the chair illustrated here are not identifiable as Chippendale, Queen Anne or Jacobean. And while the rectangular chair back hints of Sheraton, the cabriole legs and curving armrests cancel out any such attribution.

As for the oval table beside the chair, the brown-and-gold ornamental carvings remind one of red-and-gold namwood furniture. But the design of the two supporting baluster posts, connected by a stretcher and ending in splayed cabriole-like legs, is obviously English/European in inspiration. Nonetheless, eclecticism is a fundamental feature of all Straits Chinese teak furniture. Courtesy of Prof and Mrs Yusoff Talib.

above, initiated by British officials working in the service of the British government and the East India Company. As a predominantly merchant and trader community, the Babas were naturally more concerned with financial success and material acquisitions than with the art of gracious living – that came much later. Originality and trendsetting were not their forte. Hence, there is no clear evidence that the various categories of cultural artefacts which we now attribute to the Baba community were ever created *de novo* to their specifications.

Indeed, the stylistic peculiarities of these artefacts, be they porcelain, gold and silverwork, jewellery, embroidery and beadwork, furniture or even architecture, had already been established when the Babas decided to adopt them for their own domestic and ceremonial functions – the innovations, if any, having been initiated by others, including the craftsmen and artists who fashioned them. Where the Babas differed from other clients, however, was in their consistent and continual custom of these artefacts over a period of many decades, up to a century in some instances, long after others had lost interest in these things. But it is precisely this feature about Straits Chinese artefacts, namely their long and intimate association with the culture of the Babas, which gives these objects their special cultural identity.

While it is true that the Babas did not initiate the introduction of English-style teakwood furniture in Malacca, Singapore or Penang, what is significant, as just mentioned, is that they did

subsequently turn out to be the most enthusiastic customers of this type of household movable, continuing their support long after the fashions had changed. Fundamentally, the main reason for adopting English-style furniture was a strong desire to emulate the customs and manners of the *orang putih*, or the British, whom the Babas (among all other communities of overseas Chinese) admired so greatly. These included sending their boys to English schools, instead of traditional Chinese schools where they would have learnt *hua yu* or Mandarin. The more well-to-do families even hired private tutors to teach their daughters (and in some cases, their wives as well) the three Rs (reading, writing and arithmetic). When their sons grew up, they actively encouraged them to seek employment as clerks in the colonial civil service. The Babas also took to wearing apparel designed in the English style and showed no compunction about cutting off their long Manchu queues in favour of the shorter but neater European hairstyles. Up to the 1930s, as extant photographs of this period show, it was customary for English-educated, young 'Chinamen' to wear black suits (some with tail coats) complemented with starched white cotton shirts sporting upturned collars, black bow ties and black patent leather shoes. Several varieties of hats (excepting perhaps, the bowler hat) were frequently worn. I clearly remember, for example, that my father wore a hat every morning when he left home to go to work. In fact, he had several hats made of some stiffened felt material on his hatstand, ranging from black, blue and brown to dark green.

The other aspect of British customs which the Babas zealously sought to emulate, but not too successfully perhaps, concerned table manners. Traditionally, the Babas ate from plates with their bare hands – the more conservative ones stuck to chopsticks and bowl. British custom, however, prescribed the use of plates with silver or silver-plated forks and knives, and, superficially, it would appear that this was a more elegant and 'civilized' way of eating. In English customs, too, soup was to be taken out of a shallow dish by the use of a silver-plated spoon, rather than slurped directly from a bowl as it was done in China. However, such English manners could not easily be applied in Baba homes because the traditional Chinese method of serving meat, fish or vegetables in small, pre-cut morsels made forks and knives superfluous, there being nothing that needed cutting or slicing. Besides, it was considered impolite, not to say barbarous, in oriental custom to display a lot of gleaming knives and pointed forks on the dining table. So as a compromise, the Babas not only gave up the habit of eating with bare hands, but also dispensed with the presence of knives at the table, and instead adopted the more practical method of eating with forks and spoons.

Characteristic features of teakwood furniture

As with the Anglicization of their table manners, so with their adoption of English-style teakwood furniture. The traditional Babas were, alone among other communities of overseas Chinese, unrepentant Anglophiles, to whom everything about English culture was admirable and well worth emulating. Thus, it was logical that this deliberate process of Anglicizing Baba culture should include English-style, if not original English, furniture for the more well-to-do Baba

homes. For this purpose, there were, by the turn of the 20th century, many skilled cabinet-makers who were only too willing to cater to the needs of the Babas.

As noted previously, the early pieces of English-style furniture made for British clients were probably accurate reproductions of the originals. But as their products became more widely accepted by a larger clientele, Shanghainese cabinet-makers felt confident enough to improvise upon the archetypes by introducing both structural and stylistic changes which, before long, transformed the character of this type of furniture from mere imitation to a kind of Anglo-Chinese furniture unique to the Straits Settlements. Among the innovations which they instituted were: (1) modifying the structure of the original designs to suit Chinese taste, (2) substituting traditional Chinese art and religious symbols for European ornamental motifs, (3) applying partial gilding in the increasingly Anglo-Chinese pieces of furniture, after the manner of red-and-gold furniture, but borrowing the European technique of gilding, (4) using marble slabs for table tops more frequently than was customary in English (or for that matter traditional Chinese) furniture, (5) preferring cane seats and backs for chairs and couches to cushioned and upholstered seats so commonly seen in upper-class European furniture, and (6) using only one type of timber, namely teak, for the construction of this type of furniture. There are other minor differences but these will suffice for the purpose of our discussion.

Structural modifications

One of the more significant structural differences between British originals and Anglo-Chinese reproductions concerns the *height* of the chair seat. In most Straits Chinese teakwood chairs,

the height of the seat turns out to be *higher* than that of English or European chairs – the average difference being about 2–2½ inches (5–6.5 centimetres). In absolute terms, the seat of most Straits Chinese teakwood chairs (as measured from the ground) is between 18½ and 19 inches (47 and 48 centimetres), while that of most English chairs is 17 inches (43 centimetres), excluding the bulge of the upholstery where this is applicable. Traditional blackwood chairs have even higher seats – on average, the level of the seat is about 20½ inches (52.5 centimetres) above the ground.

On the face of it, a difference of two inches (five centimetres) is hardly worth mentioning. And yet its significance is clear enough when we bear in mind that, as a race, the Chinese are of a much shorter build than Caucasians. Hence, their legs must be proportionately shorter than those of Caucasians. Yet their chair seats are higher. Indeed, if a Chinese of average build were to sit barefoot on one of these Anglo-Chinese Baba chairs, the chances are that his feet would barely touch the ground. Should he sit on one of those traditional, throne-like blackwood chairs with a seat that is at least 20½ inches (52 centimetres) high, his feet would most certainly dangle several inches above the ground. In European chairs, however, the level of the seat is always constructed just high enough to enable a person sitting on it to place his feet flat upon the ground. What, then, is the reason for this curious phenomenon of the level of the seat in Chinese chairs?

One plausible explanation, as discussed in a different context in chapter two, bears repeating here. Most homes in China, unlike those in England, were generally uncarpeted. The Chinese do, of course, have silk and woollen carpets of their own, but these have always been expensive and thus beyond the reach of the vast majority of people in the country. Chinese winters in the north are extremely cold, so chairs have to be constructed in such a way that when a person sits on them, his feet do not touch the icy-cold ground. Thus, if one were to look carefully at *huanghuali* and *zitan* chairs of the Ming period, one would notice at once that the lower parts of the chair legs are braced together by four stretchers raised two or three inches (five or 7.5 centimetres) above the ground. The front stretcher, in particular, was meant to serve also as a footrest. Thus, by raising the chair seat to 20 inches (52 centimetres) and positioning the lower front stretcher at about three inches (7.5 centimetres) above the ground, Chinese chair-makers found that it was possible for a person to sit comfortably on a blackwood chair provided his feet were firmly rested upon the front stretcher. In the language of modern car-makers, this method of seating makes for improved 'ergonomics'.

This, however, applies only to blackwood chairs of the classic Ming and early Qing periods. Where Anglo-Chinese chairs are concerned, their designs are based not on the box-like structure of classic Chinese chairs, but mostly on 18th-century European models in which the front legs are cabriole-like and stretchers dispensed with entirely. One would have expected, therefore, that local Shanghainese chair-makers would have noted that the structural differences between a traditional Chinese chair and a European chair centred largely on a different kind of sitting posture which, among other things, required scaling down the chair seat to a more acceptable level of comfort. Apparently, they took this fact into consideration, for no teakwood chairs in English design come with 20 inches (52 centimetres) high chair seats. Yet most of the chairs that have come down to us today are still about two inches (five centimetres) higher than they ought to be. Is this not a case of old habits die hard? Perhaps.

Another type of structural modification concerns the design of tables, especially side tables. We begin by noting the height of Chinese tables: just as Chinese chair seats are, on the average, two to four inches (i.e. five to 10 centimetres) higher than English or European seats, Chinese tables, whether they be blackwood, red-and-gold namwood or English-style teakwood tables, are several inches taller. Thus, the height of most Chinese tables is between 2 feet 8 inches (80 centimetres) and 2 feet 11 inches (87.5 centimetres), whereas the standard height of most English/European tables is 30 inches (75 centimetres) – the difference being between five

and 12 centimetres.

But this calculation is based on the assumption that Chinese tables are freestanding. Many traditional Chinese, as well as Anglo-Chinese side tables, especially the more showy and ceremonial pieces, are not freestanding, but supported on low-rise pedestals of between six inches (15 centimetres) and 18 inches (45 centimetres) in height. For example, the *sam kai* altar table we described earlier was customarily raised upon a carved and giltwood pedestal of up to 18 inches (45 centimetres) high. By and large, crescent-shaped blackwood side tables and French-style consoles (made of teakwood) stand on low-rise carved pedestals of about six inches (15 centimetres) high.

This is a peculiarity of classic Chinese table design. Pedestal side tables (known in French as *consoles*, except that there are no pedestals in their version) are not common in English/European furniture. Most English/European consoles, commodes (side tables with flat or curved fronts and either drawers or cabinets) and other types of side tables come with freestanding legs, whether straight or cabrioled – cross or side stretchers being completely dispensed with from the 18th century onwards. Anglo-Chinese console tables are structured somewhat differently: those which happen to come with freestanding cabriole legs are invariably supported by low platforms or pedestals of up to six inches (14 centimetres) high. The feet – usually of the claw-and-ball type

– have tenons below which fit very snugly into corresponding mortises at the upper corners of the pedestal. From a structural point of view, such pedestals are, of course, unnecessary, since they merely heighten the level of the table without adding extra strength or rigidity to the legs.

As for those consoles which come with cross stretchers, pedestals are dispensed with, and from an aesthetic point of view, rightly so. But Chinese cabinet-makers steeped in the Ming tradition of cabinet-making appeared never to have been comfortable with console tables having freestanding legs. It was alien to their principles of good cabinet-making. So they dutifully fixed cross stretchers to all consoles with freestanding legs.

The other notable feature of most teakwood tables in the Anglo-Chinese style is the common (almost universal) use of marble slabs for table tops. The idea is, of course, French or Italian in origin, and most extant French or Italian consoles and commodes of 18th-century dating regularly come with marble tops. Marble tops are, however, largely absent in English side tables, either because marble was expensive in England or, more likely perhaps, that the English disliked the cold and stony qualities of marble. The Straits Babas, on the other hand, seemed to have taken a real fancy to console tables with marble tops, as most extant tables in old Baba homes invariably have marble slabs over them. Apart from the fact that French console tables and commodes made for the nobility were fitted with splendid ormolu-work, marquetry designs, inlays and gildings, the main difference between French consoles and Straits Chinese types is that the marble used in the latter, which was supplied by the Langkawi Islands, is mostly white with occasional streaks of grey or black venations, whereas French marble slabs (mostly imported from Italy) are mottled green, brown, black and beige. Marble slabs with variegated spots, speckles or complex streakings are rarely seen on Straits Chinese console tables.

One of the reasons that the Babas seemed to have taken with such alacrity to console tables featuring marble tops is that the Chinese had a long tradition of using figured marble slabs to adorn their furniture (including chairs, settees, tables and even cabinets) since the time of the Ming Dynasty. Marble was, in fact, a familiar material widely appreciated by Chinese scholars and aesthetes not only for its beauty (e.g. streakings of grey and black in Yunnan marble simulating landscapes), but also for its more obvious utilitarian advantages over timber in furniture construction. For unlike timber, marble is largely an inert mineral stone composed of calcium carbonate ($CaCO_3$). It keeps better than even most types of heavy hardwood because, among other things, it does not react to changes in weather and climatic conditions (e.g. absorbing or shedding moisture) and it is practically immune to attacks by fungi, insects and worms. It does not warp, shrink or split. It remains stable through the ages. Hence, tables which feature marble boards are more durable and infinitely easier to maintain.

On the other hand, there are people who only swear by tables which are one hundred per cent solid timber because, in their opinion, well-made and well-finished wooden table boards have a warmth and beauty which is unique to timber alone. This is especially true when the timber is hard, dense, dark, silky smooth and naturally endowed with complex streakings of whorls, waves, spirals, loops and eyes. To those who appreciate the look and touch of fine and seasoned timber, therefore, there is perhaps nothing to compare with the richly figured surface of a polished table top. And old timber tends to take on a patina and a texture which reminds timber buffs of the mellow tones of a Stradivarius violin, or perhaps a bouquet of vintage wine. Indeed, it is not uncommon for devotees of classic Ming period chairs and tables made out of old *huanghuali* to wax ecstatic over the honey tone and lustrous sheen of either *Dalbergia latifolia* or *Pterocarpus indicus*.

However, every type of wooden furniture suffers from certain fundamental defects peculiar to the nature of timber: wood can be scratched, chipped, dented, stained and burned. And no matter what one does to preserve the wood (e.g. by lacquer, oil, wax, grease and paints) even the best of heavy hardwoods is subject to certain basic phenomena which affect woody materials: shrinking, warping, splitting, cracking and rotting (caused by insects, wood-borers and worms). Only timbers which have been buried in peat swamp and river mud for years are immune to further deterioration.

In 18th- and 19th-century England and Europe, upholstered chairs were expensive luxuries which only upper-class nobility and wealthy businessmen could afford. People with more modest means had to be content (from the 17th century onwards) with cane seat and cane back chairs and settees. But when English/European furniture made its appearance in the Straits Settlements, it was expected that those luxurious and comfortable upholstered chairs and settees would have caught the imagination of the more well-to-do Babas whose love of ostentation was well known. Certainly, such upholstered chairs were more expensive than those with cane seats. But for some reason or other, those splendid pieces of furniture which traditionally graced the homes and palaces of English and European nobility never caught on with the Babas, if extant pieces of such furniture are anything to go by.

The Babas opted for chairs and settees with cane seats and cane backs.

There were good reasons for this. Cane chairs are better suited to the tropical climate of the Straits Settlement colonies, where the average day temperature is between 87°F and 90°F (31°C and 32°C), and where the humidity is often close to saturation point. As many people are aware, unless rooms are air-conditioned to bring the temperature and humidity down to a lower level, say, between 70°F and 75°F (20°C and 23°C), upholstered chairs and sofas are uncomfortable to sit on for any length of time. And incidentally, air-conditioning in offices, restaurants, department stores and homes only became widespread in the 1960s. Until then, cane chairs and settees were preferred by most people.

Also, traditionally, the Chinese have always been somewhat more spartan than the Europeans as far as comfort is concerned. The climate of northern China, for example, is bitterly cold in winter, and yet Chinese chairs from the earliest times were rarely upholstered to the standard of comfort attained by European chairs and sofas of the 18th century. Royalty were allowed to sit on cushioned chairs, but most ordinary people either sat on chairs with plain wooden seats and backs, or else chairs with cane seats.

The greatest drawback of chairs and other types of furniture with cane seats, and one which I do not happen to see mentioned in English books on furniture, is that cane chairs, particularly in the tropics, tended to harbour an obnoxious, blood-sucking and wingless insect known commonly as the bedbug (*Cimex lectularius*). This little vermin has a flat and reddish abdomen and a disagreeable odour. Most younger generations of Singaporeans and Malaysians nowadays may not have heard or even seen a bedbug. But in my childhood days before World War II, bedbugs were so common and lived in such close intimacy with human beings that nobody ever thought there was anything unusual about the presence of these blood-sucking pests. In fact, one of the common household chores assigned to teenagers in those days was to take grandfather's antique chairs out into the open and stamp them against the floor to dislodge bedbugs hidden in little holes and crevices between the matting of the cane seat.

But with the advent of DDT (dichloro-diphenyl-trichloro-ethane), which the victorious British army brought after the war, the days of bedbugs were numbered. Soon most families were using small handheld canisters of DDT to spray into the crevices of beds, benches, chairs, settees, couches and other pieces of furniture which were likely to harbour bedbugs. Within a decade or so, bedbugs, the bane of householders for centuries, had become a thing of the past.

A few words must be said about cane. Cane furniture is reputed to have been invented in India sometime in the 16th or 17th century, and this could well be true. However, there are many classic blackwood Chinese chairs, some dating back to the 15th century, which come with closely woven cane seats. Indeed, Chinese traders had been trading with the natives of Southeast Asia as far back as the Han Dynasty (206 B.C.–A.D. 220), so the art of weaving mats with narrow strips of cane stems was probably known to the Chinese for a very long time.

Rattan canes belong to a variety of climbing palms (family of *Palmae)* with long, trailing stems, punctuated at regular intervals by sharp spines and measuring several hundred feet long. Rattan canes are usually obtained from two species of such palms, namely *Daemonorops* and *Calamus*, which grew in tropical jungles in Burma, Thailand, Malaysia, New Guinea, the Philippines and Indonesia. When they are processed, seasoned and split into long narrow strips, the stems can be woven into the seats and backs of chairs. Unlike the fabrics and stuffing (mostly horsehair) used in heavily upholstered furniture, which are subject to dampness, dust, heat, fading of colours by exposure to direct sunlight and attacks by moths and fabric-eating insects, cane is light, durable and strong. Costwise, chairs sporting cane seats and backs were less expensive than those which were heavily upholstered with luxurious fabrics.

Ornamental modifications

There are other minor structural differences between Straits Chinese blackwood furniture and its European archetypes. But the points outlined above exemplify the distinct changes in the structural design. The next type of modification which local cabinet-makers wrought concerns changes to the style and content of the decorations of the furniture. As long as the English/European style of furniture was commissioned by European clients, Shanghainese cabinet-makers willingly obliged by ensuring that their reproductions were as authentic as they could possibly make, not only with regard to the overall design of the furniture in question, but also in the ornamental motifs, which include acanthus leaves, floral scrolls, fluted legs and columns, pilasters with Grecian capitals, cockles and other types of seashells, lion heads, pie-crust edges, Roman garlands, trailing grapevines, rosettes, acorn nuts, Gothic arches, reel-and-bead and twist-turn balusters, etc.

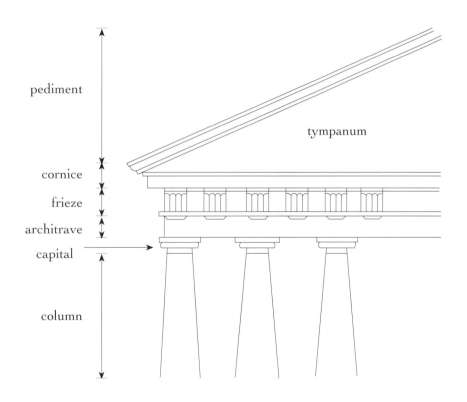

pediment

tympanum

cornice

frieze

architrave

capital

column

Guide to architectural terms and their related structures

Pintu pagar, *or the outer gate of a typical traditional Baba home in Singapore. The difference between a Singapore-type of* pintu pagar *and a Malacca one is this: the Singapore gate tapers upwards towards the centre to form a sort of pediment, while the Malacca gate is flat without any form of tapering. As for the traditional Baba homes in Georgetown, Penang, they had no* pintu pagars.

This beautiful and ornamental pintu pagar *features a combination of pierced-work and bas-relief carvings of floral and European vase-and-garland motifs. It has been meticulously restored and re-gilded. Probably made of teakwood. Private collection.*

But one suspects that Chinese cabinet-makers, still steeped in their ancient culture, never really felt comfortable with the kinds of decorations which European cabinet-makers and their clients traditionally fancied for all their furniture. For one thing, the decorations appearing in English/ European furniture seemed all rather capricious and meaningless to Chinese eyes, since they were employed mainly for ornamental purposes. To the Chinese way of thinking, the theory of 'art for art's sake' was foreign to their culture because Chinese art, like the art of ancient Egyptians, Mesopotamians, Indians and those of other civilizations (including the cave paintings of Lascaux in the south of France), was essentially a symbolic art. This simply means that the decorations which adorn any man-made artefact must always be chosen for their symbolic, religious and propitiative significance, rather than for their appeal to our sense of beauty. If anything, therefore, art for the Chinese must be for 'life's sake'. That is why the motifs of the carvings in Chinese furniture must always fit the social or religious functions which these pieces of furniture were intended to serve.

Thus, whenever an opportunity arose which enabled them to express themselves in ways that were more authentic to their culture, Shanghainese carvers used the occasion to substitute those traditional Chinese motifs for European types of decoration. They soon discovered that *their* versions of English-style furniture were readily acceptable to the Babas who, for some reason or other, did not find the appearance of phoenixes, dragons, *qilins* and peonies objectionable in their furniture. Nor, for that matter, did the Babas demur to the substitution of dragon heads for scrolled knobs on the handles of armchairs. Lotus flowers, peonies and plum blossoms, somewhat stiff and formalized, began to appear in the crestings and the splats of armchairs, the aprons and upper stretchers of tables and the panels of doors for cabinets and sideboards. Straits Chinese-style console tables soon began to sport bold carvings of *lohans*, Taoist Immortals, *qilins*, dragons, phoenixes and peonies on the frieze or aprons, while the corners of cabriole legs showed *taotien* masks instead of acanthus leaves and cockle shells. And incidentally, Chinese scrolls are quite different from English/ European scrolls. Whereas European scrolls tend to be rendered in perfect circular, spiral twists which normally terminate in a spray of acanthus leaves, with or without flower buds or acorn nuts, Chinese scrolls have a more ambiguous character about them: sometimes they resemble formalized cloud scrolls, at other times, one end terminates in what looks like a dragon head, while the other resembles the foliated tails of dragons. In any case, Chinese scrolls are never rendered in perfect circular spirals.

The net result was that Anglo-Chinese furniture began to take on a culturally hybrid appearance. On the one hand, the overall design of these pieces of furniture was obviously European in origin; on the other hand, the pervasive presence of ancient Chinese motifs gave such furniture a curiously oriental, if not Chinese, look about them. It is this curious mixture of European furniture design with the ancient Chinese style of decoration which, more than anything else, gave Straits Chinese teakwood furniture its unique character.

There are, among extant pieces of Straits Chinese teakwood furniture, display cabinets with glass doors designed in the European style. Such cabinets, known as *tu kacha*, or 'glass cabinets', were apparently intended for storing Chinese porcelain as well as old Waterford cut-glass wine decanters, wine glasses, fruit bowls and vases.

Incidentally, the Babas never adopted the European method of storing their porcelain plates by, for example, standing them flat against the back of a cupboard. In Chinese custom, plates and bowls, unless they were precious antiques, were stacked in a pile and placed upon the shelves.

Generally, the façade of these glass cabinets was so designed that it gave them a monumental and architectural appearance. This is achieved by the incorporation of such features as columns or pilasters, with or without capitals, supporting an entablature over which a pediment or arch is constructed to crown the cabinet.

There is ample evidence that, while such replicas of European cabinets were made from time to time for clients who specifically wanted them, Chinese cabinet-makers, when left to their own devices, did not particularly fancy the idea that cupboards and cabinets should, whenever possible, be designed to simulate architectural structures, particularly with regard to their facades. To them a cupboard was simply a cupboard, that is, basically an upright, rectangular case for storing things. They did not, therefore, see any particular merit in making it look like a miniature building of some kind, however appealing the idea may seem to some people.

Close-up of the pintu pagar *featured on the previous page showing the details of the gilded carvings on the pediment.*

However, if a cupboard must, for some reason or other, be adorned, the decorations should, as far as possible, serve only as frills and not as significant structural alterations to the basic form of the cupboard itself.

One has only to examine samples of extant Straits Chinese cabinets to see how Shanghainese cabinet-makers put this principle into practice: from the time of the Ming Dynasty (1368–1644), or even earlier, all Chinese cupboards were structured on the basic form of an upright, rectangular case standing on four short legs. This fundamental principle was adhered to for at least six centuries, down to the end of the Qing Dynasty at the turn of the 20th century. Decorations, whenever they appeared, were kept to a minimum and consisted largely of simple geometric mouldings to the door panels, the frontal posts and horizontal bracings. Thus, when it came to the question of adapting traditional Chinese ideas of cabinet design to European methods of constructing and designing cabinets (and they were given a free hand to do as they liked) Shanghainese craftsmen stuck uncompromisingly to this basic rectangular structure and concentrated all their decorative skills on two areas only. The first consisted of adorning the glass doors (and some broad cupboards may have as many as four doors) by fabricating gilded fretwork panels – depicting mainly formalized floral and foliated motifs – for mounting behind the glass panels. The second consisted of carving a cresting panel, again of gilded fretwork in which auspicious beasts, birds, plants, flowers and fruit are vividly depicted, for the top of the cupboard. The other minor modification consisted of substituting cabriole legs for straight legs.

These were the only ornamental concessions which Chinese craftsmen allowed to the basic structure of the cupboard. They did not attempt to slavishly imitate the European practice of incorporating decorative ornaments which overtly or covertly suggest architectural structures of some sort, as they could not perceive any analogy between the structure and function of a cupboard and those of a building. Those ornamental crestings and panels made out of gilded fretwork and which most people take for granted are, however, peculiar to Straits Chinese teakwood cabinets: they are absent in English/European cabinets.

Partial gilding

The term 'giltwood furniture' is normally used to refer to those pieces of furniture which are either completely or partially gilded with gold leaf. By and large, English furniture, upon which much of Straits Chinese teakwood furniture was largely modelled, was ungilded, except for those pieces made for nobility and which were based on 18th-century French designs. Continental Europeans, from the Renaissance period (1350 onwards), were particularly attracted by the splendour of giltwood furniture, and consequently the household movables, especially of Italian royalty and nobility, were largely gilded. The English, by contrast, were content to appreciate the intrinsic qualities of natural timber, its colours, grain and texture, without the distractions of gilding. In this respect, they resembled the Chinese

mandarins and nobility of Ming period China in their taste for the beauty of natural wood, especially as exemplified by *huanghuali* and *zitan*.

As for Chinese giltwood furniture, this seemed to have been confined mainly to the southeastern provinces of Zhejiang and Fujian, where namwood and elmwood furniture was gilded. However, gilded namwood furniture, as we have previously noted, was not utilized by the Imperial Court in Beijing until about the time of the reign of Emperor Qianlong (1735–96). Even so, court furniture was largely made out of blackwood and rosewood – the two most highly prized types of timber appreciated for their natural beauty.

Most extant pieces of Straits Chinese teakwood furniture in old Baba homes were modelled on 18th- and 19th-century English archetypes and, as was to be expected, authentic English furniture was ungilded. Yet, we notice again and again in the Straits Chinese versions of English furniture that partial gilding was applied. On the face of it, this would suggest that local Chinese cabinet-makers borrowed this idea of partial gilding from French and Italian furniture which they must have seen in books and magazines. This is entirely possible, except that partial gilding in 18th-century French furniture was mostly confined to ormolu (gilded bronze) decorations which were separately crafted by skilled metallurgists and then attached to various parts of a piece of furniture. In other words, gilding in such types of furniture was exclusively confined to metal decorations. Metal gilding employs a technique which is different from that of wood gilding. In metal gilding, the chased and repoussé decorations are thoroughly cleaned, then applied with an amalgam of gold and mercury and fired. The heating causes the mercury to evaporate and leaves the gold to adhere to the metal. This method of gilding is prohibited

nowadays because the mercury oxide given out during the firing is highly toxic and dangerous to health. Nevertheless, gilding produced by this method is exceedingly beautiful and very durable.

Straits Chinese teakwood furniture, by contrast, contains no ormolu decorations – there are no metal parts in this type of furniture other than iron nails, screws and hinges. Its decorations are carved out of a solid teak base. In French and Italian giltwood furniture, the gilding is either confined to ormolu decorations or else applied to the entire wooden frame of a piece of furniture. Chinese cabinet-makers adopted neither of these techniques. Their method of gilding furniture was *always* partial gilding, but not in the sense of the partial gilding applied in French furniture. They reserved the gilding process only to the carved decorations on wood and this technique was borrowed from Chinese gilders of Zhejiang and Fujian provinces, where red-and-gold namwood furniture originated.

There is, however, one significant difference between the technique of gilding employed by Chinese gilders and that of European gilders. Chinese gilders did not apply gesso, size, red clay or any of the typical European types of undercoating to the carvings prior to laying gold leaf over them. Chinese carvings were simply rubbed and sanded down to remove all traces of coarseness caused by the action of the carving instruments. When this was completed, a coating or two of red lacquer was applied evenly over the woodwork and allowed to stand for, say, a couple of hours (depending on weather conditions such as temperature and humidity) until semi-dry. Gold leaf was then applied over the still sticky surface of the carvings in rapid succession. Of course,

this could only be executed by skilled and experienced gilders.

In the European method of gilding, successive layers of gesso (which is a mixture of plaster of Paris and size) are applied to the raw wood and then rubbed down until all the crevices have been covered and the details of the carved motifs stand out conspicuously. The woodwork is then painted over with size and clay and the tacky surface is applied with gold leaf. Finally, when all the gilded surfaces have dried out, the gilding can be burnished by rubbing gently with soft cotton wool, or a piece of smooth agate pebble.

For some unknown reason, the gilders who were given the task of gilding Straits Chinese teakwood furniture preferred to employ the European method of gilding, which entails more work perhaps than the traditional Chinese method used in red-and-gold furniture. This can easily be ascertained by using a penknife to scrape gently on the surface of the giltwork of such English-style furniture. It will be seen that, immediately below the coating of gold leaf, a layer of white chalky substance can be detected. There is no chalky substance below the gilt carvings of red-and-gold furniture.

The era of teak

As I have already dealt with two distinguishing features of Straits Chinese teak furniture, namely the frequent use of marble slabs for table tops and the decided preference for cane chairs to upholstered ones, I would like to remark on some of the circumstances surrounding the exclusive use of teakwood for making English-style Baba furniture for at least 50 years – from about 1880 to 1930 – in the history of the Straits Settlements.

I call this 'the era of teak'.

There was, as a matter of fact, no compelling reason why teak should have been preferred to any other type of tropical hardwood for making furniture, especially when one bears in mind that the varieties of light, medium and heavy hardwoods available in tropical countries far exceed all the varieties of hardwoods available in temperate forests. And yet one finds that English and European furniture employed a whole variety of temperate timbers including oak, ash, elm, walnut, beech, birch, yew, pine, cedar, applewood and pearwood, as well as such tropical hardwoods as rosewood and mahogany. Besides, teak is not even endemic to Peninsular Malaysia: much of it came from Burma and Thailand. Nor, for that matter, is teak the hardest and most beautifully figured timber available in Southeast Asia. Indeed, the Malaysian Timber Industry Board, in its publication entitled *100 Malaysian Timbers*, 1986, listed 14 species of heavy hardwood, 36 species of medium hardwood and 47 species of light hardwood which are of economic value. There are, of course, more than 100 species of useful timber to be found in the teeming tropical forests of Malaysia and Borneo, which, according to botanists, are at least 130 million years old! But many of these otherwise excellent timber trees are not easily obtainable in sufficient quantity for economic exploitation. It is clear, therefore, that cabinet-makers a hundred years ago, could, without difficulty, have availed themselves of, say, 20 or more varieties of good timber for furniture-making – had they wanted to.

For example, the common *tembusu* (*Fragae spp*), a wayside tree which grows extremely slowly, produces a fine, hard timber of bright yellow-orange colour and attractive streaky venations. For all its apparent denseness and coarseness of grain, it is relatively easy to work with and

produces a smooth and lustrous polish. And yet it is principally used to make chopping boards for butchers because of its sheer strength and durability. Next, there is *kekatong* (*Cynometra spp.*) which belongs to the family *Leguminosae*. This is another beautiful hardwood and its heartwood varies from reddish-brown to claret-red. The richly figured grain is brown and black. *Rengas* (*Melanochyla spp.*), of the family of *Anacardiaceae*, is highly prized by traditional Malay craftsmen as an excellent cabinet wood because of its colour, which varies from dark red to deep blood-red and its streaky venations of black. It is also said to be strong and durable. Then there is *merbau* (*Intsia palembanica*), which is yellowish to orange-brown when freshly cut, but turns to a dark red-brown upon prolonged exposure. This heavy hardwood is sometimes mistaken for rosewood and has lately come to be used increasingly in Malacca (and Kuala Lumpur?) for making reproductions of antique Straits Chinese furniture. In Sabah and Sarawak, *belian* (*Eusideroxylon zwageri*), belonging to the family of *Lauraceae*, is the most valuable of heavy hardwood known to the natives. Its heartwood is bright yellow when freshly cut, but darkens to reddish-brown and even black upon prolonged exposure to the atmosphere. A strong and durable timber, it is nonetheless easy to work with and, like *tembusu*, produces a lustrous surface when polished.

There were many more of such hardwoods, including *balau* (*Shorea spp.*), *cengal* (*Neobalanocarpus heimii*), *meranti* (also *Shorea spp.*), *nyatoh* (*Sapindaceae spp.*) and *kapur* (*Dryobalanops spp.*), which were available to Chinese cabinet-makers and traditional Malay carpenters, wood-carvers and builders. And because all traditional Malay houses were made of local timbers from time immemorial, Malay builders (*tukang kayu*) were naturally very knowledgeable about the properties of different types of tropical hardwood, of their suitability or otherwise for woodwork of every type (including cabinet-making) and where they might be obtained in the dense and steamy tropical jungles. But for some unknown reason, it probably never occurred to anyone among those early British officials residing in the Straits colony that the *tukang kayu* was a mine of useful and reliable information concerning the various uses which some of these local species of hardwoods might be put to, including cabinet-making.

Teak was preferred for furniture construction largely because it was so wellknown and so highly prized in India since time immemorial as a timber of extraordinary durability. It thus was regarded as highly suitable for building construction. Indeed, teak columns found in some of the temples in Vijayanagar, southern India, are said to have lasted more than 500 years in spite of being continuously exposed to the inclemency of the tropical climate. Some of the teak beams in cave temples are said to be 1000 years old and are still in a fine state of preservation. When kept under cover, teak is virtually imperishable. It is not without good reason, therefore, that the Indians valued teak so highly.

The earliest officials of the English East India Company to be sent abroad were stationed in India, especially in Bombay, Madras, Calcutta and Delhi. Calcutta became the headquarters of the company in India by the turn of the 19th century. Thus, by the time of the founding of the Straits Settlements in the Malay Peninsula in 1867, the East India Company had traded and administered a substantial part of the Indian subcontinent on behalf of the British government. And of the numerous things which the company's officials learnt about India, the excellence of teak as a timber for both building construction and cabinet-making was common knowledge. Beams

of teak were even exported to England where shipwrights used them for laying the keels of British men-of-war. But unlike the other types of tropical and sub-tropical hardwood, namely mahogany and rosewood, it was rarely used for making furniture in England.

Officials sent out from either England or Calcutta to administer the Straits colony, as mentioned earlier, usually brought some English furniture with them for their personal use. Before long, they learnt from their counterparts in India that teakwood was an excellent timber regularly used there for making fine furniture and that it was available in large quantities from Burma. Thus, when the need arose in later years for making reproductions of English originals, the first type of timber that came to mind was teak and not any of the largely unknown Malayan hardwood I have mentioned. The import of teak for the manufacture (by hand, that is) of English-style furniture started off as a contingency measure to meet the needs of certain expatriate officers for essential pieces of furniture while they were on overseas posting. Later it became the standard practice for all subsequent officers assigned to the Straits Settlements.

What, then, are the virtues of teak which make it so highly commendable to cabinet-makers? To people who have had considerable experience in utilizing teak for making furniture, the superior qualities of *kayu jati* (to use the Malay name for teak) are obvious. Teak may not be as dense and hard (its density is only about 450 kilograms per cubic metre and thus it may only be classified as a light hardwood) as many of the local species of hardwood, but it is easy to work with and an absolute joy to the wood-carver. It does not split or warp under varying climatic and weather conditions and it does not crack (a problem with some tropical hardwoods) when iron nails or

Four-poster brass bed with three enclosure panels. However, the main structures of these beds, such as the bed frame and the four main posts, were in fact made of cast iron plated with brass. Only the railings and balusters were fabricated of pure brass. Brass beds of this type were made in England and other European countries, but those exported to the Straits Settlements for the Straits Chinese community invariably come with three enclosure panels to simulate the original alcove structure of the traditional Chinese kang. Courtesy of Prof and Mrs Yusoff Talib.

screws are driven into the heartwood. It is practically immune to every type of wood-eating and wood-boring insect, such as ground termites, because the heartwood is permeated with an aromatic oil which has proven insecticidal properties and which, for this reason, confers extraordinary durability upon the timber. This very same oil helps to keep nails, screws and metal hinges free from rust. I have, on many occasions, extracted nails and screws from old teak furniture, some of which are at least 80 years old, but they showed no signs of rust except on those parts which happened to be exposed to the atmosphere. Teak furniture datable to the turn of the 20th century shows no sign of any deterioration whatsoever other than a darker (and a more pleasing) patina on the varnish of shellac. And teak, of course, has an attractive golden-brown colour.

European styles and techniques of furniture construction

I shall, for the sake of completeness, describe briefly the attempts by Chinese cabinet-makers, from the last two decades of the 19th century to about the 1930s, to adapt European styles and techniques of furniture construction for turning out English-style furniture. This is necessary, especially when one bears in mind that traditional Chinese methods of cabinet-making are different in some fundamental respects from European techniques, and that those local Shanghainese craftsmen who fabricated the bulk of extant pieces of English-style teak furniture were in fact trained in the Chinese tradition of cabinet-making. Nonetheless, when it became expedient for them to switch to European methods of furniture

construction, they adapted very rapidly. Before long they were producing what was really an alien style of furniture with a surprising verve and assurance which hardly betrayed any evidence of false starts, tentative gropings or technical incompetence of any sort. I have yet to come across a piece of English-style teak furniture in an old Baba home which is of poor workmanship, either in the constructional or ornamental aspects.

There was, admittedly, a certain amount of awkwardness about the way Chinese wood-carvers interpreted and represented European decorative motifs. But this was largely due to the lack of familiarity with European culture and particularly with the types of motif that traditionally appealed to European tastes but were perplexing from a Chinese point of view. As previously noted, the conservative Chinese artist and wood-carver required that all ornamental motifs in a work of art should stand for something auspicious about life, such as longevity, good health, conjugal happiness, fertility, success, scholarly accomplishment, abundance (of food and wealth), good fortune, harmonious relationships and so on. However, European art motifs were primarily aesthetic rather than symbolic in their function. In Chinese eyes, therefore, they seem to be either pointless or trivial. For example, while a Chinese carver could easily appreciate the ornamental beauty of acanthus leaves and formalized floral and foliated scrolls on furniture, they could not understand why anyone should appreciate art for its own sake. Surely, they thought, the motifs employed in decorative arts and crafts must be made to serve some practical end? And what, by the way,

did Roman garlands signify? As for acorn nuts, trailing grapevines, cockle shells, lion heads, ornamental urns and rosettes, what auspicious attributes did they refer to? And if they did not stand for anything of good omen, what was the point of having them at all? When it came to representing European figures, Chinese wood-carvers (and artists as well) could only succeed in making them look at best like half-breed Chinese. As for bare-breasted women with mermaid-like caudal fins and nude figures (fortunately these occurred mostly in 18th-century French and Italian furniture rather than in English furniture), Chinese carvers avoided them altogether because of their possible pornographic suggestions. Whereas the nude has been with European art for the better part of 2500 years – if we date it back to the Athens of 5th century B.C. – it was, in

China, depicted mainly in erotic folk art meant largely for private viewing only. The nude could never be made the object of public exhibition as in many European countries.

Thus, except for some culture shock encountered by former generations of local Shanghainese cabinet-makers and wood-carvers in their initial attempts to depict and present European art motifs convincingly, no serious problems of any sort were encountered in adapting European methods of furniture construction for turning out English-style teak furniture. As we have noted previously in chapters two and three on blackwood and red-and-gold namwood furniture respectively, all traditional types of Chinese furniture were fitted together by mortises and tenons only. No screws, nails, brackets, struts, pegs or even glues were ever employed in the joinery and this meant of course that the standard of joinery required to maintain a piece of furniture in its structural integrity had to be of a high degree of precision and rigidity. For this reason, joiners had to undergo long years of apprenticeship under some demanding master joiners in order to acquire the kind of proficiency for executing a whole variety of complex tenons and mortises to meet every foreseeable type of joinery in furniture construction. One has only to consult the excellent illustrations of the principal types of joint employed by Chinese joiners in Wang Shixiang's[22] and Gustav Ecke's[23] works (Wang illustrated eight principal types of joint, while Ecke showed that at least 28 different types of joint could be detected in classic Chinese furniture) to appreciate the complex ingenuity of these joints and the skill required to execute them. Unless they are frequently moved or dragged about, the joints in antique blackwood and red-and-gold namwood furniture are likely to remain rigidly fixed and intact for up to a century or more, notwithstanding seasonal changes in weather and climatic conditions. Undoubtedly, the excellence of the Chinese art of joinery may also be attributed to the remarkable strength and density of the different species of *Dalbergia* timber which go into the making of what we describe here as 'blackwood' furniture.

Of Chinese techniques of cabinet-work, therefore, anyone who has undergone the long and arduous apprenticeship required of a joiner/cabinet-maker in China would have had little

A study of the tapered baluster legs of the dining table on page 149.

difficulty coping with the various kinds of joints commonly employed in the construction of European furniture. These included dovetail joints, tongue-and-groove joints, bare-faced joints, halved joints and lapped joints. Executing such joints was relatively easy for every well-trained joiner. The traditional Chinese art of furniture-making, however, required that every joiner should also be able to execute complex mitre joints (the distinctive feature of the Chinese art of joinery), peg-tenon joints, bridle joints, shoulder joints, etc. These are complex and difficult enough to cut with precision, but when they have to be carved by hand out of such dense and heavy woods as *huanghuali* and *zitan*, the job is made doubly demanding. For this reason, when local Shanghainese cabinet-makers were asked to make English-style furniture out of teakwood – a light hardwood which is easy to work with – using simpler types of joints than those they were customarily required to do, as well as such labour-saving devices as nails, screws, brackets and struts, they took to their new assignments like ducks to water. It was so much easier turning out English-style teak furniture than blackwood furniture, and the result was a marked increase in productivity – and in earnings as well.

This increase in productivity, significant as it was, underlined a basic difference between the attitude and practices of European cabinet-makers and those of their Chinese counterparts. Generally, European cabinet-makers, especially from about the beginning of the 19th century, when industrialization in Europe was gaining momentum, were not averse to using the latest labour-saving devices (e.g. the use of the treadle lathe for making wood-turnings, the application of brackets and struts secured by iron screws and nails rather than by tenons and mortises) to speed up and to simplify furniture construction.

Traditional Chinese cabinet-makers, however, regarded furniture construction as a form of craftsmanship in which manual dexterity guided by a sure eye was prized above mechanical efficiency. Master craftsmen and cabinet-makers steadfastly refused to sanction the use of such things as iron nails, screws and even wooden pegs and brackets as short-cut substitutes for joints and bracings because it violated a fundamental principle of furniture construction, namely that all the separate components of a piece of furniture must be crafted by hand and fitted together by mortises and tenons. They also rejected wood-turnings of any type which happened to have been executed with the aid of a treadle lathe (a very important invention in carpentry) simply because wood-turning was considered a counterfeit form of carving. All rounded members in blackwood furniture designed in purely Chinese tastes had to be carved by hand. In fact, they are more elliptical than round. Likewise, Chinese cabinet-makers avoided such mechanical improvisations whereby the construction of, say, the larger and more bulbous parts of a piece of furniture (e.g. lantern-shaped legs of large tables) is effected by pasting separate pieces of wood together and then shaping them by turning upon a lathe. In their tradition of cabinet-making, every component of a piece of furniture, whatever its shape and size may be, had to be sculpted out of solid timber.

Thus, conservative Chinese cabinet-makers avoided mechanization at all costs, not because they did not have the means at their disposal –

after all, bronze nails had been used for securing timber plankings to the hulls of sailing ships as far back as the Song Dynasty in the 10th century, while the treadle lathe was not unknown to them – but because, in their tradition of cabinet-making, craftsmanship was the hallmark of excellence.

I referred earlier in this chapter to the sense of cultural disorientation which local Shanghainese cabinet-makers first experienced when they had to adapt their traditional methods of furniture construction to making English-style furniture. The technical aspects of European methods of furniture-making presented minor problems which were simply ironed out by the wholesale adoption of European methods of carpentry, which resulted in higher productivity. But European ornamental motifs were a different matter. In order for anyone to carve and reproduce the motifs of an alien culture with the flair and conviction of native craftsmen themselves, one must first imbibe the values of that culture to a point where one can mentally and emotionally relate to these things in a meaningful way. But since it was hardly feasible in the circumstances to expect Chinese cabinet-makers as such to be literate about European culture – and European art motifs were largely meaningless and pointless in Chinese eyes – there was no way in which they could make authentic reproductions. At their very best, their imitative efforts would appear insipid and, at their worst, their products would be grotesque parodies of the originals.

How could the conflict produced by such culture shock be resolved? The answer is surprisingly simple. As discussed earlier, if one takes the trouble to look closely at Straits Chinese teak furniture, one finds that instead of labouring fruitlessly at trying to reproduce European art motifs in their reproductions of English-style furniture, Shanghainese cabinet-makers simply

substituted, wherever it was feasible, Chinese art and religious symbols for European art motifs. In this way, they removed all lingering doubts and misgivings about the propriety or otherwise of European art motifs in all their handiwork. The structural designs of these pieces of furniture remained unmistakably English/European in style, but when looked at closely, the motifs were definitely oriental in origin, for they included phoenixes, *qilins*, magpies, prancing Buddhist lions, bats, butterflies, carps, crickets, peonies, chrysanthemums, plum blossoms, lotuses and other symbols of good omen. As in everything else characteristic of Baba culture, Straits Chinese furniture was a composite of ancient Chinese and other foreign cultural elements.

Varnishes

Some remarks on varnishes are in order. Straits Chinese teak furniture in old Baba homes is varnished by what is known as the method of 'French polishing'. French polishing differs from the standard method of varnishing which uses a brush made of fine camel hairs, sable hairs or perhaps pig bristles to apply successive layers of varnish onto the polished and prepared surfaces of a piece of furniture. In French polishing, the main tool for applying varnish is a cotton pad (or rather, several cotton pads) which is dipped into a watery solution of copal, cellulose and shellac dissolved in alcohol or methylated spirit. Now shellac and copal are not fundamentally different from lacquer (the sap from the species of tree,

The kind of varnish regularly used for polishing Straits Chinese teak furniture is shellac – a light, golden-brown flake derived from the sap of the species of tree, Rhus vernicifera. *Shellac is steeped in a solution of alcohol to produce a watery varnish. Polishing is done by simply applying a cotton pad into the varnish and then gently rubbing it over the raw and cleanly prepared surface of the teak. The wood takes on a golden-brown sheen, as the* pintu pagar, *or front gate, in this photograph shows.*

Rhus vernicifera) in that they are all resins obtained from trees. However, it is well to remember that traditional Chinese blackwood and red-and-gold namwood types of furniture were varnished with lacquer by the usual method of painting with a brush.

In order to prepare the surfaces of a piece of furniture for varnishing by the method of French polishing, some essential procedures have to be carefully observed. First, the surface of the raw timber has to be sanded down by several grades of fine sandpaper to produce a smooth and polished finish. All dust and sandy particles must be removed to ensure that no coarse grains of sand or emery remain. When this is done, the painter prepares a padding of coarse cotton, as well as a dish of either fine pumice powder, lime or plaster of Paris. Next, he dips the cotton pad into a solution of alcohol to wet it, and then presses it lightly into the dish containing pumice powder so that some of it adheres to the cotton pad. He now begins to rub the cotton pad over the surface of the raw timber in a slow, circular motion to ensure that all the fine medullary pores are fully covered up. Apart from closing up wood pores, pumice powder acts as a fine abrasive which helps to impart a glossy polish to the surface of the wood. Needless to say, this operation requires skill and an experienced eye. The wood must be allowed to dry out for a couple of hours before the varnish is applied.

The piece of furniture is now ready for polishing with varnish. Incidentally, the preparation of the varnish (effected by dissolving shellac and other varieties of resin in alcohol) is usually done by professional cabinet-makers. The painter now prepares a second padding – this time of fine cotton fabric. He dips the padding into a thin solution of shellac and alcohol and gently rubs it over the prepared wood surface. When this is completed, he waits for the thin film of varnish to dry before making another pass with his dampened cotton pad. By making successive passes he gradually builds up the thickness of these transparent layers of varnish. The secret of fine polishing is to let every layer of shellac varnish dry out completely before applying another layer upon it. When the polishing is completed and the varnish has dried completely, a piece of chamois lightly wetted with varnish can be applied to the surface to give it that final coating of splendid lustre.

Michel Doussy[24], himself a French expert at restoring antiques, recommends the use of cotton pads for polishing. But according to Charles Hayward[25], an English expert in cabinet-making, Victorian polishers used a piece of rubber for applying successive layers of shellac varnish on furniture, and he attributed the wonderful lustre of French polish in English furniture to the polishing and rubbing effect which the rubber had upon the underlying layer of shellac varnish. Local Shanghainese cabinet-makers seemed to have preferred the cotton pad to the piece of rubber used by English polishers. They also used lime instead of pumice powder for closing the medullary pores in raw timber. Some people are of the view that the characteristic reddish golden brown of shellac varnish in old teakwood furniture was largely due to the reaction of lime upon shellac varnish and that this effect is absent if lime is not applied in preparing the wood surfaces. Whatever the truth of the matter, there is no doubt that old teakwood varnish has a depth and lustre which is

not reproducible in new furniture.

There is one major drawback about French polishing and that is it is not heat resistantand it blotches upon prolonged contact with water and damp places. For this reason, many old pieces of teak furniture, the surfaces of which have been exposed to heat and dampness (especially chairs and table tops and legs), invariably bear the imprints of not just heat-rings left behind by hot cups, saucers, dishes, bowls, plates, etc., but also whitish spots and pale patches, particularly on the lower parts of the piece of furniture which have been subjected to dampness.

Repertory of teakwood furniture in English/European styles

Chairs

All that remains for me to do is to run through the descriptions of the different categories of extant Straits Chinese teak furniture, drawing attention along the way to the distinctive features, including family resemblances and differences which, among other things, make them what they are, and provide a basis for making comparisons with the archetypes from which they are derived.

Of Straits Chinese teak chairs, it may be noted at once that their basic structures are largely derived from English archetypes. However, their ornamental motifs, if they happen to be floral and foliated ones, are predominantly of Chinese origin (e.g. lotuses, plum blossoms and peonies). Such Anglo-Chinese-style chairs, as we commonly find them, are mostly armchairs. In fact, there are more armchairs in old Baba homes than there are chairs of identical design without armrests. On the face of it, this is unusual because, in traditional European custom, dining tables made specifically to complement, say, eight chairs would normally feature only two armchairs at the extremities of the table, and six chairs without armrests at the sides. This practice was strictly observed by the Anglicized Babas. But there was still a surplus of armchairs in most old Baba homes which were not accounted for, if we simply assume that chairs of this type were exclusively used for the dining room.

The real explanation for the excess of armchairs is to be found in the traditional Chinese (and hence also Baba) custom of furnishing the space along the two side walls of the main reception hall with four sets of chairs, two on each side of the hall. Each set consists of two armchairs and a small, matching tea table (placed between the chairs). Readers will recall that the traditional type of furniture in the main reception hall of all well-to-do Baba homes consisted largely of a variety of squarish, throne-like blackwood chairs and small, matching tea tables, crescent-shaped display tables, benches, a set consisting of a circular tea table with four stools (set in the centre of the hall), a set of altar tables and framed panels of embroidery or brush paintings, all inlaid with mother-of-pearl decorations. By the turn of the 20th century, however, heavy and bulky blackwood furniture had begun to make way for English-style teak furniture as the Babas became more and more Anglicized in their lifestyles. The general decor of the reception hall, however, remained conservatively Chinese.

Thus, instead of squarish blackwood chairs, the Babas now installed Anglo-Chinese-style teak chairs complemented with tea tables sporting marble tops. Instead of a pair of crescent-shaped pedestal blackwood tables, each of which was placed centrally between two sets of armchairs, they now set up teakwood pedestal console tables with marble tops. And where formerly Chinese scroll paintings or embroidered panels mounted in blackwood frames hung on the side walls, the Westernized Babas now set up either enormous rectangular mirrors mounted on gilded and carved teak frames or large Bohemian-style crystal mirrors.

A peculiarity of all English-style teak furniture, as noted previously, was partial gilding – the gilding being specifically confined only to carved panels or perhaps to the more prominent parts of the ornamental-work. Chairs were no exception. However, chairs featuring upholstery of expensively woven fabrics or, say, *petit point* embroideries of the type we see in the homes of English and European nobility were conspicuously absent in old Baba homes; and since chairs of this type, which originated in the reign of Louis XIV of France, were gilded on all their exposed frames – an expensive luxury – they were never used by even the wealthy Babas. Instead, cane chairs with the seats and backs woven with a strong network of rattan cane were widely preferred, partly because they were easier to keep clean (cane seats do not collect dust so readily, nor are they prone to attacks by fabric-eating insects) and partly because the cost of replacing frayed and worn-out cane seats and backs was a fraction of what it would cost to install new silk and needlework upholstery.

Locally crafted reproductions of English chairs were rarely, if ever, faithful copies of their originals, not simply because of the tendency of Chinese craftsmen to substitute English/European ornamental motifs with traditional Chinese art and religious symbols (we have already dealt with that), but also because local Shanghainese chair-makers, when constructing *their* versions of English chairs, did not adhere scrupulously to some specific style of chair design. Instead, they borrowed the component designs of chairs belonging to different periods and different cabinet-makers as it suited their fancies, and incorporated them into the overall designs of their versions of English chairs.

The result was an amalgam of different period styles in the same piece of furniture. Thus, it is not uncommon for a Straits Chinese chair to have straight wood-turned legs in Jacobean style but which are freestanding and without stretchers, 19th-century Regency armrests and late 17th-century cresting rails surmounting the chair back. Sometimes one encounters a chair, or a set of chairs, which sports a Hepplewhite shield back with angular rhombic chair seat, but with freestanding cabriole legs in Queen Anne style, instead of kidney-shaped chair seats with straight, square-cut legs secured by lower stretchers. Chairs with double-bine, twist-turned legs (typical of later 17th-century English chairs with tall backs) invariably come with splats featuring scroll carvings typical of 18th-century

One of a set of eight chairs designed after the manner of 17th-century Jacobean period chairs. The twist-turned front legs, front posts, stretcher, back posts, as well as the fretted splat and banisters tenoned into the cresting panel and the stretcher above the seat, are all typically Jacobean in style, except for the floral motifs on the splat and cresting rail. These are formalized patterns of Chinese lotus blossoms. Teakwood. Dating: late 19th/early 20th century. Author's collection.

chairs, rather than plain cane backs. Again, it is not unusual to come across locally crafted chairs with late 17th-century features, such as high crestings, cane backs and finials on wood-turned uprights, combined with 18th-century D-shaped chair seats and freestanding cabriole legs. I used to possess a pair of what looked like reproductions of some 17th-century chairs with cane seats and cane backs, carved cresting rails, back posts with finials and straight wood-turned legs with stretchers. However, the backs were vertically straight without any raking at all. In the history of English furniture, straight-back chairs went back to 16th-century Tudor England. Obviously, Chinese cabinet-makers were blissfully unaware that the eclectic designs of their versions of English chairs were a source of irritation to the purist.

A minor feature of 17th-century English chairs which seemed to have appealed greatly to local Chinese cabinet-makers is the finial (miniature knobs, vase-like or urn-like objects) surmounting the uprights of most chairs, so much so that most extant Straits Chinese teakwood chairs have finials on their uprights. The English themselves dispensed with finials by 1700 and they did not appear again in 18th- and 19th-century chairs. Local Chinese cabinet-makers, however, were so captivated by them that they looked for every excuse to add finials to their cupboards, sideboards, washstands, dressers, hat-hangers, glass display cabinets, etc.

Certain styles of English chair never seemed to have had any impact on local Chinese cabinet-makers. The famous Queen Anne chair, so highly

Left: The ribbon-back chair was the most well known of the various types of chair design published by Chippendale in his *Director*. It is also one of the most elaborately carved types of chair, especially at the knee of the front cabriole legs. All Chippendale chairs were made of mahogany.

Right: Chippendale chairs do not always come with the characteristic ribboned splat carved in pierced-work or ornate cabriole legs with acanthus leaf carvings on the knee, ending in claw-and-ball feet. According to his famous *Director*, Chippendale also included among his various designs chairs featuring interlacing ribbon splats surmounted by yoke-like cresting rails and square legs, as this illustration shows.

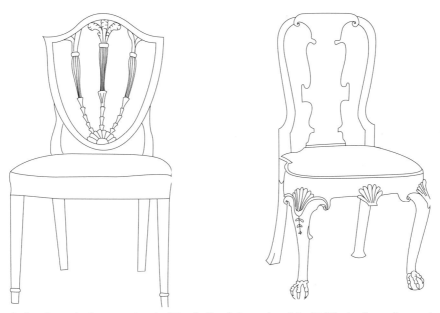

Left: Hepplewhite chair. The characteristic style of Hepplewhite chairs consists of the shield back and tapered square legs. But the classic simplicity of the design of the Hepplewhite chair belies the difficulty of how to construct the shield back in such a way that it is strong enough to withstand the pressure of a body leaning backwards against it without breaking under the strain. English cabinet-makers solved this problem by fabricating each of the back legs and back posts in one continuous piece stretching all the way from the ground to the cresting rail of the shield back. This implies that the shield back is not made in one piece and then tenoned to the back legs at the junctions just above the cushioned seat.

Right: A typical chair of the Queen Anne period (1702–14) with its distinctive vase-shaped splat, curved back rails and cabriole front legs ending in claw-and-ball feet. Ornamentation was minimal, being largely confined to shell or acanthus motifs on the knee and the front feet. Walnut was the standard timber used for crafting Queen Anne chairs.

regarded in England for the beauty and restrained simplicity of its design, and particularly for its cabriole legs with claw-and-ball feet, failed to capture the imagination of our cabinet-makers. The Queen Anne style of chair was said to have been inspired by Chinese rosewood furniture of the Ming Dynasty. If so, Chinese cabinet-makers did not seem to have shown any nostalgia for them, and very few reproductions of Queen Anne chairs are to be seen in old Baba homes. I have two of them in my collection, but they are said to have come from an old Malay house in Singapore rather than from a Baba home. Besides, the chairs seem to have been constructed out of several varieties of wood, none of which resemble teak. In any case, the Babas must have found the design of Queen Anne chairs too restrained and tame for their taste. They preferred chairs with more ornate designs.

Likewise, the highly rated Chippendale chair with either ribband or fretwork splats, freestanding cabriole legs with claw-and-ball feet and upholstered seat, which became the vogue of high quality American furniture in the 18th and 19th centuries, did not seem to have caught on with the wealthy Babas of the Straits Settlements. I have seen only one set of Chippendale-style furniture in the last 20 years: it consisted of a huge dining table made to complement 16 chairs and two buffet cupboards for crockery. The chairs had typical ribband backs and they were stained and polished to produce the dark reddish-brown colour of mahogany. I did not then, however, try to ascertain that the timber was mahogany.

One other feature of Straits Chinese teak furniture is worth noting: the seats of practically all locally made chairs are geometrically rhombic in shape, whereas chair seats of a number of 18th century English pieces (e.g. Queen Anne, George I and George II chairs) are kidney-shaped with rounded corners, or D-shaped. In some Straits Chinese chairs the front is curved but the sides are straight and angular. Now, apart from the fact that kidney-shaped and rhombic seat railings with rounded corners are harder to construct, Chinese cabinet-makers seemed to have preferred square, rectangular or rhombic-shaped chair seats – this is clearly evident in classic blackwood furniture of the Ming era.

If a general characterization of English-style teakwood chairs made to Baba tastes is required, I would be inclined to describe them as quaintly 17th century in style, notwithstanding some of the curious aberrations noted above.

Tables

There are at least seven different types of teak table traditionally found in Straits Chinese homes. These include large, extendable dining tables, also known as 'telescopic tables' (in Baba Malay they are referred to as *tok panjang* or *meja panjang*, literally meaning 'long table'); writing tables, some with rolled tops and some with drop fronts; small tea tables with marble tops (two armchairs and one tea table in between forming a suite in the reception hall); console side tables; gate-leg tables with rounded sides; card tables (which could also serve as mahjong tables); and circular Regency-style tables. Altar tables are not included among the various categories of teak table because in old Baba homes these were usually constructed out of namwood or perhaps of blackwood, with or without inlaid decorations of mother-of-pearl.

Tables meant for formal and ceremonial purposes all came with marble tops. Examples are side console tables, small tea tables with matching armchairs and large circular Regency-style tables, usually complemented by a set of four armchairs. These types of furniture were installed in the main reception hall. Marble tops were, of course, rarely used on English tables because they were never popular in England. The French and the Italians, on the other hand, had been regularly using marble tops for most of their console and commode tables as far back as the 16th century. Hence, the Babas' preference for tables with marble tops was largely influenced by European continental furniture styles. But it must be remembered that the Chinese themselves had an equally long, if not longer, tradition of using marble slabs on chair seats and backs, as well as on table tops, except that the marble slabs were always enclosed within blackwood frames or railings – never as structural components of a piece of furniture.

Regency-style tables

The most prominent type of table with a marble top to be found in the reception hall is the circular Regency-style table with a round slab of white or grey marble of about four feet (120 centimetres) in diameter, supported by either a single large pillar or by a cluster of carved pillars. In the case of the latter, there is a thick central pillar and three or four thinner pillars surrounding it, with three or four corresponding cabriole legs with claw feet and claw-and-ball feet. The cabriole legs are dovetailed into the lower sides of the central pillar, while the corresponding outer pillars are tenoned into the knees to provide additional leverage to the circular wooden frame that supports the heavy marble slab. However, where the table is propped up by only one large, central pillar carved out of rounded beams of teak of up to seven inches (17.5 centimetres) in diameter, the base support takes the form of tripod legs.

The construction of this type of Regency-style table poses a considerable challenge to the skill of the cabinet-maker. He must, first of all, ensure that the circular under-frame, which must bear the full brunt of the marble slab, does not break under the strain imposed upon it. Basically, this is done by three or four lateral braces which are dovetailed into the upper sides of the central pillar, from where they radiate outwards to connect with the inner side of the circular frame where they are tenoned. To rein-force the strength of the circular frame and its three or four lat-eral braces, corre-sponding pillars (much slimmer than the cen-tral column) are tenoned into the bottom of the braces at one end, and the knees of the cabriole legs at the other. In this way, the entire weight of the marble slab and its supporting frame is trans-ferred to the tripod or quadrupod legs below via the central and outer pillars.

But this means that the outward or side-sheering forces exerted upon the legs put considerable stress upon the joints. That is in fact so, for I have noticed, again and again, that with most antique Regency-style tables of this sort, breakage to the structure nearly always involves the legs. Subsequent attempts to re-fix the joints with screws drilled into the main pillar via the sides of the legs are rarely successful.

The original Regency tables had wooden tops lacquered or varnished to a high degree of lustre, but even with such pieces, cabinet-makers noted that considerable stress must have been exerted upon the legs below. Thus, when Chinese cabi-net-makers decided to substitute wooden tops for marble tops, they merely compounded the diffi-culties of constructing strong and durable tables of this type. It is a wonder that despite such structural drawbacks inherent in the design of this type of table, they became widely used by the turn of the 20th century, not only in the homes of well-to-do Babas, but also in most humble coffee shops in Malaya and Singapore.

Console tables

Console tables, by contrast, were never plagued by structural problems of the sort that beset Regency-style circular tables with either tripod or quadrupod legs. These types of side table with marble tops were stoutly constructed out of solid under-frames, sometimes up to three inches thick (7.5 centimetres), which were carved on three sides and supported at the corners by stout cabrioled legs. The legs may be freestanding when supported on low pedestals, or reinforced by crossed stretchers surmounted at the junctions by ornamental finials. Those types of console table which are not raised on low pedestals have longer legs – the average height of a console table being somewhere between 3 feet 2 inches (95 centimetres) and 3 feet 6 inches (105 centimetres). Incidentally, most extant teak-and-marble console tables are not of a crescent shape like their blackwood prototypes. They resemble modified quadrilaterals in which the three frontal edges are carved and shaped into a broad series of cusps and foils – not unlike foliated edges. The marble slabs (about $1^1/2$–$1^3/4$ inches or 4–5 centimetres thick) are similarly shaped and moulded to match the pattern on the under-frame, but the borders are at least one inch (2.5 centimetres) broader, so that when the marble slabs are laid upon the under-frames, they project ever so slightly outwards as to be unnoticeable when viewed from a certain distance.

Although the basic designs of console tables are recognizably French or Italian in inspiration, the ornamental motifs appearing on the three frontal sides of the under-frames are, more often than not, oriental (particularly Chinese) in origin. These ornamental motifs are depicted on the outer sides of the broad and solid under-frames in high-relief carvings, and they include Buddhist lions, *qilins*, phoenixes, figures of *lohans* and Taoist Immortals, peonies, lotuses, magnolias, etc. Among the better pieces, the carvings are bold and masterfully executed. The cabriole legs, with *taotien* masks at the corners and claw-and-ball feet, are sometimes curved in a pronounced fashion; and since they are all carved out of solid timber, a good deal of wood must go to waste in the course of cutting and shaping the table legs.

Although the majority of console tables were varnished by the method of French polishing to produce a pleasant and translucent reddish-brown colour, I have noticed that from time to time console tables appear which are varnished somewhat differently to produce a deep reddish-brown (almost black in certain instances), simulating old mahogany. Gilding, whenever it occurred, was used very sparingly. There are, of course, no Straits Chinese console tables in which the entire framework is gilded after the manner of European giltwood furniture, nor for that matter, are Straits Chinese console tables ever decorated with polished brass ormolu-work.

Most console tables are built to stand on low, matching platforms or pedestals of about six to seven inches (15 to 17.5 centimetres) high. The top of these pedestals are usually taken up by floating panels executed in lattice-work. Sometimes, however, the top panels consist of plain slabs of wood decorated with engravings of peony and other floral blossoms and outlined in gilt. To ensure that console tables are firmly secured to the pedestals on which they stand, cabinet-makers constructed tenons directly below the claw-and-ball feet so that they may be fitted (loosely) into prefabricated mortises positioned at the corners of the pedestals.

Some extant console tables are freestanding. But in such instances, the legs are slightly longer to compensate for the absence of pedestals. In most cases, the additional length amounts to an average of about six inches (15 centimetres). But the structural weakening caused by long and freestanding legs led directly to the construction of crossed braces to strengthen the legs and prevent them from wobbling. To the credit of the cabinet-makers, they had a sufficient sense of aesthetics not to make the braces look too drab and functional, but instead carved them into sinuous or serpentine curves connected at the junction by some solidly carved ornament resembling either a flower basket or perhaps a rectangular urn of archaic Shang design.

Only a pair of such console tables were traditionally required for furnishing the reception hall of a Baba home, along with other types of furniture. Following the traditional practice of laying out blackwood furniture, console tables were set in the middle of the two side walls facing each other. Each of the console tables was flanked on either side by two sets of armchairs, each of which was complemented by a small tea table.

Tea tables

The tea table is the smallest of teakwood tables with marble tops. The shape of the marble top is not, however, that of a simple rectangle or a square, as the more conservative types of tea table made of blackwood used to be. Instead, its shape may be described as that of a modified quadrilateral in which the sides are curved slightly outwards, but are squared off at the corners.

Teakwood tea tables of this type usually come with rather tall, sinuous cabriole legs which are strengthened lower down by crossed stretchers. Such tables never come with an intermediate shelf as in the case of blackwood and namwood tea tables, and tea tables were never placed in front of armchairs as they were done in English homes. Instead, a tea table was usually placed at the sides of a pair of armchairs because it was not customary in China for host and guest to sit facing each other. Thus, we have a curious situation here: while the armchairs and matching tea tables were obviously English in design, the way they were laid out was traditionally Chinese. And the Chineseness of this type of teak furniture extends to the motifs of the various carvings. Where tea tables are concerned, floral and foliated motifs representing lotuses, peonies and plum blossoms frequently occur on the aprons of the under-frame. Acanthus scrolls, or what look like acanthus scrolls, may still be found on the knees of the cabriole legs.

Antique collectors nowadays turn these tea tables into a variety of uses, such as stands for table lamps, telephone tables or even stands for large antique vases. Because of their archaic European design, they seem none the worse for the new roles assigned to them by modern devotees of Straits Chinese furniture.

Dining tables

The long, extendable dining table (or *tok panjang*) that is found in most old Baba homes was a reproduction based on an original invention of the Victorian era. The unique feature of this type of table is the incorporation of two sets of parallel sliding rails built directly beneath the two slabs of table boards fixed to the under-frame. These paired rails (the outer member is permanently secured by screws to the underside of the table boards, while the inner member is movable) are tenoned into each other side-by-side by the method of dovetailing which allows one rail to slide upon another. Teakwood, being somewhat greasy because of the presence of teak oil in the heartwood, is particularly ideal for constructing sliding rails since it reduces friction between the tenons and mortises.

The construction of such an extendable type of dining table (some of which may be 'stretched' up to 16 feet or 480 centimetres) calls for a very high degree of skill in cabinet-making. Wood, it must be remembered, expands and contracts with changing temperatures and humidity. Hence, the dovetailing of the movable and fixed rails must be so constructed that some allowance is made for unequal shrinkage and expansion of the timber. I have noticed from past experience that during hot and humid spells (especially in the tropics), the railings have a tendency to get jammed, and considerable effort is required to move them. Once the railings are extended, detachable boards can be installed within the spaces so created. Where the extensions required of a particular dining table are considerable, especially when it has to be 'stretched' to, say, 10 feet (300 centimetres) or more, a fifth leg might be installed directly under the centre of the table to absorb some of the strain imposed upon the rails by the additional slabs of table board laid upon them. This fifth leg is also useful in preventing the table from sagging in the centre.

Table legs specifically constructed for dining tables are stout and usually carved out of solid timber. In Straits Chinese *tok panjangs*, the legs are usually executed by a combination of wood-turning and carving, and the shapes so formed include lantern legs, double-bine twists, fluted balusters or even cabriole legs with *taotien* masks at the knees and claw-and-ball feet. The larger and heavier the table is, the more massive are the legs and the structure of the under-frame.

Because of their sizes (the average length of these tables when fully extended is at least seven feet or 210 centimetres, while the average width is about 3 feet 6 inches or 105 centimetres), marble slabs are never used on such dining tables. Indeed, the combined weight of the number of marble slabs required to cover a table of just seven feet by 3 feet 6 inches would impose intolerable strain to the structure of the under-frame and its supporting legs. What more when the table is 14 feet long! Size for size, wood boards weigh much less than marble slabs, and from an aesthetic point of view, wood slabs are more pleasing to the eye and the sense of touch, especially when the timber is of richly figured grain and polished to give a fine and translucent lustre.

The largest and most impressive dining table that I have seen in the last 20 years was a huge Chippendale-style extendable table over 14 feet in length (420 centimetres). It was complemented with 16 sumptuous dining chairs in typical Chippendale style with fretwork ribband-backs and varnished to produce a dark reddish-brown mahogany tint. The massive under-frame of the enormous dining table was supported at the corners and in the centre by five of the largest and most impressively carved legs I have seen.

In traditional Straits Chinese custom, especially on festive occasions such as Chinese New Year when dinner was served on the *tok panjang*, it was customary for hosts, guests, relatives and other members of an extended family to eat in relays. Protocol required that the first batch of diners to sit down at the *tok panjang* be the elderly males of the family and male (and/or female) guests. When they had eaten their fill, (and the Baba-Nonyas usually ate at a leisurely pace), they would vacate their seats, while used dishes were removed and fresh, clean ones brought in to replace them. Fresh servings of food were set upon the table, and the next batch of diners, namely the female members of the family, sat down to eat their share of the dinner. When they, too, had eaten their fill, the house servants or maids would repeat the process of clearing the table of used dishes and leftovers of food, and replace them with a fresh, clean set of plates and bowls. At the same time, another fresh serving of food would be laid out and this time the new batch of diners would be mainly children. Finally, when the children had partaken their share of the dinner, the house maids, servants and other helpers would sit down for the final round of eating.

The Western custom of serving dinner in 'buffet style' when the number of guests and family members exceeds the seating capacity of a dining table at any one time was something foreign to Straits Chinese practices. Eating in relays was their own peculiar solution to the problem of accommodating more diners than the seating capacity provided for by the *tok panjang*.

Although circular tables with marble tops were available and were in fact widely used by the former generations of Babas in their homes, it was not customary for them to dine on such tables. Likewise, circular and oval-shaped gate-leg tables were also available to the Babas – and there were many homes in which gate-leg tables were to be found. But for some reason or other, the traditional

Babas did not seem to have adhered to the customary practice of their forefathers and of the more conservative communities of Chinese of regularly partaking their dinners around circular tables.

Bureaus and writing tables

The kinds of bureaus and writing tables that one finds in Straits Chinese homes were also widely used in many government offices before World War II. There is evidence that it was the demands made by different types of clerical functions and services within the colonial civil service which (more than the whims and fancies of some wealthy individuals) determined the structure and design of desks and writing tables meant for civil servants. For example, bureaus with roll tops or tambour-fronts, and those with sloping lids which could be opened outwards to provide flat writing boards, sometimes referred to as 'drop-fronts', were commonly seen in many government offices. But bureaus surmounted by tall, rectangular glass-front bookcases with broken pediments were hardly found in government offices and only infrequently in old Baba homes in Singapore and Malacca. So, too, were those large and heavy writing tables with large flat tops and two sets of side drawers supported on low pedestals. Well-to-do Babas, who worked as merchants and traders, and who operated their businesses in their own shops and offices, tended to install such writing tables in their workplaces rather than in their homes.

Tambour-front and drop-front bureaus, as well as bureau cabinets with tall bookcases, were peculiar to the European art of cabinet-making, and, hence, there were no similar counterparts of such types of writing desk in classic Chinese furniture. The tambour-front bureau, for example, was probably French in origin, and some of the finest extant pieces of *bureau à cylindre*, the French equivalent for such roll-top desks, were made during the reigns of Louis XV and Louis XVI. However, not all tambour type covers for such desks were made out of thin strips of mahogany, birch or pine and pasted on to thick sheets of canvas to facilitate the movement of the covers sliding along the grooves. Some 18th-century French tambour-front bureaus made for royalty had solid roll-tops. But as with flexible tambour-fronts, they are loosely tenoned into grooves carved out of the inner side walls. Another feature worth noting is that the flat writing boards on roll-top desks are also movable; that is to say, they can be extended outwards by up to six to seven inches (15–18 centimetres) beyond the edge of the desk to provide for additional writing space. English as well as local Chinese reproductions of tambour-front bureaus never utilized ormolu brass decorations: all ornamental-work on such writing desks was carved on the wood itself.

The writing desk with the sloping lid which can be opened outwards to serve as a writing board was more frequently encountered in old Baba homes than the tambour-front bureau, partly because it was somewhat easier to construct. Whereas the construction of the tambour-front bureau requires that the design of the writing table incorporates a central, vacant space or recess between the two sets of side drawers to enable the sitter to insert his legs into the space below the desk top when sitting at the bureau, the drop-front bureau automatically creates sufficient leg-room when the sloping writing board is laid out flat. In this way, the upright rectangular case which incorporates the writing board preserves its structure intact as no structural modifications to the overall design are called for.

Writing tables of the type which the French referred to as *bureau plat*, that is to say, a fairly

large desk with a row of several drawers arranged laterally across the under-frame and supported at the corners by four straight and slightly tapering legs which curve somewhat at the feet, were uncommon in the Straits Chinese inventory of European-style teak furniture. This type of table was, however, not unknown to traditional Chinese cabinet-makers in China. Some extant pieces made out of *huanghuali* are shown in Kates' *Chinese Household Furniture,* figures 52 and 53. Most large writing tables, as contrasted with the secretaire-type of writing desk, with or without bookcases, are heavy pieces of furniture with table tops measuring five feet (150 centimetres) long and three feet (90 centimetres) wide. They have two sets of side drawers and/or cabinets which reach down to two corresponding sets of low pedestals at the base.

Cabinets

Teakwood cabinets of the type found in old Straits Chinese homes may be divided into two broad categories: (1) those which were used for storing and displaying expensive pieces of porcelain, silverware, crystal-ware, books and curios, and (2) those which were meant to serve as wardrobes for storing garments and apparel of various sorts, as well as other personal belongings.

Display cabinets

Display cabinets were either reproductions of European originals or else highly modified versions of European designs incorporating archaic Chinese

ornamental motifs. However, as display cabinets, they all have one obvious feature in common, namely doors with transparent glass panels which may be constructed in the form of traceried doors with small glass panels of various shapes, or whole (and thus larger) glass panels superimposed on the obverse side with carved and gilded wood panels. Generally, display cabinets with traceried doors tended to be more authentically European in their designs.

Traceried doors with small glass panes were originally necessitated by the difficulty of manufacturing glass panels in large flat sheets. But, by the 19th century, the technology in glass manufacture had developed considerably, and the production of glass panels of various thickness and strengths became a matter of course. Thus, most display cabinets in old Baba homes which were crafted from the latter part of the 19th century to the first two decades of the 20th century were fitted with whole glass door panels and even side panels in some cases.

Traceried door panes come in a variety of shapes: mostly they consist of a complex of square, rectangular, diamond-shaped or hexagonal wood panels or a combination of several types of panes, which are tenoned into the door frame to provide a solid backing of braces that are rebated on the reverse sides to allow the glass panels to be fitted and puttied in. In other instances, the supporting wooden panes are structured into a network consisting of curvatures and arches – as with traceried doors in Hepplewhite cabinets. Traceried doors with Hepplewhite-type of panes were, of course, much more difficult to execute because the crafting and fitting of curved wood structures called for greater skill and precision of workmanship.

Apart from traceried doors, European-style display cabinets also feature such architectural elements as broken pediments with ornamental urns sprouting between the gaps, fluted side pilasters topped with capitals and moulded cornices. Some of these cabinets are over six feet (180 centimetres) tall and four to five feet (120–150 centimetres) wide. The legs are usually short, freestanding and of cabriole shape. Stretchers (usually crossed close to the base) are incorporated when a cabinet happens to be very large and heavy, and when the legs have to be strengthened to absorb the strain imposed upon them.

Above: One of a pair of tall and slender display cabinets of refined elegance in the design. The Talibs use them for displaying their collection of antique silver. Height: 6 ft (180 cm). Width: about 2 ft (60 cm). Teakwood. Dating: early 20th century. Courtesy of Prof and Mrs Yusoff Talib.

Right: A large set of teak-and-gold cabinets – the gilding having been worn off with the passing of time. These cabinets are almost 7 ft (210 cm) tall and over 5 ft (150 cm) wide. Each cabinet is divided into three separate compartments rather than two, as was usual with other cabinets of this type. It is possible, therefore, that cabinets of this sort were meant more for the dining room than the bridal chamber. I have seen many such cupboards in old Baba homes in Malacca and Singapore, and they were invariably filled with crockery and other kitchen utensils. Courtesy of Prof and Mrs Yusoff Talib.

Where display cabinets tended to be more Anglo-Chinese in design, architectural ornaments in European taste were dispensed with. Instead of traceried doors, for example, the inner frames are decorated all round with a narrow border of floral and foliated carvings (which may be gilded in some cases) executed in open-work, and framed by thin strips of mouldings. Whole panels of transparent glass made to order are then rebated into the door frames from the reverse side and either puttied in, or else held in place by thin, square-cut strips of wood railed into the frame. Alternatively, fielded panels of solid giltwood carvings, depicting either floral and foliated motifs or phoenixes and tree peonies, and executed in open-work, are grooved into the door frames and sealed up by whole panels of transparent glass.

One other feature which was peculiar to Anglo-Chinese display cabinets and which clearly evinces the traditional Chinese cabinet-maker's view that cabinets were not to be regarded as miniature pieces of architecture (nor, for that reason, should their façades be made to resemble those of a building) was the dispensation of the pediment and elaborately moulded cornice and architrave. In its place was a simple cornice-like structure surmounted by a crescent-shaped piece of carved wood panelling depicting phoenixes, birds and floral and foliated motifs executed in open-work and outlined in gilt. This panel was screwed on to the top of the cabinet, but in such

a way that it tilted forwards somewhat.

Such display cabinets were mostly used to store the more expensive pieces of polychrome enamelled porcelain, and, among the wealthy Babas, dinner services sometimes came in sets of 144 pieces. Thus porcelain could take up considerable space on the shelves provided for in these cabinets. Cut-glass decanters, wine glasses, jugs, vases, ornamental fruit bowls, etc., usually of Waterford vintage, were also kept in display cabinets. And so too were silver cigarette boxes, bowls, wine ewers, teapots, plates, trophies, candlesticks and other odds and ends. Books, however, were rarely kept in such cabinets and, except for some of the more scholarly-inclined Babas, bookcases did not feature conspicuously in the furniture of old Baba homes. Occasionally, one finds a secretaire surmounted by a bureau cabinet with books in it. But generally speaking,

The Babas referred to large display cabinets, of the type shown here, with long glass panels for the doors, the sides and sometimes the shelves as well, as the tu kacha *(that is, 'glass cabinets'). This tall and handsome cabinet which has a recessed break-front for the central compartment is elegantly ornamented with border trimmings in gilt and three carved panels mounted over the cornice. Height: over 6 ft (180 cm). Width: over 5 ft (150 cm). Teakwood. Courtesy of the National Museum of Singapore.*

the habit of reading and buying books was confined to a small minority of English-educated Babas.

Wardrobes

Wardrobes may be divided into two types: (1) those which were modelled after the design of the traditional two-tiered red-and-gold namwood wedding cabinets, and (2) those which were designed as tall, upright, rectangular cabinets, with compartments equipped with hanging railings and pegs for garments, as well as shelves, movable trays and drawers for storing other types of personal belongings.

The two-tiered type of teak cabinet was meant to be an Anglicized version of the two-tiered red-and-gold namwood wedding cabinet, except that the structure was throughout constructed out of solid teakwood, while the frontage retained many architectural features, such as side columns complete with capitals supporting moulded cornices, but without pediments. The gilded carvings executed in flat open-work differed from those of traditional red-and-gold namwood cabinets. But the most distinctive feature of teakwood cabinets is the crescent-shaped panel of parcel gilt carvings which surmounts the top of

the cabinets. Red-and-gold wedding cabinets, it will be recalled, have flat tops. But in all other respects, the design of two-tiered teak cabinets – and incidentally they were intended to be used as wedding cabinets when namwood red-and-gold cabinets ran out of production in China around 1930 – resemble that of their namwood archetypes: the top cabinet has two built-in drawers and a shelf which divides the interior space into two compartments. A narrow, detachable shelf with two sets of drawers arranged in step-like fashion is also fitted to the upper ends of the top compartment.

As for the lower cabinet, its structure consists of two upper drawers and a smaller cabinet below. The glass-panelled doors are backed up by wood panels of gilded fretwork carvings mounted from the rear of the door frames. These panels are held in place by little nails driven into the door frames. In some cases, the door frames are fitted not with glass panels but with fielded wood panels ornamented with floral engravings (usually flower baskets) outlined in gilt. All such cabinets stand on short cabriole legs, braced by carved and convex aprons on the front and the sides, and a plain, square-cut stretcher at the back. The knees have gargoyle-like masks and the feet are hoof-shaped rather than claw-like. And as noted before, gilding was applied on the carvings which had

Teak-and-gold wedding cabinet. The unusual feature of this set of wardrobes is that the upper cabinet is distinctly taller than the lower cabinet. The present owner has converted this cabinet into a display case for Straits Chinese porcelain. Height: over 7 ft (210 cm). Courtesy of Mr Johnson Tan of C. K. Tan Gallery.

previously been treated with gesso and size.

There is, in my opinion, evidence that Anglo-Chinese wedding cabinets of this type did not catch on with the Babas until the latter part of the 1920s, when it became increasingly difficult for furniture importers to obtain the traditional red-and-gold namwood wedding cabinets either through Shanghai or Xiamen. By the early 1930s, when hostilities between the Kuomintang forces led by Chiang Kai-shek on the one hand, and the Communist forces led by Mao Zedong on the other, erupted into a full-scale civil war in China, the export of red-and-gold namwood wedding cabinets was brought to a complete halt. From then on, local Shanghainese cabinet-makers had to improvise by using teakwood for constructing their version of the traditional red-and-gold cabinet. This explains why most extant examples of the two-tiered teak-and-gold wedding cabinet are datable between the late 1920s and the late 1930s. The vogue for teak-and-gold wedding cabinets modelled on the red-and-gold archetypes lasted only a decade at the most. By the outbreak of World War II in 1939, their production ceased altogether, never to be revived again.

Apart from the two-tiered variety of teakwood wardrobe modelled after the red-and-gold namwood originals, there is yet another type of wardrobe which is largely European in design. The basic structure of wardrobes in this style consists of a tall, upright case (some of which are over six feet or 180 centimetres high and at least four feet or 120 centimetres wide) divided down the centre into two compartments, one of which is equipped with pegs, hooks and rails for hanging garments and apparel of various types, while the other is fitted with shelves, movable trays and drawers for storing various other personal belongings.

Since the largest exposed surface on these wardrobes is taken up by two massive doors, it is on these doors that the main decorations are concentrated. Usually, the surface of each door is so constructed that it houses two or more rectangular frames arranged vertically, and for each of these frames, a fielded panel carved with floral and foliated motifs in bas-relief is grooved in. However, the decorative carvings are not, as with those in the two-tiered cabinets, gilded. This is because the European archetypes on which these wardrobes were modelled were hardly ever gilded. In some of the finer wardrobes, the bas-relief carvings are sensitively executed, but for some reason or other, the ornamental-work on such European-style wardrobes never quite seemed to have attained the masterly quality that one finds in the better pieces of old red-and-gold cabinets.

Relief-columns topped with simple Doric capitals adorn the sides, reaching up from the base to the top to support the moulded cornice, often complete with dentils, stretching across the width of the wardrobe. However, instead of surmounting the cornice with a broken or arched pediment, the Chinese cabinet-maker substituted a crescent-shaped panel carved with tree peonies, phoenixes and perhaps magpies, executed in open-work for this architectural element.

In many extant examples of wardrobes of this type, which feature a pair of fairly large drawers placed side-by-side at the bottom of the cabinet, the lower portion, incorporating the pair of drawers and the base frame fitted together by aprons and four short, cabriole legs at the corners, usually served as a base structure upon which the upper portion of the wardrobe rested. Large wardrobes which measure up to 4 feet 6 inches (135 centimetres) across may even have an additional side compartment fully equipped with shelves, drawers and movable trays, and secured by a lockable door ornamented with floral engravings on the outside. A full-length mirror was customarily installed on the reverse side of one of the two main doors of the wardrobe.

Sideboards

The last major item of teak furniture in old Baba homes is the tall and massive sideboard which was usually placed against the far end of the reception hall, facing the main entrance to the house. With the possible exception of the four-poster red-and-gold namwood bed, the sideboard was the largest single piece of furniture in an old Baba home. The design of the Straits Chinese sideboard is a variation based on English/European archetypes, such as the 17th-century English 'court cupboard' and the Italian Renaissance cupboard which, like the English version, consisted of a cabinet surmounted by one or several tiers of shelves. However, in the hands of local cabinet-makers, many details in the structure were altered, with improvisations of one sort or another being incorporated over the years so that the eventual design of the Straits Chinese sideboard looks very different from its European originals.

Thus, the Straits Chinese sideboard as we find it today bears no resemblance at all to the

homely English court cupboard, which is simply a rectangular cabinet surmounted by two tiers of shelves propped up by bulbous struts. Nor, for that matter, is it structured like one of those modest-sized Victorian sideboards featuring marble-top cabinets and gilt-framed mirrors, or in some cases, featuring looking glass and open shelves. The Straits Chinese sideboard is, in most instances, a massive piece of furniture with a break-front or bow-front cabinet, topped with a huge marble slab stretching up to six feet (180 centimetres) across, and a high backboard which rises (in step-like fashion) up to a height of nine feet (270 centimetres) above the ground.

The weight of the marble slab, six feet (180 centimetres) long, two feet (60 centimetres) wide and at least 1½ inches (four centimetres) thick, can well be imagined. On average, it weighs in excess of 60 kilograms. But the most remarkable feature of the Straits Chinese sideboard is the size of the backboard which rises about five feet (150 centimetres) from the top of the cabinet. Heavy as it is, the backboard is mounted with frame mirrors of various shapes and sizes, pigeonhole trays propped up by wood-turned struts and small cabinets. Three or four tiers of pigeonhole trays and cabinets rise from the bottom of the backboard in step-like fashion, and the topmost tier is crowned by a cornice featuring a crescent-shaped panel of carving executed in open-work.

Obviously the stability of the backboard, with its assortment of mirrors, shelves, cabinets, carved spandrels, and its cornice and crowning carved panel, cannot be maintained without it being firmly secured to the cabinet on which it rests. For one thing, the larger and heavier the backboard, the greater is the tendency for it to fall backwards or forwards. To prevent this from happening, cabinet-makers attached three or four stout wooden bars to the rear of the sideboard, in such a way that each of the bars, secured by screws, bestrode the backboard and the cabinet. These braces can be unscrewed to detach the backboard when the sideboard has to be moved from one position to another.

Despite its great weight and cumbersome structure, these sideboards are supported at the base by four (sometimes six) stumpy cabriole legs of rather modest proportions. They are, however, rather sturdily built, for most apparently old sideboards that I have seen in Baba homes in Singapore and Malacca (and some of these were probably made at around the turn of the 20th century) were always found with their legs intact, even though the shellac varnish had deteriorated with the passage of time.

Miscellaneous items

Among the miscellaneous items of teak furniture extant, we may include large, parcel-gilt framed mirrors, washstands, dressers, card tables, benches, reclining chairs or day beds and bedside cabinets. Of these, I should like to refer briefly to the framed mirrors and dressers.

The large bevelled **mirror** (usually a pair of them hung on the side walls of the main reception hall), mounted on a broad and elaborately carved teak frame, is the local Anglo-Chinese version of European wall mirrors. Some of these Anglo-Chinese mirrors (there is a pair in the collection of Katong Antique House dealer Mr Peter Wee) are massive objects measuring over six feet (180 centimetres) high and 3 feet 6 inches (105 centimetres) wide. The mirror itself may measure up to five feet (150 centimetres) high and 2 feet 6 inches (75 centimetres) wide.

The ornamental motifs carved in high-relief on the frames are a mixture of traditional Chinese and European art symbols. Side columns executed in relief are invariably carved onto the side frames, while the top frame takes the form of a cornice of some sort supporting an arched or triangular pediment broken in the centre – the gap thus created being filled up with a floral basket or an elaborately ornamented vase. Those mirrors whose frames are lacquered in dark brown (almost blackish in tone) have all their carvings rendered in gilt. But the more ordinary run of teakframed mirrors are simply varnished with shellac solutions by French polishing.

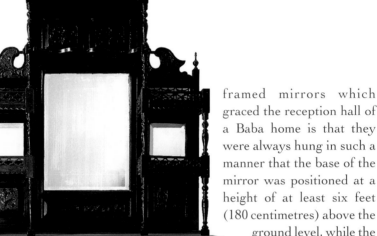

Among the more well-to-do Babas, it was fashionable, at around the turn of the 20th century, to install Bohemian mirrors of polished and mirrored glass. Most of these mirrors were of an oval shape and rather modest sizes, and they were usually hung on the wall in the kitchen area above the washstand or, perhaps, the kitchen dresser. But occasionally a pair of large rectangular mirrors with arched headings would be seen in the reception hall of some old Baba home. The vogue for Bohemian mirrors did not last very long and they soon went out of fashion. Teak-framed mirrors of local provenance continued to be produced until about the early 1930s.

One of the peculiarities of these massive teak-framed mirrors which graced the reception hall of a Baba home is that they were always hung in such a manner that the base of the mirror was positioned at a height of at least six feet (180 centimetres) above the ground level, while the top of the mirror tilted forwards at an angle of 10° or 15° from the wall. Now, the forward tilting of the mirror is rendered necessary simply because it was mounted well above eye level; and while this was not the customary manner of hanging mirrors in most European homes (most wall mirrors being mounted flat against the wall and at a height whereby the centre of the mirror is positioned at average eye level), it was certainly a baroque custom employed in palaces in Italy during the 18th century. Whether the traditional Babas hung their massive mirrors thus in conscious imitation of some antiquated European custom is hard to say. But they must have been advised by makers of mirrors that this was the 'correct' method of hanging large mirrors.

When grooming themselves, the older and more conservative generations of Straits Nonyas employed the carved red-and-gold variety of namwood **dresser** (which we mentioned earlier), on which stood a separately crafted gilt-framed mirror stand. Traditionally, the red-and-gold dresser came with the bridal trousseau and, over

the years, this article of furniture became a treasured family heirloom. However, with the advent of English-style teak furniture from about the 1880s, the later generations of more Anglicized Nonyas began to use English-style dressers which reflected the changing fashion of the time.

The Victorian-style dresser is really a simple affair: it consists basically of a table measuring about 3 feet 6 inches (105 centimetres) long, 1 foot 6 inches (45 centimetres) wide and about 2 feet 6 inches (75 centimetres) high. It features two drawers constructed directly below the table top and low railings on the back and the two sides. The legs are either of plain bobbin or reel-and-bead turnings and freestanding, or else are of twist-turnings with lower stretchers spanning the legs 'H' fashion. The mirror is usually of modest dimensions, say, 14 inches (35 centimetres) by 10 inches (25 centimetres), and it is separately mounted on a box or a plain slab of wood with the aid of two upright posts. Two special metal devices attached to the posts and the outer frames of the mirror enable it to swing forwards or backwards.

By about the turn of the 20th century, the mirror stand and the dressing table were no longer separate entities, but constructed in one whole. Even the mirror had grown larger. It was mounted on moulded teak frames with arched or triangular headings featuring carved motifs in high-relief, and held between upright posts secured to the back of the dresser by screws. As before, the mirror could be swung forwards or backwards.

Above: This teakwood dressing table is somewhat unconventional as it comes with two tiers of drawers under the table instead of the usual single set of drawers. The mirror, centrally positioned on a carved backing, is also fixed rather than swivelled, while the legs and stretchers feature 17th-century barely-twist carvings. Dating: early 20th century. Courtesy of Prof and Mrs Yusoff Talib.

Left: Teakwood dressing tables of this type, featuring a central rectangular mirror which swivels in and out, side compartments and drawers beneath the table, were already used in traditional Baba homes by the opening decade of the present century. But by the 30s, when the supply of namwood red-and-gold furniture from Fujian Province declined considerably as a result of the mounting civil war in China, local cabinet-makers began to turn out large quantities of teakwood furniture made according to British/European designs to meet the shortfall in traditional namwood furniture. Such dressing tables are about 4 ft (120 cm) long, 1 ft 6 in (45 cm) wide and 6 ft (180 cm) high. Courtesy of Mr Peter Wee, Katong Antique House.

~ *chapter five* ~

Patina and the Dating of Old Furniture

Patina should not be confused with dirt which has accumulated on old furniture, and it is certainly not artificial dirt which has been smeared on reproductions of antique furniture and then painted over with treacle-like varnishes. It is the cumulative effect of a number of different factors all of which contribute to the gradual ageing and mellowness in the appearance of a piece of antique furniture. For example, the peculiar lustre and colour of some types of furniture (e.g. *huanghuali*, mahogany and teak) in which the wood has turned to a honey tone is actually brought about by countless years of constant polishing either with beeswax or linseed oil, together with any accidental dirt and grime which happened to have been rubbed in. This, and the natural process of ageing which all timber undergoes, is what contributes to the peculiar colour and charm of old furniture, so much so that it is difficult for those of us who are used to

living with such furniture to imagine what it must have looked like when it was new. In any case, we would probably be disappointed were we presented with modern reproductions of this type of furniture, even assuming they were pretty well-made. For one thing, the shine of new lacquer or French polish does not have the characteristic sheen and colour of old varnish. The timber directly beneath the polish would be much too fresh and clean. It would not bear the markings of age and the hurly-burly of constant usage, such as scratches, minor bruises, stains, dirt and other blemishes. In this sense, therefore, patina is not something that can be instantly and artificially created in a piece of furniture.

For this reason, too, the craze for stripping an old piece of furniture of all its varnish and patina by the indiscriminate application of powerful acid paint-removers and caustic soda solution, as many people do nowadays, is a deplorable practice. The patina of old furniture which takes decades and even centuries to develop is irretrievably lost in a few hours of frenzied paint-stripping. Besides, if an old piece of furniture were stripped to bare timber, its antique value is lost forever because there is no distinction now between the wood surface and texture of an old piece of furniture

Sideboards of this design, with short frontal posts modified to look like ornamental vases, two tiers of drawers directly underneath the shelves and a central compartment, have their origins in 17th century English furniture. They are often referred to as 'Jacobean furniture', but this sideboard was crafted locally by Chinese cabinet-makers probably at the turn of the present century. Length: 5 ft (150 cm). Height: 5 ft 6 in (158 cm). Courtesy of Prof and Mrs Yusoff Talib.

and that of a new one. Unless, therefore, a piece of old furniture has been subjected to ugly and frequent repainting with varnishes which leave behind a treacle-like effect that conceals the natural colour and grain of the timber, there is no merit at all in stripping the original polish from a piece of furniture simply for the sake of removing some minor scratches, blotches and stains. But many among the newer generation of antique furniture collectors seem to be very anxious that those pieces of old furniture which they purchase from an antique shop and which are intended for their new apartments be thoroughly cleaned and rid of all the vestiges of age and usage.

About 15 to 20 years ago, many expatriate collectors of antique Chinese and Anglo-Chinese furniture in Singapore and Malaysia initiated the trend of stripping off the varnishes from all old furniture which they happened to have acquired from antique shops. The rationale behind this curious practice (and I even fell for it at one time) was to remove the original varnish completely so that the bare wood with all its natural colour and grain would be shown to advantage. It was recommended, therefore, that furniture which has been cleansed of its original varnish and patina should be thoroughly waxed and polished, or alternatively, that it should be rubbed down with linseed and other varieties of oil and allowed to dry out. According to this view, furniture which has been polished with wax or oil took on a beautiful lustre of its own. And so it would seem for a time, except that many collectors who had fallen for this wax-and-oil fad soon discovered that before long (within a month or two in fact) most of their waxed and oil-polished pieces of furniture were covered over with unsightly

blotches and splotches of greyish-white mould. If this was left unattended, the mould would leave permanent and ugly markings on the wood itself, which no amount of subsequent repolishing could remove completely. The fact is that the warm and humid climate of the tropics is highly conducive to the growth of different varieties of fungus, some of which thrive on wax and oil. Needless to say, no one who had experienced this unexpected phenomenon ever again recommended the use of wax or oil on unvarnished and unlacquered surfaces of wood furniture.

In colder and more temperate climates, polishing furniture with wax and linseed oil is a time-honoured practice which has proven beneficial effects upon the gradual ageing and preservation of old furniture. And the problem of moulds and mouldiness which we encounter in the tropics apparently do not affect furniture in temperate countries.

While it is generally accepted as a rule-of-thumb by knowledgeable people who appreciate antique furniture that the colour and patina should not be tampered with indiscriminately, the fact remains that some pieces of old furniture are not particularly pleasant to look at, while others are certainly not pleasant to live with. For example, an old chair seen in an old house may look attractive and charming enough with its patina and blemishes of age in its somewhat dingy surroundings. But when it is transferred to an entirely different setting, such as the interior of a modern apartment, it may appear utterly wrong and out of place. Hence, some kind of cleaning and sprucing-up may be necessary to remove unsightly scratches, dents, dirt and blotches, and to clear up any blackish scum which conceals the

original varnish and wood-grain. Nowadays there are many commercial brands of chemicals for cleaning old furniture in order to show up the primary colour and tone of the underlying varnish and wood-grain without doing harm to the patina. Obviously, the work of cleaning and restoring an antique piece of furniture should be left in the hands of experts who have a healthy regard for the role that patina plays in the aesthetics of old furniture.

Unfortunately, most of the repairs and restoration carried out by many expert craftsmen in Singapore and Malaysia that I have seen in the past 20 years have been less than satisfactory. For one thing, the tendency among many of these craftsmen was to effect a thorough spring-cleaning

of most pieces of antiques entrusted to their care. There was hardly any attempt at judicious cleaning to remove dirt, grime and other blemishes on the furniture with a view to brightening it up and to revealing the original colour tone and patina of the varnish and, where possible, the underlying beauty of the wood-grain. That this could be followed up with gentle polishing and the final application of a thin coating of lacquer or varnish to protect the original paintwork and patina, and that the net result was far more satisfying for having restored the glow and mellowness to old furniture, was rarely appreciated.

Instead, most of these otherwise skilled craftsmen resorted to using powerful detergents (e.g. caustic soda and borax solutions) and acidic paint-removers to strip an antique piece of furniture of all its original varnish and lacquer till the underlying raw wood was laid bare. This would be followed by a thorough sanding and polishing process to remove all vestige of scratches, dents and bumps, and finally several new coats of lacquer and/or varnish. The result was as expected: most of these antique pieces of furniture that emerged from these restorers' shops looked so fresh and new that they could have been made the previous day! Upon seeing their antique chairs or cabinets completely transformed into what looked like brand new pieces of furniture, most customers usually expressed satisfaction, while the restorer beamed with pleasure and everybody was happy – all, that is, except the person who really values antique furniture for what it is.

I have often asked, rather discreetly, of these skilled craftsmen who undertook restoration work on antique furniture why they always insisted on removing the original varnish completely and what advantages, if any, accrued from the application of fresh coats of lacquer on a particular piece of furniture. Would it not have been better, I suggested, if they had retained as much as possible of the old-world charm which characterized antique furniture by preserving the colour and patina, while removing only the dirt, grime and other minor blemishes? 'Yes,' they said, 'but our customers always like it this way. They want all their antique furniture to look clean and new!' And they made it clear to me that there was no gainsaying the customers' wishes.

Perhaps. But we can certainly learn to preserve antique furniture in the way the Europeans do theirs, and that is, not to tamper, as far as possible, with the colour and patina of old furniture. Any refurbishing undertaken should be handled by skilled craftsmen and be carried out with the sole aim of restoring the underlying varnish and grain by a judicious removal of excess dirt, grime and minor blemishes, without doing violence to the peculiar patina that age and usage have wrought upon the furniture in question. Contrary to popular belief, what makes a piece of old furniture authentic is not simply its special structural design nor the fact that its ornamental-work is handcrafted. In fact, very often these characteristic features *can* be reproduced by present-day skilled craftsmen using a combination of power tools and sophisticated carving tools, should the demand for such a type of furniture justify it. Rather, what makes an antique piece of furniture genuine is the characteristic patina which, as I have already pointed out, is the accumulated effect of time, of frequent polishing down the ages over dirt and stains on the furniture, and of the natural process of ageing to the wood and the varnish. This is not something that a piece of furniture acquires overnight, despite the ingenious efforts of some people who deal in fakes and forgeries.

Dating

If the presence of natural patina is the touchstone not only of the originality of craftsmanship, but also of age, then the first step in dating a piece of furniture is to determine whether it displays the natural patination that comes with ageing and passing time. Once this is ascertained, we may proceed in trying to establish its approximate age by studying its structural design and the details of the carved ornaments – assuming, that is, that most pieces of antique furniture are unmarked, unsigned and undated. Comparisons based on affinities (and differences) in stylistic features will then enable us to tell whether the piece of furniture in question belongs to the style of a particular period and thus can be dated to that period.

This, however, is easier said than done. Where the three categories of Straits Chinese furniture we have dealt with previously are concerned, we encounter several problems. Firstly, in the case of traditional Chinese furniture, we are up against an inherent conservatism of attitude and practice which led Chinese cabinet-makers of blackwood and red-and-gold furniture to persist in turning out the same types of furniture, using practically the same types of timber (e.g. *huanghuali, zitan,* namwood and elmwood) for centuries on end, without so much as deviating from the original designs of the pieces of furniture in question. Thus, for even the astute student of blackwood furniture, there is virtually no apparent difference between, say, a chair or a lute table made at the beginning of the Ming Dynasty (circa 1400) and a similar chair and lute table made in the middle of the Qing Dynasty (circa 1770), though the time interval between the making of the two types of furniture is about 370 years! The experts may, of course, detect certain subtle changes in the designs. But dating based on stylistic considerations is at best conjectural. More likely than not the age of the furniture in question is determined by other independent criteria (e.g. information about the original owner and his biographical data).

Three-and-a-half centuries may not be sufficient to produce significant changes of any sort in furniture development in China. But in the history of English or European furniture, even one-and-a-half centuries would represent a long and eventful period of change in the styles and techniques of furniture construction and development. Look at, for example, the great differences between a late 16th-century Tudor period chair, with its square and box-like structure, and an early 18th-century Queen Anne chair, with its characteristic cabriole legs with claw-and-ball feet, its vase-shaped splat and the subtle curves of the cresting rail and uprights. And in between, there were (1) the Jacobean chair with twist-turned legs and uprights, scrolled armrests, carved seat and back, and carved front stretcher, and (2) the William and Mary chair of Dutch origin somewhat similar to the Jacobean chair except for its upholstered seat and back, and crossed stretchers. And yet the interval which separates these different styles of chair is barely 150 years. Likewise the period spanning the creation of the Queen Anne chair and that of the shield-back Hepplewhite chair, or the ribbon-splat Chippendale chair, was a mere 60 years or so. And yet the changes that were wrought in chair designs were so far-reaching that they continued to influence English furniture designs for a century thereafter.

It is clear, therefore, that dating a particular category of antique furniture (in which the structural designs remained unchanged for several centuries) purely on stylistic considerations presents obvious problems. With regard to classic blackwood Chinese furniture, we encounter this difficulty in many instances where the designs have shown no modifications whatever for at least 100 years or more. Fortunately, the variety of blackwood furniture traditionally used by the Straits Babas, namely the type with inlaid mother-of-pearl decorations, appeared rather late (probably in the latter part of the 18th century) in the history of the development of blackwood furniture. Besides, we know, based on circumstantial evidence, that most extant pieces of blackwood furniture with inlaid mother-of-pearl decorations in old Baba homes are datable to the 19th century. I have not met anyone in Malacca thus far who claims that the blackwood furniture in his family's *rumah abu* (or ancestral home) can be dated back to the 18th century, even though this is entirely possible, given the fact that there are Baba families in Malacca who can trace their ancestry back to the Ming Dynasty. Why this should be so is not easy to explain. After all, some pieces of late 17th- and 18th-century Dutch furniture may still be seen in some old homes and in the collection of the former State Museum of Malacca. But given the chequered history of the Chinese settlers in Malacca, especially the depredations which followed the conquest of the city by the Dutch in 1641, plus the total cessation of trade with China until Malacca was handed over to the British at the end of the Napoleonic Wars in Europe (about 1800), it is hardly surprising that no significant collection of blackwood furniture pre-dating 1800 survived to this day.

The same may perhaps be said of red-and-gold namwood furniture: it would be difficult indeed to chance upon a piece of this variety of Chinese furniture made largely in Zhejiang and Fujian provinces in southeast China which predates 1800. Most extant pieces are either datable to the latter part of the 18th century or the turn of the 20th century, according to circumstantial evidence associated with the family histories of their present owners, the age of the house in which such pieces of furniture were found, bills of purchase, etc. The structural designs and ornamental motifs of red-and-gold namwood furniture are probably more archaic than those of blackwood furniture. But they remained unchanged even into the 20th century.

The other extreme situation is where the furniture designs consist of a hodge-podge of structures and patterns drawn from furniture belonging to different historical periods and cultures. Locally-made Straits Chinese teakwood furniture incorporating Anglo-Chinese designs and structures is a good example of furniture displaying such an admixture of styles.

Superficially, Straits Chinese teakwood furniture with an English/European style looks curiously archaic. To those who are familiar with the history of the development of English furniture in particular, the designs of many of these extant pieces of teak furniture appear very similar to those of 17th-century English archetypes. For example, chairs featuring caned backs and seats, double-bine, twist-turned legs and uprights and/ or tapering square legs with stretchers and scrolled armrests are characteristically Tudor or Jacobean in style. On the other hand, we may come across a chair with typical 17th-century turned legs but without bracers (in other words, a combination of 17th- and 18th -entury features), Regency armrests (early 19th century) and a caned back with arched or pointed crestings and cane seats (obviously 17th-century characteristics). How should we date this chair on purely stylistic considerations?

In the same way, we are bound to encounter sooner or later, in some old Baba home, a sideboard which resembles one of those 17th-century court cupboards featuring a lower cabinet with framed and panelled doors. However, instead of the usual straight, squat feet that one expects of 17th-century court cupboards, it sports late 18th-century ogee feet, with their characteristic serpentine curves. What is even more interesting, it incorporates a large framed mirror in the backboard, a feature found mainly on sideboards made during the Victorian era (1837–1901). Is this sideboard then, datable to the 17th, 18th or the 19th century?

Most people may not be aware of it, but many extant writing desks or bureaus in old Baba homes, whether the tambour (also known as 'roll-top') type or the less frequently encountered drop-front secretaire type surmounted with a tall cabinet featuring an arched or broken pediment, were largely modelled on 18th-century French archetypes peculiar to the reigns of Louis XV and Louis XVI, except that the local versions have no brass ormolu ornaments and marquetry-work, nor were they made out of mahogany. To make matters a little more complicated, the Babas commissioned a type of console table with shaped and moulded marble slabs which was basically of French and Italian inspiration, but which incorporated chinoiserie-like features, such as high-relief carvings on the front and side railings depicting Taoist Immortals, stags, *qilins*, phoenixes, peony blossoms and even *taotien* masks on the knees of the cabriole-like legs! Chinese cabinet-makers also added a low support or pedestal for many of these console tables with freestanding legs. French console tables were mostly of 18th-century dating. But we would be wrong in attributing an 18th-century dating to the Straits Chinese variety of console table. For all the various types of English- and/or European-style teak furniture are, in fact, datable only to the latter part of the 19th century at the earliest.

Thus, the dating of furniture by applying stylistic criteria can be misleading, even when carefully considered. There is, of course, no question about dating directly by reference to such things as signatures, shop marks, date marks and/or reign marks, stamped or engraved upon these pieces of furniture. This is because, as we have mentioned before, it was not customary for traditional Chinese cabinet-makers to stamp their personal seals and date marks on furniture made by them or their workshops, in the way that the scholar-painter regularly did on his brush-paintings and his calligraphies. In ancient China, the scholar-gentleman belonged to the privileged class of educated gentry, while craftsmen, along with jade-carvers, wood-carvers, potters, sculptors, bronze-casters, goldsmiths, silk-weavers and architects, belonged to people of lower social standing – 'lesser mortals' so the saying goes. The practice of attesting their signatures upon their handiwork was a privilege largely reserved for the scholar-gentleman and court officials, and hence denied to artisans. For this reason, the student of Chinese (or even Straits Chinese) furniture will not discover the counterparts of Boulle, Weisweiller, Leleu, Hepplewhite, Adam and Chippendale, even among the masterpieces of Chinese furniture.

We must, therefore, fall back on circumstantial evidence to enable us to determine the likely age and provenance of a particular piece of furniture. We must, in other words, look for sources of information which happen to be directly or indirectly related to the furniture in question. These include the names and dates associated with the original owners of these artefacts, the names of the cabinet-makers or the workshops

from which such pieces of furniture were purchased, invoices and receipts where available, the approximate date of the completion of the house, etc. The aim here is to try and link the furniture with some other objects, people or events about which we can assign some definite dates. If we assume further that the furniture in question was in some way contemporaneous with these other objects, people or events, we should be able to make useful conjectures about the dating.

With regard to Straits Chinese teak furniture modelled along English/European designs, it is not necessary to do much detective work because the history associated with the making of such furniture is relatively recent. As indicated elsewhere, it became popular with the Baba community many decades after the British had consolidated their administration of the Straits colony of Penang, Malacca and Singapore – in the 1870s or 1880s, although we cannot be precise about the dates as no documentary evidence is available. While it is not possible to definitely identify any piece of old teakwood furniture as belonging to the beginning of the 19th century purely on stylistic considerations or circumstantial evidence, it is at least possible to distinguish the original archetypes from later reproductions by noting that furniture of English and European provenance was usually constructed out of non-tropical woods such as beech, oak, walnut, ash, pine and yew, with the exception, of course, of mahogany and rosewood which were varieties of semi-tropical woods. The local types of Anglo-Chinese furniture, by contrast, were exclusively made out of teakwood.

But, apart from the problems associated with dating based on stylistic considerations, we can now surmise on the basis of the various sources of circumstantial evidence available to us that the bulk of English-style teakwood furniture extant was made only towards the closing decades of the 19th century, when teak imported mainly from Burma (and later Thailand) became cheaply available to local cabinet-makers. But by the 1930s, production of teak furniture ceased, when supplies were greatly reduced by the onset of World War II.

One final observation is pertinent here: to the traditional Chinese art connoisseur, European art historians and collectors seem to be overly fussy about dates and attribution. There is a tacit assumption on the part of the latter that any work of art which is not signed or inscribed and dated by the artist, craftsman or artisan concerned is either a piece of forgery or a work of inferior quality. While this attitude may be justifiably defended when one happens to be dating and assessing the authenticity and even the quality of European art objects, it cannot be applied consistently for the purpose of dating and evaluating Asian and, particularly, Chinese art objects. This is because in China and elsewhere in Asia, it was neither customary nor obligatory for artisans, sculptors, architects, cabinet-makers, potters, jade-carvers and metal-casters to sign or inscribe all their handiwork. In any case, most of them were illiterate. Thus, if inscriptions or date marks must, for some reason or other, be added to their handiwork, these were usually done for them by other people (scribes and calligraphers) specially trained to write their inscriptions in a clear and legible fashion.

For this reason, Chinese art connoisseurs tend to pay much less attention to such things as dates, names, seal marks and inscriptions than their European counterparts. Instead, they concentrate on those features of the work of art (or craft) that really matter, namely mastery of medium, excellence of craftsmanship, originality of form and design, and beauty of colour and texture. If an artefact is well executed, that is really what matters; names and dates are only of secondary importance. An unmarked and unsigned artefact of fine workmanship is more to be appreciated than one which is signed and dated but of mediocre or indifferent quality. In fact, some very fine and original works of art in China were unmarked and unsigned, for example *huanghuali* classic furniture of the Ming Dynasty and 14th-century blue-and-white porcelain. Hence, works of art which are ostensibly old and of fine workmanship are rarely rejected simply because they happen to be unmarked and undated.

However, the preoccupation of European art connoisseurs with dates, signatures and attribution is not a passing fad of some kind, but a practice which is deeply entrenched in their culture. In fact, it goes a long way back to medieval times when guilds or associations of people engaged in similar trades and professions were formed for the protection of mutual interests and for maintaining standards. Where arts and crafts are concerned, the time-honoured method by which a guild went about protecting its reputation and the quality of products turned out by its member craftsmen and artisans was to stamp, mark and assay its products in some distinctive manner so that patrons could refer to these marks as an assurance of quality and authenticity. Artefacts of a similar type which did not carry the hallmarks or shopmarks and the assayers' marks of the guild in question were considered forgeries or else of doubtful origin.

Existing side-by-side with the traditional guilds were individuals (some of whom were of great talent and experience) who had originally trained with some guilds, but who subsequently left to set up shops of their own in order that they might produce artefacts of distinctive characteristics. These maverick artists and craftsmen also adhered to the traditional practice of signing and dating their works. There were many such independent artists, sculptors, cabinet-makers, bronze-casters, goldsmiths, glass-makers, etc., in Europe since the Middle Ages and some of them acquired great reputations for themselves. However, it sometimes happened that some craftsman or artist went unappreciated in his lifetime (e.g. Vermeer, the 17th-century Dutch painter) and was suddenly rediscovered by some scholar or critic whose writings helped to bring posthumous fame to the artist or craftsman in question.

Now, the traditional method of making and dating art objects which applied so well in European arts and crafts, and which had its basis in the system of hallmarking and assaying initiated by the guilds, breaks down when applied to Chinese art. This is because guilds of the sort which had existed in Europe since the Middle Ages (476–1453), and which observed rigid standards, integrity and quality control, did not exist in China. The Chinese had their own peculiar method of dating and hallmarking their products. However, Chinese date marks are never stated explicitly, except by reference to the reign names of certain emperors and of the dynasty to which they belonged. The names of the individual artisans or craftsmen were practically never used,

except in two special instances, namely brush-paintings and calligraphies of scholar-gentlemen. The latter alone were privileged to put their names against their works. But even so, this was done by way of seal marks rather than signatures. The result was, of course, that the works of a famous artist or calligrapher tended to be copied extensively down the ages by lesser-known artists who tried to palm off their more inferior works as those of the master himself.

Where the reign names are concerned, it so happened that the reigns of certain emperors were associated with, say, enamelled porcelain of excellent quality, while those of others were associated with jade carvings of fine workmanship. This fact alone would provide sufficient incentive to tempt imitators to turn out porcelain and jade which duplicated the characteristic features of the original archetypes, together with the specific *nianhaos*, or imperial reign marks, found on them. In China, it must not be forgotten, the art of imitation itself had become a fine art! For the unwary collector, therefore, simply checking the authenticity of a piece of porcelain or jade by reference to the *nianhaos* is far from being a foolproof test.

In comparison, because ancient Chinese furniture is very rarely marked or dated, it forces attention to be focused on more relevant considerations, such as the structure and design, the quality of the finish (including colour and patina) and the types of timber employed. The dating and attribution of a piece of furniture will have to be made, and rightly so, on stylistic considerations, as well as on sources of circumstantial evidence connected with it.

Notes

1.   Handler, Sarah and Wang Shixiang (transl.). *Classic Chinese Furniture*. London: Han-Shou Tang Ltd, 1986.

2.   Ecke, Gustav. *Chinese Domestic Furniture*. Tokyo, Rutland: Charles E. Tuttle Co.; Vermont: Hong Kong University Press, 1962. Originally published by Henri Vetch, Beijing, 1944.

3.   It is not easy to identify the species and genus of a particular variety of wood used in antique blackwood furniture simply by noting the colour, grain and texture of the timber. With regard to *zitan* and *hongmu* (Chinese trade names for several varieties of very hard, dark, dense and heavy tropical hardwood), it is difficult to tell what species or genera they belong to. The experts are of the opinion that they belong to either *Pterocarpus santalinus* or *Pterocarpus indicus*. They may well be right, except that there are many species and genera of tropical hardwoods which have properties rather similar to those of *zitan* and *hongmu* but belong to very different species and genera of trees. For example, ebony resembles these two varieties of blackwood in several respects, but is identified as *Diospyros ebenum*. In Malaysia, red *balau* has a rich red-brown for its heartwood, but it belongs to the family of *Dipterocarpaceae*. Likewise, *chengal* has a heartwood of dark purple-brown and rust-red, and it is dense and heavy. But it also belongs to the family of *Dipterocarpaceae*. *Kekatong* is red-brown streaked with black in the heartwood, but it belongs to the family of *Leguminosae*.

4.   This statement is not based on documentary evidence, but on personal observation of the types of furniture found in the imperial quarters of the Forbidden Palace, or what is now referred to as the 'Palace Museum' in Beijing. In recent years, the Chinese authorities began to grant foreign institutions and scholars access to the interiors of many imperial quarters which hitherto had been denied to outsiders. In particular, the private chambers of the Empress Dowager, Cixi, and those of her even more famous predecessor, Qianlong, were allowed to be photographed and published in learned and popular books on the legends and splendour of Beijing. These photographs provide a very useful insight into the kinds of furniture and fixtures used by the Qing royalty.

5.   In Schulyer Cammann's *China Dragon Robes* (Ronald Press, New York, 1952), the author made the same point. But Professor Cammann was alluding to the colour of the emperors' imperial dragon robes which the Qing royal house had decreed was yellow. This was to distinguish the imperial colour of the Qings from that of the Ming emperors, which was red. Even with regard to the official robes of their royalty, the Qings were concerned that nothing should be done, wittingly or unwittingly, to revive the memory of the Ming Dynasty in the minds of the people.

6.   Roderick MacFarquhar in Chapter 4 of *The Forbidden City* (Newsweek, New York, 1979) gives a vivid description of Beijing and its history under the various Ming emperors.

7.   Kates, George N. *Chinese Household Furniture*. New York: Dover Publications Inc., 1962.

8.   Ecke, Gustav. Op. cit.

9.   Wang, Shixiang. Op. cit.

10. Apart from the fact that padding chair seats and chair backs with stuffed cushions was not a traditional practice in China, I suspect that the avoidance of mounting stuffed cushions was largely related to the kinds of wood (e.g. *zitan* and *huanghuali*) used in furniture-making. *Zitan* and *huanghuali* are extremely hard and brittle timbers which tend to split when iron nails are driven into them. As for brass tacks, they are much too soft and often bend under the impact of the hammer.

11. Chinese scholars state confidently in their writings that the high-back armchair, of which the earliest extant pieces are dated to the Ming Dynasty in the 15th century, was already fully developed by the time of the Song Dynasty (960–1279). This means, of course, that it was already in existence during the preceding Tang Dynasty (618–907), although perhaps in a more experimental stage of development. And yet the curious fact is that not a single example of a chair dated either to the Song or the Tang Dynasty survives to this day. What, then, is the evidence for their claim that the chair was in existence by, say, the 10th century? None other than from paintings depicting the interior furnishings of Chinese homes which are datable to the end of the Tang Dynasty.

12. *Antique Furniture.* London: Sun Books, Hamlyn, 1971; p. 133.

13. How much credence can we give to depictions of ancient furniture portrayed in Chinese paintings? Can they be regarded as accurate drawings of the furniture of their times? Some writers warn us not to take paintings of ancient furniture depicted in old scrolls as authentic representations. According to them, the artists' renditions are not accurate but garbled and imaginary creations.

While this is entirely possible, I am inclined to credit Chinese artists with a sharper and shrewder sense of observation than others are prepared to admit. For one thing, the structure of the various components of a piece of furniture, be it a *k'ang*, a high-back chair, a stool or even a low table, seems to be quite accurately portrayed in some of these old paintings, e.g. Gu Hongzhong's *The Night Revels of Han Xizai* and Zhou Wenju's *Concert at the Palace*, both of which are authenticated to be of the Five Dynasties period (907–960). There are, as far as I can make out, no technical or structural blunders in these drawings, which would have occurred if the artists had allowed their imaginations free rein. Besides, if the painting of the interior of a house purporting to be of the Tang Dynasty was also executed during the Tang period, there is no reason for doubting that the artist actually saw and knew what the interior of a Chinese home looked like. The only catch here is when a painting purporting to be the portrayal of the interior furnishings of a Chinese home during, say, the Song Dynasty, was in fact painted by an artist 500 years after the demise of that dynasty. Then we have every reason to suspect that the artist was recreating an interior setting which he had never seen with his own eyes.

There are many popular woodcuts datable to the 19th century which depict the interiors of Chinese homes, purportedly dating back to the time of the Three Kingdoms (220–280, after the Han Dynasty). These woodcuts characteristically employed blackwood furniture of the 17th to

19th century styles for decorating the interiors of homes which existed over 2000 years ago – long before such styles of furniture came into existence! But most people who are not students of Chinese furniture are obviously unaware of this fact.

14. There are many authoritative and learned discussions of the three opium wars fought between China and Britain, but a short and more matter-of-fact account is given in Kenneth S. Latourette's *The Chinese, Their History and Culture* (MacMillan Co., New York, 1951, Chapter 10). I find, however, that K. M. Pannikar's *Asia and Western Dominance* (George Allen and Unwin, London, 1993) contains a more passionate and exciting description of the causes of the opium wars. Undoubtedly, Dr Pannikar was a more partisan historian and the tone of his discussion was more polemical. But his account in Chapter 2 makes for more interesting reading.

15. J. C. Fergusson. *Survey of Chinese Art*. Shanghai: The Commercial Press, 1939.

16. *Chinese Household Furniture*. New York: Dover Publications Inc., 1962.

17. For a more detailed account of how gold leaf is manufactured, the reader is referred to the *Encyclopedia Britannica*.

18. These scrolled carvings usually feature dragon heads at one extremity and foliated tails at the opposite end. They bear great resemblance to the serpentine motifs painted on lacquer vessels, silken panels and embroidered articles of clothing datable to the Han Dynasty. The cloud and dragon scrolls seen in the funeral objects of Madam Lixiang of the Western Han Dynasty are excellent examples from which the carved and scrolled motifs in red-and-gold furniture were probably derived. Such scrolled carvings usually occur in the aprons and frieze panels of tables, couches (opium beds), settees, chairs and cabinets.

    It is interesting to note that while wood-carvers in Zhejiang and Fujian provinces working on red-and-gold namwood furniture freely incorporated such archaic motifs in their cabinet-work, the Xuzhou school of cabinet-makers, which worked exclusively with *huanghuali* and *zitan*, largely avoided them.

19. I must qualify this somewhat: the so-called 'high backs' of red-and-gold settees are not quite like those high upholstered backs of the 18th- and 19th-century European sofas or settees, which rise well above the head of the sitter. The back and side panels of red-and-gold settees vary between 15 and 18 inches (37.5 and 45 centimetres) and reach only up to shoulder level. Their height is only relative to those benches with low backs and side panels of about seven inches (17.5 centimetres) in height.

20. In blue-and-white Chinese porcelain of the 14th and 15th centuries, but more specifically in the porcelain of the 15th and early 16th centuries especially made for the sultans and nobility of countries like Turkey, Iran, Syria and Iraq, the floral and foliated motifs tended to be more formalized. This was done to conform to the Koranic injunction forbidding artists from making representations of naturalistic objects, which suggested idolatry from a doctrinal point of view.

But even so, the floral and foliated motifs depicted on these pieces of porcelain never quite lost that sense of naturalism which has always been typical of Chinese painting. The Chinese were never quite able to represent naturalistic oblects in a purely conventional and hieratic manner completely shorn of any vestige of realism.

21. See Buckley, Charles Burton, *An Anecdotal History of Old Times in Singapore,* University of Malaya Press, 1965. The original edition of this work was published in 1962 in Singapore and printed by Fraser and Neave. See pp. 672, 350, 378.

22. Wang, Shixiang. Op. cit.

23. Ecke, Gustav. Op. cit.

24. *Antiques*. London: Pan Books, 1973.

25. *Antique or Fake? – The Making of Old Furniture*. London: Evan Brothers Ltd, 1970.

Glossary

acanthus A stylized kind of leaf ornament which probably originated in ancient Greece and was extensively used for decorating the capitals of Corinthian columns. This ornament became very popular with French cabinet-makers during the 18th century and was widely used in their ormolu (see 'ormolu') brass fittings and carvings.

alcove A recess or partly enclosed space connected to or forming part of a bedroom.

apron A shaped bar of wood set immediately below the seat rail of a chair or settee, or below the frieze of a table, and which stretches between the legs, partly to reinforce the effect of the stretchers and partly to provide an ornamental skirting. Aprons in ancient Chinese furniture (e.g. blackwood and red-and-gold namwood furniture) are usually ornamented with elaborate carvings in pierced- and relief-work.

arabesque Decorations of flowing and meandering lines composed mainly of foliage and scrolls, and occurring largely on borders or panels.

architrave The lowest part of the entablature, i.e. the lintel above the columns.

artemisia Any one of the various plants which belong to the genus of *Artemisia*, and these include sagebrush and wormwood. In ancient Chinese art, the symbol of the artemisia leaf occurs mainly in porcelain marks of the Kangxi period (1661–1722). It is also occasionally seen in the carvings of furniture.

baluster The term refers to the streets supporting a rail or balustrade and it is often found in chair backs of the Jacobean (see 'Jacobean') period.

bas/relief This refers to shallow carvings which raise the decorative motifs only slightly above the background matrix of the wood panel. From an aesthetic point of view, however, bas-relief carvings can be just as pleasing as high-relief carvings, especially when they are executed by a master craftsman. The only difference is that high-relief carvings require more labour.

bevel In cabinet-work, the term refers to the slanting or sloping of the edges or borders of a panel of wood. This 'bevelling' of the edges is done partly to decrease the apparent size of a panel and to allow for the play of light and shade.

bow-front Also known as 'swell-front' or 'bombé-front'. It means a curved (and sometimes a swelling scallop shell) front in furniture, especially in sideboards, commodes and console tables.

brace Also known as 'stretcher' in cabinet-work. It refers to a horizontal bar of wood joining and strengthening the legs of chairs and tables.

break-front The term refers to a set of chests, a cabinet or bookcase in which the centre section projects outwards or is recessed backwards.

buffet A French word for a sideboard of the two-tier type (*buffet à deux corps*) and known in 17th-century England as a 'court cupboard'.

cabriole A type of furniture leg characteristic of those found during Queen Anne's reign (1702–14) and in Chippendale furniture. The cabriole leg curves outwards and then narrows downwards in a kind of elongated S-shape into an ornamental foot which is either of the hoofed type or the claw-and-ball type. Some experts think that cabriole legs were of Chinese origin as many 15th- and 16th-century Ming period blackwood chairs, tables, couches and cabinets have the characteristic cabriole shape.

commode A commode is also a kind of furniture (in this case, it is simply a chest-of-drawers) meant to be placed against a wall.

console table An 18th-century table (largely of French origin, though the Chinese had such tables as far back as the 14th or 15th century) which is intended to be placed against a wall.

cornice A horizontal or moulded projection which surmounts a cabinet. It is the topmost member of the entablature.

cresting This term refers to the ornamental top rail of a chair or settee, or perhaps the topmost decorative panel which crowns the cornice (see 'cornice') of a cabinet. A cresting panel is usually carved with motifs in relief or pierced-work.

Dalbergia This term refers to a large genus of tropical and subtropical tree from which rosewood is obtained. It is estimated that more than 12 different species of *Dalbergia* have been used in cabinet-making since the 12th or 13th century in China. Among these are D. *hainanensis*, *D. latifolia* and *Ormosia hennyu*, which, according to Wang Shixiang, were used for making some of the finest blackwood furniture in China from the Ming Dynasty to about the beginning of the Qing Dynasty during the latter part of the 17th century. The Chinese terms for blackwood of the finest varieties are *huanghuali*, *zitan* and *hongmu*.

dovetail joints These refer to fan-shaped tenons which form tight interlocking joints when fitted into corresponding fan-shaped mortises. Such joints were used for fixing together the walls of drawers.

dowels Wooden pegs (usually round) used for joining and strengthening component parts of a piece of furniture.

drop-front The term refers to the writing flap or board in a secretaire (see 'secretaire') or writing bureau which can be lowered to form a writing surface.

fielded panel A raised panel with bevelled edges.

fretwork Ornamental carvings executed in geometric open-work (see 'pierced/open-work') or 'frets'. This means an ornamental design carved on a wood panel along the borders and it consists generally of symmetrical and geometrical forms repeated in a serial order.

Gothic style The term, as used in the literature of English furniture, refers to a 19th-century style of furniture in which the principal decorative motifs, especially on chair backs, balusters and hand rails, etc., are depicted in the form of the pointed arch, or variations of the pointed arch.

high-relief This term is used in cabinet-work to refer to carvings which are executed almost in the round to convey the impression of three-dimensional solidity. This can be done in two ways: (i) by pierced- or open-work, a method in which the craftsman uses his chisel to cut through those empty spaces between the decorative motifs, and (ii) by carving the various motifs almost in the round without allowing his chisel to pierce through the matrix which forms the background.

huanghuali The Chinese trade name for several species of wood belonging to the genus of *Dalbergia* and which were used for the making of blackwood/rosewood furniture in the Ming Dynasty (1368–1644). Experts are not quite agreed on which particular species of *Dalbergia* went into the making of the best of Ming furniture. Some think that *D. hainanensis* was used, while others contend that *D. latifolia* and *Pterocarpus santalinus* seemed more likely.

Jacobean The term refers strictly to the reign of James I of England (1603–25). More loosely, it refers to the style of furniture which was made in England throughout the 17th century.

k'ang A large Chinese alcove bed. In north China, it was a platform built of bricks and the space below was heated by a fire stoked from the outside. In the milder climate of south China, however, the *k'ang* was deliberately fashioned out of wood. Many paintings of Chinese interiors dating from the Tang to the Ming dynasty show such raised platforms.

lacquer Any of the various clear or coloured synthetic coatings made by dissolving nitrocellulose or other cellulose derivatives together with plasticizers and other pigments in a mixture of solvents. In fact, it is used nowadays to refer to any glossy material of a resinous sort used as a surface coating (e.g. the sap from the lacquer tree).

marquetry Decorative veneer of wood or of other materials, including ivory, tortoise shell or mother-of-pearl, in which the sheets are cut to form delicate flowers, figures and landscapes in the woodbase of a piece of furniture. Floral marquetry includes trailing leaves and flowers with birds and butterflies. Marquetry was greatly appreciated in 17th- and 18th-century European furniture, and many excellent pieces of furniture with marquetry are still to be seen in Europe.

mahogany Any of the various American trees (of tropical and semi-tropical regions) belonging to the genus of *Swietenia*, valued for their hard reddish-brown and richly figured wood. Some of the best mahogany wood used for making 18th-century European furniture was said to have come from Cuba. Mahogany, however, has one drawback from the viewpoint of the cabinet-maker: it splits easily when nails are driven into the wood. Several species of African mahogany are also used for making furniture. The Dutch brought saplings of Honduran mahogany to Java during the 17th century and stands of Honduran mahogany are still to be found in Java.

mitre joint A joint made by bevelling each of two surfaces to be joined, usually at a 45° angle, to form a 90° corner.

mortise A cavity or recess (usually of a rectangular shape) in a piece of wood, stone or any other material specially cut to correspond to another projection (of the wood, etc.) similarly shaped, and known as a 'tenon' (see 'tenon').

mouldings The term refers to contours or outlines worked upon the edges or other parts of the woodwork with a view to decorating a plain piece of wood panelling.

ogee A double curve in the shape of an elongated 'S'. In cabinet-work, it often refers to a moulding that has the profile of an S-shaped curve.

ormolu The term refers to metal ornamentation attached to 18th-century French furniture. The metals were alloys of zinc and copper used in the ratio of 75% copper and 25% zinc.

pedestal A base or plinth on which something is set to show off or raise it. The term is used variously in European cabinet-work to refer to a type of large writing desk probably made popular by Chippendale during the 18th century, and which is characterized by a central vacant space below the table top, flanked on either side by two sets of drawers reaching to the ground. It was also used to describe a kind of circular table supported by a single column or pillar anchored into a plinth or, alternatively, tenoned into tripods. I use the term to refer (in Chinese cabinet-work) to a low base stand crafted specifically to raise the level of an altar table or some other type of ceremonial table.

pediment A triangular or arched form surmounting a classical cornice. In cabinet-work, the term refers to the triangular or arched cresting surmounting the top of a cabinet, secretaire or bookcase.

pie-crust mouldings These are notches and curves with parallel grooves carved into the sides of table tops for consoles and other side tables.

pierced/open-work An ancient method of wood-carving in which the craftsman executes the various designs on a wood panel by chiselling right through the matrix of the wood where there are all those vacant spaces between the various motifs. The aim of this method of carving is not merely to make the various details of the design stand out more clearly, but also to impart a sculptural quality to them.

pilaster A rectangular column with a capital and a base executed in relief. It is usually set against a wall or backing as an ornamental motif.

Queen Anne In the vocabulary of cabinet-makers in England, the term refers to English furniture made during the reign of Queen Anne (1702–14).

rail A horizontal bar supported by vertical posts or struts; a balustrade. It also refers to any of the horizontal narrow components used in a piece of furniture.

rake The angle of a chair back. Any piece of furniture (especially the back of a chair) which is inclined away from the perpendicular.

relief The projection of figures or forms from a flat background or, as in painting, where such a projection is apparent only by the use of the technique of *chiaroscuro*.

secretaire A French term which is used to refer to a writing desk or bureau with either a drop-front or roll-top front, and which is surmounted by a tall, glass-fronted bookcase. Sometimes, the term is also used to mean a bureau cabinet.

settee An extended seat made to accommodate at least two people and having armrests and a back. The early Queen Anne settees were literally double chairs. From the latter part of the 18th century, most settees were made with upholstered seats and backs.

shellac A purified lac formed into thin yellow or orange flakes, or often bleached white and widely used in varnishes. The term is also generally used to refer to a thin varnish made by dissolving flake shellac in denatured alcohol and used as a wood coating.

spandrel The triangular space between the left and right exterior curve of an arch and the rectangular framework surrounding it.

spiral or twist-turning This is a method of wood-turning executed upon a treadle lathe in which a continuous spiral groove is carved into the wood. It is also known as 'cockscrew' or 'barley twist'. See 'turning'.

splat A slab of wood often shaped and carved, especially in European furniture, which forms the centre section of the chair back between the uprights or backposts. In the classic Chinese chair made out of *huanghuali* (a type of rosewood of the genus of *Dalbergia*), the splat was a simple concave slab of wood.

stile A vertical member of a frame or panel as in a door or window sash.

stretchers Components of a piece of furniture which function as braces between the legs.

taotien mask The origin of the taotien mask in Chinese furniture dates back to those mask-like motifs regularly seen in Shang and Zhou period bronze vessels. But for some unknown reason, Chinese furniture from the Tang Dynasty (618–907) right down to the Ming Dynasty (1368–1644), which was made for the Imperial Court and for mandarin officials, was all of simple, functional design, with ornamentation being reduced to the barest minimum. However, in the southern coastal provinces of Zhejiang, Fujian and Guangdong, ancient art motifs dating from the Shang Dynasty (1766–1122 B.C.) to the Han Dynasty (206 B.C.–A.D. 220) continued to survive unchanged in red-and-gold namwood and blackwood furniture.

tambour-front This is another name for 'roll-top' and is used to refer to bureaus in which the shutter was made out of thin strips of wood, glued to a backing of canvas. Some types of roll-top bureau have solid shutters – the cylindrical-front variant.

tenon A projection at the end of a piece of wood, shaped (usually in a rectangular form) for inserting into a corresponding recess, namely the mortise (see 'mortise').

tester Literally, the term refers to the canopy of a four-poster bed. But it is also used to refer to any bed with posters and a canopy. The 'half-tester' is a bed with two posts at the extremities of the headboard and a canopy which extends over half the length of the bed.

tongue-and-groove joint In this kind of joint, a long projecting strip is carved out of one or both sides of a panel of wood, which can be fitted into a corresponding recess on another wood panel specifically carved to receive it.

top rail The highest horizontal member of a chair back.

trestle A horizontal beam or bar held up by two pairs of divergent legs and used as a support. In classic blackwood Chinese furniture, many tables were constructed with trestle legs.

turning A method of carving the legs, arms or stretchers of chairs or tables by means of a revolving lathe, usually operated (before the 19th century) by a foot pedal.

uprights Another term also used to refer to the two back posts which form the outer supports of the chair back. In traditional cabinet-work, whether of European or Chinese origins, the back post and its corresponding back legs are crafted in one continuous piece of timber to give strength and rigidity to the chair back.

Bibliography

B. Caseinsley, Herbert. *English Furniture – from Gothic to Sheraton*. New York: Dover Publications, 1968.

Bradford, Ernle. *Antique Furniture*. London: Teach Yourself Books, 1970.

Chang, Queeny. *Memories of a Nonya*. Singapore: Eastern Universities Press, 1981.

Cheo, Kim Ban. *A Baba Wedding*. Singapore: Eastern Universities Press, 1983.

Doussy, Michel. *Antiques*. London: Pan Books, 1973.

Drury, Colonel Heber. *The Useful Plants of India*. Delhi: Periodical Experts Book Agency, 1873.

Ecke, Gustav. *Chinese Domestic Furniture*. Tokyo, Rutland: Charles Tuttle Co., 1963.

Ferguson, J. C. *Survey of Chinese Art*. Shanghai: The Commercial Press, 1939.

Fry, Plantagenet Somerset. *Antique Furniture*. London: Hamlyn, 1971.

Gottshall, Franklin H. *How to Design and Construct Period Furniture*. New York: Bonanza Books, 1989.

Hayward, Charles C. *Antique or Fake? – The Making of Old Furniture*. London: Evan Brothers Ltd, 1970.

Hayword, Helena (ed). *World Furniture*. London: Hamlyn, 1965.

Ho, Ruth. *Rainbow Round My Shoulder*. Singapore: Eastern Universities Press, 1975.

Ho, Wing Meng. *Straits Chinese Silver – A Collector's Guide*. Singapore: Times Books International, 1984.

Ho, Wing Meng. *Straits Chinese Beadwork & Embroidery – A Collector's Guide*. Singapore: Times Books International, 1987.

Hobson, R. L. *Chinese Pottery and Porcelain*. New York: Dover Publications, 1976.

Honour, Hugh. *Cabinet-makers and Furniture Designers*. London: Weidenfeld and Nicolson, 1969.

Iuri, Gabriel. *Victoriana*. London: Hamlyn, 1969.

Jenyns, R. C. and William Watson. *Chinese Art*. Vol. 2. 4 Volumes. London: Oldbourne Press, Minor Arts, 1963.

Juliano, Annette. *Treasures of China*. New York: Richard Marvek Publications, 1981.

Kates, George C. *Chinese Household Furniture*. New York: Dover Publications, 1962.

MacFarquhar, Roderick. *The Forbidden City*. New York: Newsweek, 1979.

100 Malaysian Timbers. Malaysian Timber Industry, 1986.

Palacios, Alva Gonzalez. *The Age of Louis XVI*. London: Paul Hamlyn, Cameo Books, 1969.

Price, Bernard. *The Story of English Furniture*. London: British Broadcasting Corporation, 1978.

Wang, Shixiang. Handler, Sarah and author (transl.). *Chinese Classic Furniture*. London: Han-Shou Tang, 1986.

Wanscher, Ole. Hohnen, David (transl.). *The Art of Furniture – 5,000 Years Of Furniture and Interiors*. New York, Amsterdam: Rheinhold Publishing Corp, 1966.

Willis, Geoffrey. *Classical English Furniture*. Edinburgh: John Bartholomeow & Sons, 1974.

Yap, Yeng. Cotterell, Arthur. *The Early Civilization of China*. London: Weidenfeld and Nicolson, 1975.

Index